The New Policing

Eugene McLaughlin

Los Angeles | London | New Delhi
Singapore | Washington DC

First published 2007

Reprinted 2009 (twice)

SAGE Publications Ltd
1 Oliver's Yard
55 City Road
London EC1Y 1SP

SAGE Publications Inc.
2455 Teller Road
Thousand Oaks, California 91320

SAGE Publications India Pvt Ltd
B 1/I 1 Mohan Cooperative Industrial Area
Mathura Road
New Delhi 110 044

SAGE Publications Asia-Pacific Pte Ltd
33 Pekin Street #02-01
Far East Square
Singapore 048763

British Library Cataloguing in Publication data

A catalogue record for this book is available from the
British Library

ISBN 0 8039 8904 0   978 0 8039 8904 7
     0 8039 8905 9   978 0 8039 8905 4

Library of Congress control number available

Typeset by C&M Digitals (P) Ltd., Chennai, India
Printed on paper from sustainable resources
Printed in Great Britain by CPI Antony Rowe, Chippenham, Wiltshire

FSC
Mixed Sources
Product group from well-managed
forests and other controlled sources

Cert no. SGS-COC-2953
www.fsc.org
© 1996 Forest Stewardship Council

Contents

List of Figures

Preface

There are already many books in circulation that are able to provide readers with overviews of the core subject matter of police studies, such as the historical origins and development; roles and responsibilities; the legal powers of police officers; recruitment, socialization and career progression processes; the occupational dynamics of policework; police-community relations; the organizational structure of control and accountability; the work of specialist units; and crime control issues facing the police in the twenty-first century. There are also a multitude of empirical reports that present findings on critical operational issues confronting contemporary policing. The police remain an intriguing research site because it is the most visible representation of the state's sovereign authority in civil society and police officers are authorized to use their considerable powers to take action against crime and disorder in a manner that is both fair and impartial. Sitting alongside this corpus of police-centred work is a rapidly expanding literature that locates 'the police' within a broader framework of policing, security, regulation and governance. My intention has not been to replicate these texts but to reconsider some of what I view to be the defining concerns of traditional police studies and work within the transformative approaches of the new police studies. The story I tell is from a British perspective but it also touches upon much broader shifts that are restructuring the Anglo-American policing model.

This book remains very much a work in progress for the following reasons. First, it cannot claim to be a comprehensive survey of the bewildering number of 'nooks and crannies' of contemporary policing. Space limitations and analytical interests have required me to make some difficult choices about what to include and what to neglect. Second, it is extremely difficult to sift out what is of long term significance in policing in a moment of contradictory transformation. During the past decade exceptionally well publicised claims have been made with regard to numerous state-of-the-art policing policies and tactics. As demands for punitive 'law and order' measures have become an ever more important feature of the tabloid political culture, there are intense pressures to announce new crime control strategies. The contemporary landscape of policing is as a consequence littered with various initiatives that have been disposed of once they fulfilled a particular public relations function. Hence it is increasingly difficult to distinguish between rhetoric and reality. In addition, there seems to be an increasing gap between what police scholars and police officers understand to be 'really' significant. This is compounded by the sheer organizational complexity of contemporary police forces, constituted as they are through overlapping institutional configurations and networks. Third, I remain ambivalent about whether we can refine further the conceptual tools necessary to research this rapidly changing institutional field of study. I have been attempting to understand policing for many years. My overall analytical understanding of the state of British policing is constituted through researching those high profile crisis moments when an aspect of policing has to be examined, explained and 'resolved' in the political realm. This includes the Scarman report (1981) into the riots of 1981; the Sheehy report (1993) into the organizational structure and rationale of the police; the Macpherson report (1999) into the racist murder of Stephen Lawrence; the Patten report (1999) into the future of policing in Northern Ireland and the more recent Independent Police Complaints Commission examination (2006) of the shooting of Jean Charles de Menezes. Such incidents and controversies tend to cast long, unresolvable shadows over how we understand and evaluate policing.

This approach is supplemented by analysis of various overarching governmental projects to reform police structure, powers and accountability and, at a more local level, attending public meetings about neighbourhood policing issues. Some of these are routine and some are organized by single issue campaign groups who have mobilized around a specific cause for concern. It is in such fora where one can witness the conflicting shifts in policing. It is also where one learns to interrogate the contradictory multi-tiered realities that are an inevitable part of contemporary policing. It can also be a deeply depressing experience to hear the latest generation of well-intentioned senior police officers attempt to explain why something did or did not happen; respond to public concerns and manage public expectations; or detail the local implications of the latest round of top down organizational reform and modernization. A final reason why this is very much a work in progress is that the theoretical registers that one has to analyse and offer explanation seem to be increasingly inadequate to the task. During the past 30 years our understanding of the police and policing has undergone major transformations. Re-reading the classic texts of the Anglo-American sociology of the police one has a sense that they are both obviously familiar and strangely unfamiliar. Going behind 'the blue curtain' generated a research energy that is, for the most part, difficult to realize in contemporary police studies. These studies of patrol work as culturally crafted practice are remarkably self-contained with a relatively secure set of assumptions about 'the police', 'police officers', 'police character', 'police work' and 'the policed'.

The carefully situated findings of previous generations of researchers are by no means redundant and future generations of students of policing should be encouraged to read them in the original. However, an underlying theme of this book is that the academic context within which contemporary police studies takes place is radically altered. Now there is an expectation that police scholars can produce work that on the one hand demonstrates theoretical connections to broader intellectual shifts and on the other meets the policy demands of professional policework. This 'disciplining' has produced a notable schism within police studies and a re-profiling of police scholarship. There are an increasing number of contracted researchers and consultants who use managerialist methodologies to evaluate police personnel, practice and procedure and turn out 'what works' reports. The aspiration to move from an ad hoc administrative police studies to a fully-fledged police management science is supported by the decisions of funding bodies. There would seem to be less room for those scholars who wish to work from the outside to interrogate the state institution that is expected to symbolize and guarantee public safety and a civil society. And yet it has never been more important to forge a critical police studies that is capable of conceptualizing policing developments against socio-cultural, economic and political transformations. It remains the case that studying the police in the broadest contextual manner is of vital importance because, as we shall see in the course of this book, postmodernity seems determined to beat out its particular complex of volatile tensions and anxieties resultant from everything from consumerization, cultural differentiation, social fragmentation through to a global war on terror on the 'police anvil' with a merciless vengeance.

The structure of this book is relatively straightforward. Each of the chapters has a distinct focus, namely, popular cultural history, sociological origins, traditional perspectives, new perspectives, crime control, culture and accountability. Chapters 1 to 4 seek to provide readers with a systematic overview of the origins and development of key theoretical perspectives in police studies. The origins of chapter 1 lie with my engagement with the work of police historians on the peculiarities of the 'uniquely mild' system of English policing. I did not want to repeat the 'distant past into the present' narration of the parish constable, watchmen and 'bobbies'. Nor did I wish to recount the influence played by late eighteenth and early nineteenth century reformers on the development of the 'new constabulary' or arguments between scholars on the relationship between the police and state (national and colonial) formation. I decided to locate my historical analysis with the cultural work that went into producing PC George Dixon, the iconic 'bobby on the beat'. The complex of cultural images and associations articulated through this powerful national popular representation pre-dates sociological interest in the British police and in unpredictable ways arises like a phoenix from the ashes to insert itself in contemporary debates. Sooner or later we have to confront and make sociological sense of the interpellative powers of the Dixonian policing imaginary.

This chapter is also intended to strengthen the case for culturally based analysis of the mass mediated nature of police representations.

Chapter 2 is the result of an increasing concern to locate, remember and rethink the sociological origins of police studies. The intention is to provide readers with an in-depth analysis of one of the first sociological analyses of the police. Along with the seminal research of William Westley, Michael Banton's, *The Policeman in the Community* (1964), represents the breakthrough in post-war police studies. Both authors presented a convincing case as to why 'the police' should be a legitimate research topic for sociologists. They also demonstrated what is distinctive and significant about a sociological approach as opposed to numerous legal-constitutional, public administration and historical studies. Although their work was inspirational for a generation of Anglo-American police scholars, both authors have now been reduced to the dust laden status of the bracketed footnotes (see Westley, 1951; 1953; 1970 and Banton, 1964). This is remarkable given that they bequeathed a distinctive field of inquiry, a 'knowledge structure' replete with key sociological concepts and research questions and a distinctive methodological approach. They also created two fundamentally different conceptualizations of policing, one 'profane' and one 'sacred'. William Westley insisted that conflict and violence were intrinsic and indeed defining aspects of US policework while Michael Banton identified the conditions that produced consensual, benign policework in Britain. Banton's explicitly comparative focus also introduced a vitally important analytical bridgehead between the UK and US police studies. In more recent times, such transatlantic ties have been less concerned with comparative academic research matters than with the introduction of American police discourse and practice into British policing. As with every other field of public policy, it seems that Britain is willing to import policing policies from the United States.

Chapters 3 and 4 are intended to provide a tentative framework through which to organize the key perspectives that constitute both traditional and new police studies. Although there is of course an arbitrariness about this framing and there is also the danger of over-simplification, I feel it is important to recognize that there are distinctive perspectives influencing police studies. Chapter 3 outlines the four theoretical perspectives that characterize traditional police studies: ethnographic; Marxist; administrative and left realist perspectives. Although they work with different domain assumptions, explanatory concepts, research concerns and methodologies, each has been influenced by the others. We start with the first wave of eclectic ethnographic police studies that sought to expand upon the concerns of Westley and Banton. The aspiration to represent the inner realities of policing meant that the expressive culture, active agency and organizational identity of the street cop were the primary focus as was the drama of 'doing' policework. These studies also identified the complexities and contradictions of the police function in liberal democratic societies. The dominance of ethnographic approaches was challenged by a Marxist police studies underpinned by the insistence that 'the police' be defined, first and foremost, as a political category. This allowed for the opening out of a structuralist interrogation of the policing of Western capitalist societies. Analysing how specific class interests are written into policing broke dramatically with ethnographic studies, centering the experiences of those subjected to policing and constructing a set of politicised research interests around the question of the true function of the police in a capitalist society. More recently, administrative and left realist perspectives have concentrated on identifying the highly localized role police can and should play in responding to public fears and concerns about crime, disorder and anti-social behaviour. This chapter stands as a reminder of just how influential police-based scholarship has also been to a much broader based criminological conversation. The study of 'the police' and 'policing' inevitably touches upon a complicated range of core philosophical, sociological and governmental issues. It is hard, for example, to over-estimate the broader impact of Hall *et al's* 'authoritarian state' thesis and Wilson and Kelling's 'broken windows' theory.

In chapter 4 I attempt to pull together and organize a variety of perspectives that have been generated as a result of a widening of the analytical lens from state-bounded conceptions of police sovereignty to 'policing', 'security' and 'governance'. The mutually conditioning relationship between nation state and police is under severe strain. This new police studies draws upon broader debates about the turbo-charged implications of the shift to postmodernity. This has stimulated 'thinking at the limits' consideration about the disaggregated, pluralized, patchworked, 'pick n'mix' shape of 'future policing' resultant from the impact of (a) pluralization of local policing and security activities and (b) the de-bordering of national policing, security and intelligence interests. There is enough evidence to suggest that this expanded conceptual imagination associated with the pluralist and transnational thinking has inaugurated a fundamental paradigm shift in police studies. I will leave it for readers to review the different perspectives and to work through the co-existent dislocated futures of policing laid out in this chapter. To further clarify the 'newness' of the new police studies, chapter 4 also considers the work of a small group of scholars who have argued that the transformation of police-media relations is arguably one of the most important analytical and methodological challenges currently facing police studies. Because of public obsession with crime, flashing blue lights and wailing sirens dominate the 24/7 news headlines and entertainment media schedules. This allows the media to play a powerful role in shaping public understanding of the 'spectacle of policing' and the criminal justice process. Some writers would go so far as to argue, for example, that hard and fast 'real' and 'fictional' representational regimes are now so intimately inter-connected and inter-textualized that the borders between the two have all but collapsed, creating a multitude of synthetic policing imaginaries. This is compounded by the fact that realizing 'instantaneous' legitimation requires the police to impress themselves increasingly on the public imagination through a range of pro-active communication, public relations and image manipulation strategies. Finally, as shall be noted in several chapters, the newsmedia can also provide an invaluable, if unpredictable, form of public scrutiny in controversial policing incidents. The political ramifications of the wrap-around prime timing presence of the 24/7 global media on policing and the disintegration of the representational regime of policing requires much more detailed consideration than is currently given.

A central intention of chapter 4 is to suggest that no single theorization is capable of dominating our understanding of contemporary developments in policing. And to a considerable degree, this is little more than a reflection of the dislocated condition of a core state institution that is being compelled to re-imagine itself on the sharpest edges of radical transformation. This is the basis for the much more grounded and specific discussion that takes place in chapters 5 to 8. The British police have never looked more professional, techno-rational, outward looking and progressive in thinking and operationally transparent and police performance is now measured and evaluated to an unprecedented degree. And yet there is a sense in which wave after wave of reforms have produced a hollowed out shell of a distinctive policing model that once was and could have been. Living as it is within the wreckage of futures that might have been, might explain why the British police seems to be incapable of generating a persuasive, legitimating, and durable 'home grown' philosophy of policing. Such a philosophical vacuum means that it is extremely susceptible to being hegemonized further by US policing discourses and ideas of 'how to police' crime. In chapters 5 to 7, I use a case study approach to examine three critical issues confronting the British police in more depth. My empirical reference point, for the most part, is the Metropolitan Police, the British police force with the most complex, pressurized, multiply symbolized working environment. In recent years it has found itself under relentless pressure to fast-forward strategies to demonstrate that it can: re-police crime, disorder, incivility and anti-social behaviour (Chapter 5); re-culture the organization so that it reflects the multi-cultural global city it is responsible for (Chapter 6); and re-structure modes of accountability so that they are capable of connecting with the security needs of myriad neighbourhoods and communities (Chapter 7). In the competitive globalized market place of policing, securitization and crime control, the Metropolitan Police must contend not just with the private sector but being increasingly evaluated against the aggressively branded NYPD's 'zero tolerance'/'quality of life' policing model and the Chicago Police Department's community oriented policing model.

The concluding chapter addresses concerns that even the new police studies will become analytically redundant as a result of the fallout from the mass casualty terrorist attacks on New York and Washington on 11 September 2001. Britain's integral partnership with the US in the global 'long war' – unlimited in time and space – against Islamic terrorism has unknown implications for internal policing and security. Initially, those concerned with civil liberties and human rights in Britain managed to rein in demands for new police powers and counter-terrorism methodologies that were deemed to be vital to deal with the increased threat of mass casualty violence. They did so by reference to the Northern Ireland experience and claiming that the terrorist threat was being overstated by authoritarians wishing to manipulate public fears and insecurities. However, the political and newsmedia terms of the policing debate changed dramatically in July 2005 with the no-warning suicide bomb attacks on London's transport system, the subsequent failed attacks and the fatal shooting of Jean Charles de Menezes by Metropolitan Police officers. This chapter is anchored by Sir Ian Blair's high-profile November 2005 BBC Dimbleby Lecture. This touchstone – 'What kind of police service do we want?' – lecture reflected on some of the key issues and debates raised in Chapters 4 to 7. Long term, we now have to give sustained attention to the construction of a critical police studies that is capable of engaging analytically and politically with the multi-tiered national security policing modality that seems likely to emerge during the next decade.

Acknowledgements

In writing this book I have been fortunate to have had the encouragement and support of a number of colleagues and friends. A particular debt of gratitude and friendship is owed to John Muncie and Karim Murji. Over the time this work has been developing John and I have concluded many criminological publishing projects with Sage. Throughout he always reminded me that at some time I would have to settle my account with police studies and move on. For many years Karim and I produced numerous papers about the impossibilities and refusals of policing and some of the core chapters in this book could not have been completed otherwise. Gordon Hughes and Sarah Neal have helped to work through different futures of policing, community safety and crime prevention and governance. Many of the arguments that are central to the book reflect engagement with the work of: Michael Banton, Maureen Cain, John Clarke, Adam Crawford, Adam Edwards, Clive Emsley, Stuart Hall, Frances Heidensohn, Paddy Hillyard, Simon Holdaway, Gordon Hughes, Tony Jefferson, Anja Johansen, Les Johnston, Michael Keith, Ian Loader, Barry Loveday, Agon Mulcahy, Pat O'Malley, Tim Newburn, Maurice Punch, Robert Reiner, Phil Scraton, Jim Sheptycki, Joe Sim, Betsy Stanko, Kevin Stenson, 'Tank' Waddington, Louise Westmarland and Lucia Zedner. I am indebted to Pat O'Malley, Robert Reiner, Betsy Stanko and Tank Waddington for reviewing the manuscript. The usual qualification applies of course: any errors of fact or analysis remain my responsibility. I would also like to thank colleagues at the Open University and City University who have required me to think beyond police studies. Alison Wakefield kept reminding me of the limitations of a state centred conception of policing, whilst Chris Greer has been instrumental in making me think seriously about the under-researched relationship between the police and the 24/7 information age. At a key moment, Winifred Power deployed her incisive editorial skills to help me make sense of police theory.

I wish to also express my sincere gratitude to Caroline Porter, Miranda Nunhofer, Louise Skelding, Ian Antcliff and the editorial team at Sage for their unfailing patience, general support and advice at key moments. This includes clearing the permission to reproduce in chapter 1 some of the material that appeared originally in 'From Reel to Ideal: the 'Blue Lamp' and the cultural construction of PC George Dixon', *Crime, Media and Culture: an International Journal*, 2005, 1 (1): 1–32. I would like to acknowledge Canal Plus Image UK and Getty Images for permission to use the photographic images used in Chapters 1 and 2 and the Police Federation and the Gay Police Association for providing the images used in Chapter 6. Finally I would like to thank Kate Lowe. Needless to say, without her continuing support and friendship *The New Policing* would not have been possible.

The Cultural Construction of the Police

This chapter considers how a very particular cultural representation of the British police was established prior to and in many respects anticipated sociological analysis of policing. Today, the police constable, or 'bobby on the beat' can be found in virtually every tourist gift shop in London in a bewildering number of formats: postcards, key rings, puppets, dolls, teddy bears, coffee mugs, T-shirts all carry this instantly recognizable image of the English police. An avuncular 'bobby' has even featured on the front page of brochures for holidays in London. No other European capital carries such an array of police-based tourist trinkets. We must look to North America for comparable merchandising of the police officer. The Los Angeles Police Department (LAPD) registered its initials as a trademark in August 1998 in an attempt to halt the proliferation of cheap 'tacky' imitations of the force's badge and other symbols that the Commissioner of the LAPD believed created confusion and threatened 'to dilute the authority of LAPD officers' (*Guardian*, 6 August 1998). In 1997 the Royal Canadian Mounted Police took similar action in relation to 'Mountie' merchandise proclaiming that every souvenir company wishing to use the instantly recognizable 'redcoat' image would have to clear copyright approval with a special licensing body. The Canadian government supported fully the new regulatory framework on the grounds that the 'Mountie' was not just an important police image but in certain respects the most expressive self-image of the Canadian nation. The process of public relations management was completed with the Disney Corporation acquisition of the licensing rights to all products bearing the image of the 'Mountie' (Gittings, 1998), generating accusations that the Canadian government was supporting the 'Disney-fication' of policing. And post 9/11, the image of the NYPD has been culturally and commercially revalued as illustrated by a new wave of heroic representations on sale. A general point to note, therefore, is that, within certain societies, the police officer can acquire a representative status that stands at the very centre of the popular cultural imagination (Ericson, 1989; Loader and Mulcahy, 2003).

What is truly significant is that the English 'bobby' has been culturally constituted through a set of popular cultural storylines which underscore his essential 'difference' from the police officers of other countries (McLaughlin and Murji, 1998). Numerous publications continue to assert that he is the finest police officer in the world: a faithful, incorruptible public servant who is unwavering in his commitment to the community; part of the 'thin blue line' that marks out an orderly society from a disorderly one; unarmed because he works with broad-based public consent and respect but 'armed' with prestige and street wisdom rather than power (Radzinowicz, 1955; Critchley, 1967; Ascoli, 1979). This 'exceptionalist' discourse has also exercised a powerful hold over police scholarship.

As we shall see in later chapters, sociological interest in the UK police force in its own right was to come later. For now, we need to look at how the police were depicted in contemporary press, fiction, film and TV in order to throw light on how the 'bobby' came to be such an important icon of 'Englishness'. To date most discussion of the origins of the positive image of the English 'bobby' reproduces the discourse of the 'native genius' of far-sighted reformers who created him and the unique constitutional settlement and bureaucratic processes that legitimated the police mandate in England. According to this perspective, the English not only laid down a unique policing model but devised a constitutional framework within which policing, civil liberties and social order could not just be reconciled but interwoven as an exemplary form of liberal democratic citizenship. This chapter seeks to complement and complicate this 'national feeling for policing' perspective by focusing on the intersecting popular cultural practices that re-imagined the police constable from being the most un-English of ideas into a multi-dimensional icon of English national identity.

This chapter does not propose to re-tell and re-argue the history of the British police. Suffice to say that a considerable amount of political work had to take place in order for 'the police' (this most 'un-English') of institutions to be first of all sheltered from popular resentment and hostility and gradually transformed into one which could be ideologically celebrated as the epitome of Englishness (Critchley, 1967; Ascoli, 1979; Gatrell, 1990; Emsley, 1991; Reynolds, 1998). Newman (1987) argues that in the course of the nineteenth and early twentieth century we witness systematic efforts to constitute a mythological 'Englishness'. The quintessential characteristics and values of 'Englishness' materialized in a variety of political, cultural and institutional settings. The English character was seen to be marked by robust common sense; a sense of fair play and humour; decency; self-restraint; pragmatism; a sense of duty; chivalry; an individualism bordering on eccentricity;

under-statement; and team spirit. Moreover, the English were seen as *patriots* rather than nationalists – patriotism being defined as an unconscious individual predilection and nationalism a consciously expressed collective sentiment (Colls and Dodd, 1986). What is interesting is that Hobsbawm and Ranger (1983) have detailed how quintessential markers of 'Englishness' were initially denounced and rejected as unacceptable departures from 'English' practice and custom. The police provide us with one of the most striking examples of this process of cultural metamorphosis. As we shall see, initial public responses to the 'bobby' did not envisage him as a defining representation of the English character.

The cultural construction of the English police constable

It is hard to convey the depth of resistance to the idea of 'police' in late eighteenth- and early nineteenth-century England. Available evidence suggests that, because of public sensitivities, considerable attention was paid to the image and styling, demeanour and status of the new police before they finally joined the parish watch (the 'Charlies') on the streets of central London at 6 p.m. Tuesday, 29 September 1829 (Lyman, 1964; Miller, 1977; Palmer, 1988; Hay and Snyder, 1989; Reynolds, 1989; Beattie, 2002; Harris, 2004). As Clive Emsley notes because of the English antipathy to a standing army quartered at home, Metropolitan Police constables did not, in any way, look continental or military. They were dressed in:

> top hats, uniforms of blue, swallow-tail coats with the minimum of decoration, in contrast to the short scarlet tunics with colour facings and piping of the British infantry; the constable's weaponry was limited to a wooden truncheon, though cutlasses were available for emergencies and for patrolling dangerous beats, and inspectors and above could carry pocket pistols. (Emsley, 1991, p. 25)

The new force's officially defined mandate was crime prevention, and constables were given written instructions stressing the need to be civil and obliging to people of every rank, and to respect private property at all times. The force was headed not by a government minister but by two independent commissioners. Even though the 'new police' were drawn from the 'ordinary classes', they faced considerable derision, public hostility and violent resistance to this most 'un-English' of innovations from many different sectors. Well-attended public meetings, placards, posters and petitions demanded the abolition of the 'robin redbreasts', 'crushers', 'bluebottles', 'bobbies', 'coppers', 'raw lobsters' and 'Peelers'. The middle classes protested against having to pay for a public service that both lowered the tone of their neighbourhoods and they did not believe would succeed. The working class objected to the clampdown on leisure pursuits and the unprecedented regulation of public space. London parishes took issue with central government control while police magistrates complained about their loss of power. Political radicals and nascent trade unions objected to the introduction of an 'alien' force of *gendarmerie*, spies and uniformed troublemakers (see Storch, 1975; Reynolds, 1998). The press, both popular and otherwise, highlighted controversial police actions, with *The Times* commenting that the new police was an instrument 'for the purposes of the arbitrary aggression upon the liberties of the people' (*The Times*, 10 January 1842).

Indeed, such was the depth of public animosity that at the conclusion of the inquest into the murder of PC Robert Culley during a political riot in Clerkenwell on 12 May 1833, the coroner's jury brought in a verdict of 'justifiable homicide' (see Thurston, 1967). The jurors concluded 'that no Riot Act was read nor any proclamation advising the people to disperse; that the Government did not take proper precautions to prevent the meeting assembling; and that the conduct of the Police was ferocious, brutal and unprovoked by the people' (quoted in Gould and Waldren, 1986, p. 14). The jurors were feted as public heroes – indeed, a coin was minted to commemorate 'this glorious victory for English liberty'.

There was further public outcry when the police began to expand: for instance, when the Metropolitan Police established a detective department in 1842 and when new police were introduced into other cities in the course of the nineteenth century. In certain parts of the country the new police were forced physically from the streets (see Storch, 1975, 1976; Philips and Storch, 1999).

'One of us': popular cultural representations of the new police

The foregoing is not meant to serve as a definitive survey of the public controversy surrounding the introduction of the new police. However, it does suggest that a considerable amount of very basic cultural as well as political work would have to take place in order for this most 'un-English' of institutions to be first of all sheltered from popular resentment and gradually transformed into one which could be celebrated as 'a very *English* institution ... and the envy of less fortunate people – a reassuring symbol of all being well and tranquil in the world' (Ascoli, 1979, p. 3). Three key measures were needed in order to achieve this.

First, the new police required sustained political patronage and judicial protection. A pattern was established where the authorities refused to investigate allegations of police violence, corruption or malpractice or established commissions and inquiries which either supported the police version of reality or opted for a 'rotten apple' theory to explain acts of deviance and asserted on every possible occasion that the English police was the finest in the world. The judiciary passed exemplary sentences on those who dared to attack or obstruct a constable carrying out his duty.

Second, as historians have established, the police had no choice but to negotiate often 'unspoken' contracts with various social groups. For example, police constables learned to 'turn a blind eye', as far as possible, to middle-class indiscretions and to respond as quickly as possible to their demands. In turn, the urban middle classes began to see the advantages of a routinized and predictable police presence. Political commentators noted with barely disguised relief how the Metropolitan Police handled the great Chartist demonstration in London 1848 and compared this with the mob violence that had engulfed other European capitals (Emsley, 1991). The new police were also forced, because of lack of organizational resources, to reach settlements with elements of the working class. Critical concessions included institutionalizing contacts with informal social control systems and leaving working-class neighbourhoods to police and order themselves (Storch, 1975; Humphries, 1981; White 1986). In certain parts of London, for example, there was virtually no police presence. The real site of struggle was control of movement of the disreputable working class on the main thoroughfares and public squares. The working class also came to realize that not only were the police not going to be abolished but that their presence could be useful in 'sorting out' local disputes. Evidence of this gradual transformation in attitudes can be found in the murder of PC Frederick Atkins on 22 September 1881, which resulted in unprecedented positive press coverage and public sympathy for the police (Gould and Waldren, 1986).

Third, and equally important I would argue to the stabilization of the new institution, was the rapid incorporation of the police constable into Victorian popular culture where he became a normalized presence. Popular cultural representations personalized the general and the abstract, concentrating not on the organization but on the character of the individual constable (Kift, 1986). The formal establishment of the Metropolitan Police detective department in 1842 attracted widespread attention in the popular press and was crucial to both the development of the English detective novel and eventually the myth of Scotland Yard. Prior to this, as Julian Symons has pointed out, crime stories had tended to bestow criminals (operating outside the law and on their own terms) with heroic status. Charles Dickens' public support for the new detective force is very significant – extolling its worth stood in contrast with his barely hidden disdain for virtually every other public official (Collins, 1964; Welsh, 1971; Ousby, 1976; Haining, 1996). The 'Penny Dreadfuls' and 'Yellow Back' novels also provided Victorian readers, of all classes, with exciting stories which foregrounded the deeds of fictional Scotland Yard detectives. The detective novels barely mentioned the uniformed police constable. Even then, the detective is not portrayed as 'all powerful' and needs a cast of other characters to help him do his job (Symons, 1992).

Dickens' Inspector Bucket of *Bleak House* (1853) was the first fictional English police detective and was based on Inspector Fielding of Scotland Yard. There was also the Night Inspector in *Our Mutual Friend* and his detective stories in *Household Words*. Dickens left an unfinished detective novel *The Mystery of Edwin Drood* (1870). For him, the exploits of the new detectives and their villainous foes and rivals were the repository of the most exciting tales of the city. The detectives also provided the author with safe passage when he wanted to visit London's notorious rookeries. Not surprisingly, the reader's understanding of the criminal underworld and police work was constructed through Dickens' detective based perspective.

The first full-length English language detective novel, Wilkie Collins' *The Moonstone* (1868), introduced Victorian England to Sergeant Cuff, who was based on the Scotland Yard detective Jonathan Whicher. In the introduction to a 1998 reprint of *The Moonstone*, Trodd argues that Sergeant Cuff's presence 'has all the social and moral ambiguity surrounding the new detective force appearing to those around him as thief taker, spy, domestic servant and public guardian'. Indeed, Collins positioned his detective very carefully: Sergeant Cuff is neither the main protagonist nor the narrator. He is professionally competent but socially unacceptable to the novel's upper class characters. The local police are represented as socially acceptable but incompetent. The author's intention may have been to accommodate middle-class fears of creating a too effective police force that does not know 'its place'. Sergeant Cuff is also bestowed with an eccentricity that is intended to emphasize that he is not just a crime fighter but quintessentially English. He has an interest in gardens and is an ardent admirer of the virtues of the English rose. Importantly, Sergeant Cuff does not solve the crime, thus reassuring readers that the new detective police were fallible and needed to rely on the help of others (Ashley, 1951).

Marginalization of the public detective took place during the golden age of 'cluedo' detective novels. The police detective and uniformed officer are, for example, quite clearly subordinate to Sir Arthur Conan Doyle's amateur but master sleuth Sherlock Holmes, the most enduring representations of 'English' detective genius (see Miller, 1981; Kayman, 1992).

However, the constable had also acquired his own cultural patrons. *Punch* magazine, established in 1841, was resolutely pro-police and can be seen to have played a pivotal role in popularizing and traditionalizing 'the bobby'. This was done by smothering him in representations of 'Englishness' and constituting him as the embodiment of the national temperament, periodically reminding readers that his creator, Robert Peel, was the epitome of English genius.[1] By 1925, a commentator on police affairs could note: 'if fear of the police is, in England, less acute than it might be and there is culpability in the matter, Mr Punch's artists are to blame … since the days of Leech, whose policemen wore top hats, *Punch* has been busy in delineating the Force with kindliness … geniality and tolerance' (Pulling, 1964).

Crucially, *Punch* took the uniformed constable out of his urban origins and imagined him quintessentially as the avuncular 'village bobby', comparing him favourably with his continental counterparts. *Punch* even managed the tricky public transition when it was decided to replace the constable's top hat with a Prussian style helmet in the late nineteenth century. Emsley (1992) has documented how in this time period popular ballads, street songs and later music hall routines poked fun at the constable and highlighted his liking for tea, beer, cozy resting places, and kitchen maids. And of course Gilbert and Sullivan produced a comic portrayal of the constable in the *Pirates of Penzance* and provided popular culture with the instantly recognizable refrain: 'A Policeman's Lot is not a Happy One' (see Disher, 1955).

The serious press in this period also published editorials which began to extol the unique virtues of the English police. It is also worth noting that the first official history of the organization, written by Lee in 1901, celebrated the uniqueness of a very English institution, tracing the lineage of the constable back to Anglo-Saxon concepts of mutual pledging, collective security and common law (Lee, 1901). The book extolled the genius of Sir Robert Peel and the first two commissioners and exaggerated the faults of the old system. It was stressed that the police of England, unlike other police forces, were *of the people* and supported *by the people*. Lee also emphasized the unique orderly nature of English society that made the success of the new police a foregone conclusion, completely ignoring the extent and nature of local hostility and opposition. This text is significant because subsequent popular studies of the police uncritically reproduced Lee's Whiggish version of history.

It is important to keep in mind, however, that popular resentment of the police endured well into the late nineteenth and twentieth centuries. Ford and Harrison (1983) unearthed a remarkable photograph of the effigy of a much-disliked village policeman, PC Rover, about to be burnt at the Stebbing, Essex 'Guy Fox' bonfire of 1880. The front-line public order role played by the police in the social and economic conflict which characterized 1918–1940 de-stabilized their relations with virtually all sections of the working class. During the 1930s, violent confrontations with the police were endemic in certain parts of the country. Moreover, revelations of police corruption, public scandals over the use of 'stop-and-search' powers and the police role in the enforcement of the new Road Traffic Act of 1930 threatened to rupture carefully cultivated relationships with the middle classes.

There were also forces intensifying the by now 'traditional' representation of the English 'bobby'. Unqualified political support was forthcoming from the governments of the day and the police also found new political backers in the form of the parliamentary Labour party who were desperate to prove their acceptability and credibility. Virtually all shades of upper- and middle-class opinion mobilized behind the police in the aftermath of the shoot-out with anarchists in Tottenham in January 1909 and the Sidney Street Seige, Stepney in 1911 (Rumbelow, 1988), with many joining the special constabulary during the 1926 General Strike. BBC radio broadcasts and cinema newsreels edited incidents of police violence heavily and went to remarkable lengths to cast the police as 'the thin blue line' or caught in the middle of extremists. During the General Strike the media were responsible for disseminating one of the defining images of a benign police force – police officers playing football with strikers (see Emsley, 1991, p. 169)

By now the police were also in a position to produce and disseminate their own self-authenticating narratives:

1 Ex-police officers wrote a series of autobiographies/memoirs and popular histories which were overwhelmingly positive in orientation (see, for example, Dilnot, 1930; Adam 1931; Cornish 1935; Tomlin, 1936; Gollomb, 1938). Each publication built uncritically upon the previous one and effectively reproduced the same Whiggish storylines, all of which steeped 'the bobby' in 'Englishness'. They asserted that the English had found the secret to effective law enforcement because England was governed through 'common law' rather than the Napoleonic Code. Indeed, some of the more extreme narratives attributed the success of the British police to the racial characteristics of the Anglo-Saxons: the English had a 'flair' for law and order in the same way as the French had a natural flair for criminality and cooking! Police officers also gave advice to the generation of authors responsible for the 'golden age' of detective novels.

2 The formation of the Police Federation in 1919 as the negotiating body for rank and file officers was also significant. From the outset, the Federation concerned itself with policing its past and projecting *a particular representation* of the English police officer. In doing this, the Federation constructed an historical narrative that idealized the identity of constable by reproducing the 'best' of the popular cultural representations, available histories, and political statements which emphasized that England had the finest police force in the world.

3 The centenary anniversary of the founding of the Metropolitan Police was marked by the publication of its first official history (Moylan, 1929) and numerous newspaper articles detailing the origins and uniqueness of 'the bobby'. Official acknowledgement of the event was forthcoming in the form of an inspection by the Prince of Wales in Hyde Park. This was vital in the further traditionalizing of the force and the inception of organizational traditions.

4 In 1929 Scotland Yard appointed a full-time press office to brief crime reporters and Home Affairs correspondents. In the same year, in an unprecedented move, PC Harry Daley gave a series of talks on the radio on the life of an 'ordinary copper' (Emsley, 1991). This was reinforced by the emergence of what became known as a Reithian conception of the historical uniqueness of the British policing system (see Reith, 1938; 1943):

The new cinema was, not surprisingly, a key site of struggle in representations of the police. The forces of law and order undoubtedly benefited from the hand-in-glove relationship between the British film industry and national institutions and the fact that strict censorship 'ensured that British crime films kept a respectable distance from the sordid realities of the underworld. No reference to drugs or prostitution was permitted, scenes inside prison were forbidden, depiction of criminals carrying out crime in a realistic way was discouraged' (Richards, 2001). Nonetheless, there were unflattering depictions. In 2005 the BBC broadcast restored versions of films made by Sagar Mitchell and James Keynon, the pioneers of British commercial cinema. The reels included incredible documentary footage of late Victorian and early Edwardian Manchester police officers and comedies which featured constables being made fun of by youths. To the annoyance of some police officers, American Mack Sennett's ever popular slapstick *Keystone Kops* was joined by English films such as *Blue Bottles* (1928), *Ask a Policeman* (1939) and *It's That Man Again* (1942) which continued to reproduce the 'good-hearted-but-dim-witted' comic celluloid representations of 'the bobby':

> Although the old type of policeman has gone, the public are not allowed to believe it, because in the most recent films, in stage plays, and more especially on the radio, the policeman is always portrayed as a kind of 'country yokel', with no brains, a Somerset accent, and a most horrible lack of manner or common sense. In the modern detective novels and plays the private detective always clears up the crime in less time than a 'copper' can fill his pipe. There are frequently unjust and mean jibes at the police, but no retaliatory measures are taken ... the policemen get far too much criticism and too little praise. (Aytee, 1942)

As a result, between 1829 and 1939, on the various stages of popular culture the uniformed English police constable was actualized via a whole series of characteristics, many of which were unflattering. As was noted previously, popular culture portrayed 'the bobby' as an incompetent, harmless, benign, good natured, deferential individual, partial to a drink and a pretty girl's smile. His counterpart – the village constable – was illustrated in even less flattering terms. However, in the long run, as Emsley argues, these 'indulgent' popular cultural representations humanized and individualized officers and one suspects went a considerable way to deflating popular suspicion and resentment. They also reaffirmed that the English could laugh at themselves, would not stand for pomposity in its public officials and had nothing to fear from a police officer.

The second part of this chapter will analyse how the Ealing Studio film *The Blue Lamp*, ruptured pre-war representations and re-assembled, in the form of PC George Dixon, the iconic depiction of the English 'bobby' on the beat. This film would have an immense impact on popular perceptions of the police giving rise to the spin off BBC television series *Dixon of Dock Green* which consolidated the representation of the 'Iconic PC' that would become a enduring part of English culture. And as we shall see in the next chapter, this representation would also provide the crucially important context for the first sociological studies of the British police.

The iconic police constable: the cultural construction of PC George Dixon

In the immediate post-war period, English national identity underwent an unprecedented crisis, lurching between a sense of embittered anti-climax because daily life was burdened by rationing, austerity and bureaucratic red tape; a sense of deep loss, yearning for the past and fear of the future; and self-deception and illusions of grandeur in the form of dream-like forecasts of the coming of a 'New Jerusalem' (Hopkins, 1964).

Nothing exemplified the national identity crisis more than the output of the English film studios. During the Second World War, they had played a crucial role in defining and communicating the essential characteristics of the 'English' way of life that people were being asked to defend (Furhammer and Isaksson, 1971; Hodgkinson and Sheratsky, 1982; Richards and Aldgate, 1983; Hurd, 1984; Taylor, 1987; Coultras, 1989; Landy, 1991; Chapman, 1998). In the decade after the war, many of the studios, in an attempt to hold the national audience that had flocked in their millions to the cinema during the war years, produced self-authenticating celebrations of 'the people as collective hero' as well as broadening connotations of national identity (Richards, 1997). A 'traditional' look was adopted in order to make a spate of post-war films resemble those made during the war years, 'deliberately obscuring the passage of time, and continuing to visually merge the documentary and fictional traditions that was a notable feature of 1939–1945' (Ramsden, 1987). The nostalgia present in some of these films is heart-rendering with pre-war 'England' becoming an 'imagined community' of long, hot summer days, village greens, quiet meadows and cricket matches.

In the same historical moment, English society felt itself under siege from a violent crime wave and unchecked juvenile delinquency (Mannheim, 1946; Taylor, 1981; Morris, 1989; Thomas, 2003). Mark Benney, the *Daily Mirror's* crime reporter, captured the unfolding crime crisis in the following terms:

> The crime wave for which the police have been preparing ever since the end of hostilities is breaking upon us. Armed robberies of the most violent and vicious kind feature daily in the newspapers. Even the pettiest crimes are, it seems, conducted with a loaded revolver to hand. And well-planned robberies, reminiscent of the heyday of Chicago gangsterdom, have relieved Londoners of £60,000 worth of jewellery in the past week alone. Holdups of cinemas, post offices and railway booking offices have already become so commonplace that the newspapers scarcely bother to report them. To deal with the situation the police are being forced to adopt methods more akin to riot breaking than crime detection. (Quoted in Murphy, 1993, p. 89)

The consensus was that the war had created the conditions in which criminality could flourish. There was also a very real concern that post-war youngsters would be much more prone to delinquency and anti-social behaviour than previous generations (Hodgkin, 1948; Smithies, 1982; Hebdige, 1988). Particular attention was paid to the supposedly corrupting influence of a spate of popular Hollywood gangster and homemade 'Spiv movies' which flourished between 1945 and 1950. The former were a cause for concern because of their heightened 'ripped-from-the-headlines' realism and the blurring of the boundaries between villain and hero (Doherty, 1988; Clay, 1998; Arthur, 2001; Spicer, 2002). Low-budget, commercially viable British 'riff-raff realist' movies were also criticized for their representation of that most transgressive of characters, the Spiv:

> ... the grinning 'Spivs', the 'wide boys', the barrow boys and the 'wheelers' gradually endeared themselves to the general public. The archetypal 'Spiv' wore yellow shoes, a wide lapelled suit and a wide tie, and sported a shifty little trilby pulled rakishly over the forehead. He symbolised a flashy flaunting of authority and petty regulations – especially towards the end of the war when people were long tired of self-denial and the many wartime restrictions ... (Minns, 1980, p. 160; see also Sarto, 1949; Deacon, 1980; Hughes, 1986; Clay, 1998; Wollen, 1998)

Film critics and social commentators condemned Spiv films for the casting of charismatic actors as violent, 'Americanized' hero-villains; the glamorizing of sordid, petty criminal lifestyles and the depiction of the police not just as comic but as cynical and corrupt. Alongside moves to censor the Spiv film were demands that British film studios redress the balance by producing socially responsible and morally uplifting films which would condemn criminality and delinquency, project positive role models for the nation's youth and mobilise public support for the forces of law and order (Murphy, 1999). It was in the context of an intensifying moral panic about the wave of real and celluloid 'gangsterism' and delinquency supposedly sweeping the country that Ealing Studios began work on *The Blue Lamp*. It is not surprising that the film would relate in complex ways to both the stylistic shifts in the crime film genre and the social turmoil of the immediate post-war era.

All those involved in the production of *The Blue Lamp* were conscious of their social responsibilities. Only Ealing Studios was capable of realizing such a cultural project. The studio's instantly recognizable 'national narrative' style, which finally came together during the 1940s and first half of the 1950s, combined conventional cinematic structures with 1930s' documentary realism. Ealing's high-quality films had good entertainment value, included a degree of escapism and, despite the fact that the studio operated under the control of the Ministry of Information, 'softened' the visually and emotionally excessive propagandistic elements. However, there could be no doubt that the films produced by Ealing Studios were 'rooted in the soil' and sensibilities of the nation (Balcon, 1969; see also Kardish, 1984; Harper, 1994; Richards, 1997; Drazin, 1998; BBC, 2002).

The inspiration for the film lay with the murder of Police Constable Nathaniel Edgar on 13 February 1948. He was the first Metropolitan Police officer to be murdered after the war and the hunt for his killer and the funeral dominated the front pages of the popular newspapers. An army deserter, Donald George Thomas, aged 22, was found guilty of the murder but because the death penalty had been suspended was committed to penal servitude for life (Christoph, 1962). Sydney Box, a Gainsborough film producer, assigned Jan Read, Gainsborough's script editor, and Ted Willis to work up a script specifically recounted from the point of view of police officers (Aldgate and Richards, 1999). As part of his initial research Willis immersed himself in the everyday routines of police work, thus anticipating the methodology that sociologists of the police would use. Willis spent a considerable amount of time in the company of an Inspector Mott, an 'old time copper' who became the inspiration for the central police character of the proposed screenplay. Scotland Yard was assured that Ealing Studios' heroic dramatization of the English police constable would shatter the one-dimensional comic depictions of the constable prevalent in pre-war films. Willis noted that he was only too aware that:

> Up to that time the British policeman had usually been portrayed as a bumbling simpleton who habitually licked the stub of a pencil, was respectful to the Squire and left the investigation and solution of serious crime to brilliant educated amateurs like Sherlock Holmes and Lord Peter Wimsey. (1991, p. 70)

Completion of the screenplay coincided with the unexpected closure of Gainsborough Studios. Michael Balcon, the head of Ealing Studios picked up the script and to the disappointment of Read and Willis it was handed on to T.E.B Clarke for refinement. The choice of Clarke, Ealing's most influential post-war script writer, to work on the film was significant because it 'suggests the importance attached to finding a screenwriter who was politically reliable. As an ex-War Reserve Constable, Clarke fitted the bill admirably' (Chibnall, 1997). Clarke's inside knowledge of the police meant that his re-drafting of the script deepened the already police-centred perspective. The producer–director team was Michael Relph and Basil Dearden, whose films consistently tried 'to grasp the totality of England as a unity, a family structure: local solidarity and mutual responsibility writ large' (Barr, 1980, p. 83).

Careful attention was paid to choosing a cast that would be instantly recognizable to the film-going public. Jack Warner, the former East End vaudeville star, was the obvious choice to play PC George Dixon since he had appeared as the personification of working-class paternal values in several films. It was assumed that audiences would instantly side with 'his warm, natural humour and common sense' (Clarke, 1974, p. 158). Another music hall star, Gladys Hensen, was cast to play his wife. Jimmy Hanley, who played the typical boy next door or friend to the hero in a series of films, was cast as the new recruit PC Andy Mitchell. Dirk Bogarde, hitherto a romantic lead, was given his first 'heavy' role as Tom Riley, the embodiment of a new generation of reckless young criminals threatening the nation. Basil Dearden was in no doubt about Bogarde's role telling the actor that he need 'a weedy type' to play 'the snivelling little killer. Neurotic, conceited, gets the rope in the end.' (Bogarde, 1978, p. 128). In its narrative construction, particularly after the British Board of Film Censors had finished editing the script, the role of hero would be shifted from the 'Spiv' to the police constable (Robertson, 1985; Aldgate, 1992).

During shooting, the film-makers were provided with unparalleled Metropolitan Police co-operation, advice and facilities. In fact, the actors were tutored by senior Scotland Yard detectives and police officers also appeared as extras. Jack Warner notes how there were probably more real policemen than actors in *The Blue Lamp*. In addition, the production crew was provided with unique day and night access to locations across London and to the inside of police stations. The hard-edged streets of Paddington, Ladbroke Grove, Maida Vale and White City provided a suitably urban backdrop.

Ealing's publicity campaign for the film even used noir style posters and realist straplines to suggest that *The Blue Lamp* was a frenetic crime thriller movie: 'The battle with the post-war gun man blazes to life on the British screen for the first time'; 'The unending battle of the city streets'; 'Scotland Yard in action as death stalks the streets'; 'The street is their 'no-man's' land'; 'Scotland Yard at grips with post-war crime'; 'The greatest murder hunt the screen has ever shown'; 'Secrets of Scotland Yard on the screens for the first time'; '999- and the hunt is on'; 'Through fear he shot a policeman. Through fear he was betrayed'; 'The inside story of Britain's crime wave'.

An action-packed opening sequence does not disappoint viewers. It starts with the police pursuing criminals in a high-speed car chase through the bomb-damaged streets of London. The car driven by the hoodlums crashes and they shoot an innocent shopkeeper as they attempt to flee the crime scene. Aldgate and Richards (1999) argue that audiences would have been immediately reminded of the gunning-down of a passer-by in central London while he was trying to stop a burglary on the Tottenham Court Road in 1947. The urgent realism is heightened by the flashing of 'crime wave' newspaper headlines across the screen: 'Murder in the streets; father of six killed by gunman'; '70mph police chase ends in crash'; 'Stolen car strikes woman in West End crash'; '2 women fight bandits in London street'; 'Bank gunman found dying'; 'Double murder tests by CID'; 'Gunman holds up shop girl'.

The narrator informs the viewer that:

> To this man until today, the crime wave was nothing but a newspaper headline. What stands between the ordinary public and this outbreak of crime? What protection has the man in the street against this armed threat to life and property? At the Old Bailey, Mr Justice Fidmore in passing sentence for a crime of robbery with violence gave this plain answer: 'This is perhaps another illustration of the disaster caused by insufficient numbers of police. I have no doubt that one of the best preventives of crime is the regular uniformed police officer on the beat'.

Figure 1.1a   PC George Dixon: the iconic constable

The voiceover continues: 'Veterans like George Dixon with 25 years service and now PC693 attached to Paddington Green and young men like Andy Mitchell who has just completed his training'.

PC George Dixon of Dock Green

Moving on from pre-war representations, a range of meaning is constructed around the figure of PC George Dixon. He is portrayed as an uncomplicated, down to earth, seen-it-all London 'bobby' who knows his 'manor' inside out and who is called upon to police the everyday rather than serious crime. Because of his devotion to 'the job' he enjoys the respect of senior officers and all sections of the locality, including the petty criminal elements. The film's press book explains that:

> He is representative of all policemen throughout the country, steady going, tolerant, unarmed, carrying out a multitude of duties. He directs traffic, helps kiddies across the road, moves on the barrow boys, keeps an eye on property.

When crimes take place his investigations are soon taken over by Scotland Yard, but there is always the danger of armed thugs, planned hold-ups, smash and grab raids.

As one of his last responsibilities before retirement, a reluctant PC Dixon is given the role of 'puppy walking' Probationary Constable 814D Andy Mitchell and familiarizing him with the manor in which he will be working. We see them intersecting and interacting with a complex range of human behaviour and predicaments. Drama is clearly not the stuff of 'welfare policing'. The many supporting characters who populate the film are used to show that the white working class community's attitude to the police ranges from respect through to wariness and resentment. Dixon gradually takes a protective interest in the young constable and their relationship unfolds as a model of father–son closeness. The audience is familiarized with not just the day and night routines of working the street and the ebb and flow of local crime and disorder but also with the informal 'canteen culture' and the warm and humorous home life of George Dixon. The basis of the relationship between him and 'Ma' Dixon is companionship and the shared experience of public service and the war. His off-duty character is fleshed out via his devotional tending to his plants and flowers, which of course is reminiscent of Sergeant Cuff. The probationary constable, who is not a Londoner, is offered lodgings and he quickly becomes a replacement son. As Barr notes:

> What Mitchell has been absorbed into is a family. First a literal one: he finds lodgings with Dixon and his wife, and comes to fill the place of their son of the same age who has been killed in the war. Second, a professional family: the close community of the police station in Paddington, characterised by convivial institutions; canteen, darts team, choir; and by bantering but loyal relationships within a hierarchy. Third, the nation as a family, which may have its tensions and rows but whose members share common standards and loyalties; in a crisis, the police can call upon a general respect and will to co-operate. This sense of national family ... is built very profoundly into the structure of the film. (1980, p. 84)

In time-honoured Ealing fashion, *The Blue Lamp*'s many sub-plots present the audience with the world of ordinary people in the neighbourhood, workplace and the family. As various commentators have noted, the film spells out the moral basis of this imaginary community: restraint, self-sacrifice and emotional understatement. Social stability is reproduced through a web of intimate, differentiated relationships generated by the bonding routines of work, family and communal off-duty activities. This critical context highlights the need for young men to be absorbed into traditional work relationships where they can learn to understand the importance of duty, obligation and responsibility. This commendable 'in-built' world of the cultural values and 'structures of feeling' of 'old' London is contrasted starkly with the representation of young children running wild in bomb-scarred neighbourhoods, over-crowded, dilapidated tenement blocks and gangs of youths congregating in the garish 'wild' West End. The narrative repeatedly invokes newspaper discourses about dangerous young tearaways and violent criminals on the road to ruin, a police force stretched to the limits, fractured post-war communities and the influence of London's 'square mile of vice' (see Tietjen, 1956; Kohn, 1992).

The criminal threat

Dirk Bogarde's character, Tom Riley and his sidekick 'Spud' are constructed to exemplify a very different youthful masculinity to that of the respectable PC Mitchell. The voiceover tells us that:

> These restless and ill-adjusted youngsters have produced a type of delinquent partly responsible for the post-war increase in crime. Some are content with pilfering and petty theft, others with more bravado graduate to more serious offences.

We then get the first glimpse of the Spiv-like Riley and Spud lighting cigarettes in Piccadilly Circus before making their way to a dimly lit snooker hall to seek the support of the local crime boss. The voiceover informs us that they are:

> Youths with brain enough to plan and organise criminal adventures but who lack the code, experience and self-discipline of the professional thief, which sets them as 'a class apart'. All the more dangerous because of their immaturity. Young men such as these two present a new problem to the police. Men, as yet, without records or whose natural cunning or ruthless use of violence has so far kept them out of trouble.

As the film progresses, the characters of Tom Riley, Spud and Riley's girlfriend, Diana Lewis, offer the audience a view of what happens when traditional forms of informal social control break down and repressed desires are allowed to play out in an unregulated manner. The film implies that the excess of individualism and hedonism of these wayward youths is threatening the very fabric of the fabled Ealing Studio's version of the community and indeed the nation. The criminal machinations of Riley and Spud and the suggested sexual relationship between Riley and Lewis in their dingy bedsit magnify the permissiveness threat they represent to the social order.

Tom Riley is portrayed as a threatening, immature young man (with no stable family home or settled class or community context) acting out scenes from his favourite gangster movies. He is also outside London's ordinary, decent professional criminal community whose ethos is depicted as 'dishonest but decent, shady but entirely predictable. They stick to their accepted territory: the billiard hall, the dog track, like a stamp to a letter, adopting a deferential manner to the police, and even assisting them when mutual codes are violated' (Chibnall, 1997, p. 140). In one scene, Mr Randall, the crime boss, rejects Riley's attempt to involve them in their plans: 'What happens if you get done? You little layabouts are all the same. You'd scream your 'ead off. Then the bogeys get on to me. Stick to gas meters sonny'.

All Tom Riley has to depend on is a 'flashy' materially oriented West End emergent youth subculture that despises broader communal bonds and looks on the code of London's traditional criminal fraternity and the police with disdain. The relationship between the conscience-free, arrogant Riley and the 'hysterical' peroxide blonde Diana Lewis is tension ridden with an ever-present petulance and petty jealousies. When the camera first alights on 17-year-old Diana she is walking through a crowded neon-lit London street, jazz playing in the background. The voiceover tells the audience that she is 'a young girl showing the effects of a childhood spent in a broken home and demoralised by war'. Her desire for self-esteem and a more exciting life leads her to declare to a female police officer that she would kill herself rather than go back to the dismal, brutal home environment that she has run away from. As the film progresses, we see that Diana Lewis is obsessively attracted to the good looks and edgy attitude of Riley and the bright lights of the West End.

The Sacriligious act: the murder of PC Dixon

Tom Riley's do-whatever-it-takes-to-prove-yourself graduation from petty crime to armed robbery and murder develops its own terrible momentum. His willingness to use violence is made clear early on in the film when he 'coshes' a police officer who has disturbed their first big robbery. The emotionally charged 'moment of truth' in *The Blue Lamp* originates roughly halfway through the film when PC George Dixon confronts Tom Riley as he attempts to flee from the scene of an armed robbery of the Coliseum picture house that has gone dreadfully wrong. This pivotal scene is stretched out to make sure the audience witnesses just how vulnerable the unarmed police officer is when faced with this new generation of gun-toting young criminals. Dixon tells Riley not to be a fool and to drop the revolver.

> *Tom Riley*: Get back!
> *PC Dixon*: Drop that and don't be a fool. Drop it, I say!
> *Riley*: I'll drop you!

> *Dixon walks forward despite Riley's panic.*

> *Tom Riley*: Get back! This thing works. Get back! Get back, I say! Get back!

Then, in an unprecedented moment in English cinema, the masked teenage gunman panics and fires two shots at point-blank range into PC Dixon. For the first time an audience has been allowed to bear witness to a close-up cold-blooded shooting of a uniformed police officer. The drama of this violent

Figure 1.1b   Tom Riley confronting Dixon: from delinquent to 'cop killer'

interruption contrasts sharply with the banality of the setting: PC Dixon on his night beat just after informing his colleagues that he has decided to postpone his retirement and a couple squabbling in the foyer of the Coliseum picture house. The audience is forced at this moment to recognize that this film, in line with the conventions of *film noir*, is not going to have a conventional happy ending. Dixon will not survive the operation to save his life. Riley's desperate eyes convey a terrible truth: his cowardly act has shattered the hopes of a consensual post-war social democratic order and generational relationships. Jack Warner was clearly aware of the potential impact this dramatic moment of self-sacrifice would have on audiences: 'I realized that the murder of the policeman, far from eliminating him, really gave him a martyr's crown as a man never to be forgotten and that any audience would readily understand the spirit of the film and the message it conveyed' (Warner, 1975, p. 54; Warner, 1979).

One of the most poignant moments in the film comes when PC Andy Mitchell has to tell 'Ma' Dixon that her husband has died in the hospital. She is getting ready to go the hospital with a bunch of George Dixon's flowers from the garden when she realizes 'he's dead'. She puts the flowers in water before breaking down and crying on Mitchell's shoulder. PC Mitchell swears to her that they will apprehend the killer. Her dignified response allows the audience to understand the enormity of the crime of murdering an unarmed bobby on the beat.

The restoration of social order

The gunning-down of PC Dixon transforms the film into a classic 'police hunt down violent criminals' crime movie. We witness the behind-the-scene assembling of the Scotland Yard operation to catch 'the bastard that shot George Dixon'. There will be no escape for the juvenile Spiv-turned-cop killer. Justice will prevail because Scotland Yard CID – the world's most professional crime-fighting machine – has been mobilized. In addition, even the most anti-police sections of the community are shocked by the murder of a 'copper'. A street trader who we have already seen Dixon moving along declares to PC Mitchell that although he does not have much time for 'coppers' he does not approve of shooting them. This theme is exemplified by the detectives' encounter with Queenie, the tough little street urchin who has found the murder weapon. Initially she refuses to co-operate telling them that her dad has warned her against talking to 'coppers'. The conversation gradually moves to a more focused question:

> Detective: Do you know what a murderer is?
> Queenie: Someone who gets hanged.
> Detective: That's it. We think you can help us catch one. We want you to show us where you found that revolver. Will you take us there?

After Queenie shows them the canal where she found the revolver she asks 'will you be able to hang him now?' The detective quietly replies 'We'll see Queenie. We'll see'.

His growing realization that the police are closing in leads Tom Riley to go voluntarily to the police station in an attempt to clear his name. However, his over-confident attitude and contradictory answers arouse the suspicions of the detectives who interview him. He survives a hastily convened ID parade but is tailed. He finds Diana in Spud's lodgings and when she refuses to accompany him Riley tries to strangle her. A detective bursts through the door with Diana screaming 'He shot that copper. He was the one that killed him. Tom Riley killed him'. He steals a car, and in an extended car chase, that echoes the films opening scenes radio-controlled squad cars block every possible escape route. Eventually the stolen Buick crashes, Spud is badly injured or dead and Riley flees on foot across the railway tracks with PC Mitchell in pursuit.

In a remarkable sequence filmed at London's White City greyhound stadium, a desperate Riley thinks he has found anonymity and safety among 30,000 milling race fans. However, he is isolated and captured as a result of the co-operation between the stadium management, the gangsters (who control the betting) and the police. The cornered cop killer pulls a gun on advancing police officers but is pushed to the ground as the crowd rushes to leave the stadium. PC Mitchell removes the revolver from Riley. The film does not tell the audience what happens to Riley after his capture. For Medhurst (1986,

p. 300), it may seem odd that a film so concerned with criminal justice fails to include a concluding trial scene with Riley being sentenced to death, 'but the punishment has already been dealt out, in far more iconographically powerful terms, as the stadium crowd close in on the individual transgressor'. In classic Durkheimian terms, the film thus re-creates the fabled moral boundaries of the communal order. The penultimate scene shows footage of Andy Mitchell, now a veteran police officer, walking George Dixon's old beat giving advice to a member of the public. The film closes with a shot of the 'the blue lamp', the symbol of law and order, hanging outside Paddington police station. The final message would seem to be that you can murder a human being but not a sacred social institution.

Critical perspectives on the *The Blue Lamp*

Precise audience reception of *The Blue Lamp* is impossible to measure in any systematic manner, not least because it is now difficult to separate the film from its own mythology and because we do not have available evidence. We do know that the film was a box office success, and won the Best British Film of the Year award, with *Motion Picture Herald* voting Jack Warner Top British Male Actor for 1950. However, we do not have evidence of how younger members of the audience responded to what was in effect a film that had been scripted to exploit the public fears and anxieties about materialistic, sexually active juvenile delinquents. Certain film historians cannot believe that Ealing Studios expected the nation's youth to side with the 'drab, bland and neutered' character of PC Andy Mitchell over the 'compelling, thrilling and above all erotic' character of Tom Riley, played by Dirk Bogarde (Medhurst, 1986, p. 347).

We need to keep in mind that Bogarde was at the forefront of redefining English male roles in the post-war British cinema and his star quality and good looks gave him 'heart throb' status in the 1950s (Coldstream, 2004). Despite the best efforts of the Ealing Studios, the Metropolitan Police and the British Board of Film Censors, Bogarde's dramatization of Riley's pent-up rage and murderous desires renders him a much more noirish, glamorous villain than may have been intended. Morley (1999, p. 40) comments that his cocky performance destabilizes the heroic centre of the film because he manages to communicate 'the sexiness of evil'. An extended scene in which Riley shows a very frightened Diana Lewis how he is going to use the newly acquired revolver he is playing with to get what he wants intimates the link between sexuality and the thrill of violence.

> *Diana Lewis:* Do you ever get scared?
> *Tom Riley:* Yeah, course I do. It's a kind of excitement.
> *Diana Lewis:* You mean you like it?
> *Tom Riley:* It makes you think quicker. You're all keyed up and afterwards you feel terrific like ...

The scene ends with the one wildly passionate embrace in the film. Bogarde was in effect allowed by Ealing Studios for box office reasons to play one of the first British examples of the street-smart, violent young criminal already on view in Hollywood. And of course in his attitude he anticipates the Teddy Boys, the first fully-fledged English youth subculture of the post war period (Rock and Cohen, 1976).

Police reaction to the film was positive. Sir Harold Scott, then Commissioner of the Metropolitan Police, approved of the final product, describing it as 'a faithful picture of the policeman's life and work ... [and] a valuable means of spreading a knowledge of the efficiency and high traditions of the Metropolitan Police' (Scott, 1957, p. 100). Indeed, after the film's premier, the Metropolitan Police presented Jack Warner with a casket and scroll.

Across a broad range of political leanings, the press (though not all as we shall see below) responded well to the film – it was welcomed by *The Star* 'as an overdue apology for that flat-footed squad of "What's all this 'ere?" semi-comic policemen who have plodded through so many British films' (*Star*, 20 January 1950). *The Times* (20 January 1950) congratulated the film-makers on their 'sincerity' and 'realism': 'it is not only foreigners who find the English policeman wonderful, and in composing this tribute to him, the Ealing Studio are giving conscious expression to a general sentiment. The tribute is a handsome one'. *The Daily Worker* (21 January 1950) informed its readers that 'We have been told so often that our policemen are wonderful that it is not surprising that someone should have made a film to prove it once and for all'. *Cine Weekly* (12 January 1950) lauded the film as a 'gripping and intensely human "crime does not pay" melodrama' which is 'a worthy and eloquent tribute to our policemen'. On the other side of the Atlantic, *The New York Times* (9 January 1951) described it as 'a warm and affectionate tribute'.

However, some contemporary reviews winced at the one-sidedness of the film and criticized the sentimental representation of the police and its overall nostalgic orientation. The *Spectator* (20 January 1950), for example, described the film as a 'sincere if slightly sentimental' homage to 'that portion of our police force which wears a helmet, tells us the time, and accuses us of being an obstruction: the constable, in fact ... the production encourages us in our belief that all policemen are courteous, incorruptible nannies'. Some film critics argued that the film's limitations were symptomatic of the failure of British films to get to grips with their subjects. *The Times* (20 January 1950) film reviewer noted that:

> When the camera shifts to the persons of Police Constable Dixon and Police Constable Mitchell there is no longer the certainty of reality accurately observed and accurately presented. There is the indefinable feel of the theatrical backcloth behind their words and actions. Mr Jack Warner and Mr Jimmy Hanley do all that can be done, but the sense that the policemen they are acting are not policemen as they really are but policemen *as an indulgent tradition* has chosen to think they are will not be banished

Film Monthly (Jan/Feb 1950) and *Sight and Sound* (Enley, 1950) were scathing in their views on the tired, hackneyed nature of the Warner/Hanley partnership. Reviewers also noted that the film's ideological celebration of the Metropolitan Police compromised the very possibility of realism as did the lament for the national unity and community spirit exhibited during the Second World War.

Conclusion: the long shadow of the iconic police constable

This chapter has analysed the many ingredients that went into the popular cultural making and remaking of the English 'bobby', and he was ideologically nurtured with great care. The on-screen murder of PC George Dixon represented the final step in the English 'bobby's' transformation into an idealized representation of Englishness. The cultural project inaugurated by the Ealing Studios was concluded on 9 July 1955 when 58-year-old Jack Warner was miraculously resurrected as PC George Dixon in the BBC TV series *Dixon of Dock Green*. Ted Willis and Jan Read had retained the stage rights for the film script and a version of the film was subsequently staged at theatres in Oxford and Blackpool before playing at the London Hippodrome between November 1952 and March 1953. Willis took responsibility for scripting an initial six-episode television series that would afford audiences the happy ending that he had deprived them of in *The Blue Lamp*. The new police drama was commissioned to replace *Fabian of Scotland Yard*. Every Saturday evening the programme opened with the theme music and PC Dixon's warm-hearted 'Evening, all'. The nation was presented with an overwhelmingly benign view of police work and police–community relations in 'Dock Green'. The early shows ended with Dixon walking down the steps of the fictional East End police station – 'within earshot of Bow Bells and hard by Old Father Thames' – summing up the solved case under the 'blue lamp'. He would salute the audience and stroll out of shot whistling the old music hall song 'Maybe it's because I'm a Londoner'. Because Jack Warner felt that PC Dixon should be representative of 'the bobby' on the beat of any English town or city, rather than the nation's capital, the theme tune was subsequently changed to 'An ordinary copper', one of the BBC's classic evocative tunes (see Clarke, 1983; Sydney-Smith, 2002; Cooke, 2003; BBC, 2006)

Certain television critics and social commentators were shocked that the BBC could have chosen to revive what one described as the sentimental 'reassuring, never, never, world of "hearts of gold" coppers and "cor blimey crooks"' (see Vahimaji, 1994, p. 48). However, the comforting representations and reassuring moral epilogues established an intimate rapport between viewers at a time when television was still something of a novelty. In 1961 it was the second most popular programme on television with an audience of almost 14 million viewers (Willis, 1964). By this time viewers could also purchase *Dixon of Dock Green: My Life by George Dixon* which provided background information on his

East End childhood and why he joined the police (Willis and Graham, 1964; also Edwards, 1974). Dixon, who was finally promoted to sergeant in 1964, policed his 'Dock Green' manor until May 1976 and 'Evening, all' had become a national catchphrase. The success of the new breed of 'realist' police officers in *Z Cars, Softly, Softly, The Sweeney* and the first wave of US cop shows did force the programme makers to update the programme's storylines and characters. And, as we shall see in Chapter 4, subsequent film-makers and television companies would use frantic, restless camera work to present 'celluloid cops' in deconstructed forms and expressions that were a far cry from *The Blue Lamp* and *Dixon of Dock Green*.

Ealing Studios and the BBC produced, in the form of PC George Dixon, the authoritative black-and-white image of the 'bobby on the beat', providing the cultural parameters within which post-war English policing would be understood and debated. In June 1981 14 officers from the Metropolitan Police and Kent constabulary formed a guard of honour at Jack Warner's funeral with Assistant Deputy Commissioner George Rushbank noting that the force had a 'warm affection' for the actor immortalized as *Dixon of Dock Green*: 'he was our kind of policeman'. A wreath in the shape of a 'Blue Lamp' had been placed on top of the coffin. The BBC broadcast an episode of *Dixon of Dock Green* as a tribute. Nonetheless, in that same year television cameras were transmitting images of London police officers using dustbin lids and milk crates to shield themselves from rioters hurling stones and petrol bombs and police vehicles speeding through burning neighbourhoods. How policing had moved 'from Dixon to Brixton' was the pressing question that a bewildered British establishment had to face.

The Dixonian myth continues to haunt contemporary debates about policing. As we shall see in later chapters, calls for the modernisation of policing to meet the challenges of twenty-first-century global criminality are routinely accompanied by the declaration that it is time to exorcise once and for all the 'once upon a time' – Dixonian policing model. In 1997, for example, a *Police Review* article – 'Dispelling the Dixon myth' – concluded that 'as we head towards a new century, we owe it to the old boy to cut him adrift and consign him to his place in history' (Hicks, 1977). However, when politicians and commentators seek to summon forth a lost 'golden age' of 'Englishness' marked by national unity, cultural cohesion, neighbourliness and law and order they now reach – intuitively it seems – for pre-1960s images' of county cricket grounds, village greens, red telephone boxes, rose-trellised gardens, warm beer and of course PC George Dixon pounding his beat. 'Dixonian' is now routinely evoked as a form of shorthand to define the traditional values of English policing and society.

And what is truly remarkable is that we continue to hear calls to bring back *Dixon of Dock Green*. In 1999, Malcolm McLaren, the Svengali of contemporary British youth culture, promised voters that if he was elected Lord Mayor of London, a hologram of a digitalized PC George Dixon would flash over the city to reassure law-abiding Londoners and criminal elements that they were being watched over! Sir John Stevens, the then Metropolitan Police Commissioner, conceded in February 2003 that the force had made a terrible mistake in removing bobbies from the beat. Newspapers carried the story under 'It's time to bring back Dixon' headlines with the obligatory photograph of PC George Dixon. In June 2005, 50 years after BBC television launched *Dixon of Dock Green* and 55 years after *The Blue Lamp* PC George Dixon was back in a series of Radio 4 plays based on the original TV scripts. Newspapers enthusiastically greeted the news with 'Dixon returns to Dock Green' type headlines. Later in the year, a news item on Paddington Green police station produced the following letter in 'The Job', the staff newspaper of the Metropolitan Police:

> I was very pleased to read the article about the Blue Lamp at Paddington Green police station. It brought back memories of my first station, the old Paddington Green. I must have gone under the lamp many times. In 1947 I was posted there as a probationer. During the making of *The Blue Lamp*, we were told to co-operate with the film company as the Commissioner thought the film would be good propaganda for the service. I do not agree with the comment that the film showed an idealistic view of British policing. Maybe I look back through rose tinted glasses, but I saw it as a true reflection of the situation at Paddington, maybe with a few embellishments for entertainment purposes.
>
> On my first two days out on the street, I was shown around the ground by a PC with about 20 years service. Like several other senior PCs at the station he could have been Dixon. Everyone had great respect for him, even the villains, and he knew all of them in the area ... . He was a marvellous policeman and taught me how to be a practical policeman. I know the enthusiasm, camaraderie and team spirit at this busy station kept me in the job in those early days. May the lamp continue to shine for the next 140 years as a symbol of law and order. Yours sincerely, John Solway.

Hence, despite all attempts to modernize and professionalize policing, the core British police identity remains profoundly dependent on a fictional image of the 'bobby on the beat' projected by Ealing Studios in 1950. In Chapter 2 we will see how the first British sociological study of the police by Michael Banton reinforced the idealistic cultural image of the 'bobby' by defining the British police as a sacred national institution.

Finally, a reflection within a reflection about the transformations engulfing English society between the making of *The Blue Lamp* and the screening of *Dixon of Dock Green*. By 1952, according to contemporary newspapers, 'young toughs' and 'cosh boys' were stalking London's streets and alleyways. A climax was reached on the evening of 2 November 1952 when PC Sidney George Miles was killed during an exchange of gun fire between Metropolitan Police officers and one of the two young burglars who were attempting to break into a warehouse. The youths were Christopher Craig aged 16 (who was armed with a revolver) and Derek Bentley aged 19. Sensationalist headlines in the next morning's newspapers declared that a Chicago-style gun battle had raged on the streets of south London. As with PC Edgar's murder four years earlier, this shooting stoked public anxiety about the threat posed by violent crime to British society (Selwyn, 1988). Craig, because he was under the legal age for hanging, was sentenced to life imprisonment. The jury added a plea for judicial mercy. The mentally subnormal Derek Bentley was executed on 28 January 1953 for inciting Craig to free the fatal shot by shouting 'Let him have it, Chris'. Yallop noted at the time that this expediently demonstrated the government's 'termination to solve the problem of juvenile crime, particularly crimes of violence, once and for all. The Executive felt that Bentley's death would encourage the youth of this country to think twice before they went out armed with revolvers, knuckle dusters, coshs, knives, razors and chains ... His death in fact, was a categorical statement of intent to all delinquents, 'if this death does not encourage you to mend your ways, then take care; you may be next to hang' (Yallop, 1971, p. 96). Derek Bentley had become the scapegoat for a whole generation. The Bentley family campaigned relentlessly to have this miscarriage of justice acknowledged by the British authorities and the case played a pivotal role in moves to put an end to capital punishment. Finally, in July 1998, the Court of Appeal overturned the conviction on the basis that Lord Chief Justice Goddard had denied Derek Bentley the possibility of a fair trail. Bentley was also granted a full posthumous pardon. A memorial service at Southward Cathedral on 28 January 1999 was attended by approximately 250 people. It took place the day after the Home Secretary signed the sixth protocol of the European Convention on Human Rights which formally abolished the death penalty in the United Kingdom. The simple inscription on Bentley gravestone reads: *Here lies Derek William Bentley: a Victim of British Justice.*

Note

1. It is worth noting that the constable had already been constructed as a comic character by William Shakespeare. We have Anthony Dull in *Love Labour's Lost*; Elbow in *Measure for Measure* and most famous of all Dogberry in *Much Ado About Nothing* (see Roberts, 1974).

The Sociological Construction of the Police

2

In his essay 'Why read the classics?' Italo Calvino (2001) defines classics as books that 'are treasured by those who have read and lived them', 'exert a peculiar influence' and have 'never finished saying what they have to say'. They simply 'refuse to be eradicated from the mind and conceal themselves in the fold of memory camouflaging themselves as the collective or individual unconscious'. J.M. Coetze (1993, p. 13) notes that 'the classic defines itself by surviving. Therefore, the re-examination of the classic, no matter how critical, is part of its history 'inevitable and even to be welcomed. ... rather than being the foe of the classic, criticism and indeed criticism of the most sceptical kind, may be what the classic uses to define itself and ensure its survival'.

Though Calvino and Coetze are writing about literary works, certain socio-logical texts are also adjudged to be classics. Academic conventions mean that such texts are more likely to be valued for their ground-breaking analysis and methodological approach, rather than according to literary style and cultural significance. Nevertheless, in terms of influence and approach, particular texts and authors gain canonical status. In Britain, at least, the study of policing that has come closest to being bestowed with classic status is Michael Banton's (1964a) *The Policeman in the Community*. How and why this came about and what role Banton's book had in the formation of the distinctive academic sub-field of police studies are the subject of this chapter.

What makes *The Policeman in the Community* a classic? As we saw in Chapter 1, until the 1950s police officers in the UK were not the subjects of social scientific research. Historians, constitutional lawyers, former police officers, jour-nalists and novelists wrote about policing but not social scientists (Brett, 1979). Many of these texts reproduced the idea of the British police as exemplifying a narrative of national progress, stability and order. However, contemporary newspaper reports on the abuse of police powers, unnecessary force, corruption and controversial incidents began to shine a spotlight on policing on both sides of the Atlantic, triggering government commissions and inquiries and reform programmes. Intensifying official acknowledgement of the social problems and tensions associated with policing created the justification for the first sociological studies of the police in both jurisdictions.

Michael Banton's *The Policeman in the Community*, sitting alongside American sociologist, William Westley's, doctoral thesis, can be seen as the first sociological studies of Anglo-American policing. These pre-dated the flurry of sociological research on the police that would take place in the 1960s and 1970s. *The Policeman in the Community* was a pioneering sociological understanding of the policeman's occupation which was grounded in its social context. When the book was first published, it garnered extensive reviews because it was not just one of the first qualitative studies of the police officer but one of the first comparative sociological studies of the police.

Reiner (1995) notes that it was a 'pathbreaking study [which] was responsible for many ideas and approaches which have been repeatedly returned to', and Holdaway (1983) comments that, with the publication of the book, 'one of the foundation stones of the sociology of the police was set in place'; it was 'the first sociological study of the English police. Many features of police work that have been the subject of continuing research were identified in it' (see also Holdaway 1995). The book had three key premises. First, Banton recognized that the police are just one small element of a complex system for maintaining public order and regulating deviant behaviour. Second, he demonstrated that uniformed officers could be seen not as crime fighters or law enforcers but as multi-tasked 'peace officers' intimately connected to and dependent on informal social controls. Third, he showed that an ongoing transatlantic conversation would be necessary if researchers were to find a comparative filter through which to make sense of policing philosophies, practices and innovations (see Manning, 2005).

Through Banton's qualitative fieldwork data and the first comparative analysis of the emergent US literature on issues such as police discretion and police–community relations, he demonstrated why sociologists should study the police. As will be discussed more fully in the concluding section of this chapter, he provided a knowledge structure for future sociological investigations. He handed down a naturalistic methodological approach – rather than using just surveys or interviews, and he focused on the officer 'working the beat'. Banton also bequeathed an ethical stance for future generations of police researchers: instead of making sensationalist claims or seeking (in the manner of the investigative journalist, to 'blow the whistle' on misdemeanours and malpractice), he emphasized that the professional sociologist should be a neutral chronicler who studiously avoids taking sides.

As we will discuss in the next chapter, a generation of sociologists would test and develop Banton's ideas by collecting observational data on:

- what police officers actually do when they are on duty;
- how patrol officers make sense of their work;
- the formal and informal sources of the police officer's authority;
- how, why and with what effect officers use their discretionary powers;
- how officer/citizen interactions produce and shape policework;
- the defining features of the working personality of the police officer; and
- the characteristics and function of the rank and file occupational culture.

I have been fortunate in researching this chapter to be able to draw upon unpublished information supplied by Michael Banton as well as his answers by email and in person to many questions (see also Banton, 2005).

Michael Banton: the making of a sociologist of the police

Michael Banton is probably best known for his extensive writings in the field of ethnic and racial studies. Indeed, those most familiar with this body of work might even be surprised to find that he has also published so extensively on policing. Before looking at *The Policeman in the Community* in detail, there are some aspects of Michael Banton's intellectual formation that are useful in setting the book and his approach in context. After serving in the Royal Navy, Michael Banton enrolled at the London School of Economics (LSE) in 1947, intending to study economics. Banton notes that it was his 'great good fortune' in his first year to have as his tutor the Chicago sociologist Edward Shils, who had joined the LSE the previous year to help 'bridge the gap of eight years during which there had been practically no communication between Europe and America in the field of sociological studies' (Shils, 1949, p. 1). For Banton (1964a, p. 104), Shils 'played the part of the outsider in challenging scholarly conventions. He taught us that sociology as a subject was still in the making and that we could help shape it (see also Rumney, 1945; Sprott, 1957; Kent, 1981; Abrow, 1989; Halsey, 1997; Kumar, 2001).

Shils had a significant influence on *The Policeman in the Community* and subsequent sociological research of the police. First, he emphasized the importance of theory informed empirical research. Second, he insisted that sociological research was a living practice. Third, he encouraged the first generation of professional sociologists to concentrate their research on their own society. Fourth, it was through Shils that Michael Banton became familiar with the concept of 'sacredness'. Shils and Young (1953) had used the Durkheimian concepts of 'ceremony' and 'ritual' to argue that the coronation of Queen Elizabeth II in June 1953 was an act of 'national communion' that had 'touched the sense of the sacred' in the people, heightened a sense of solidarity and affirmed common moral values. Shils and Young made the important point that 'authority which is charged with obligations to provide for and to protect the community in its fundamental constitution is always rooted in the sacred'. Finally, Shils, as an outsider, emphasized the uniquely consensual nature of British society. The successful integration of the working class into the 'moral consensus' of British society had transformed the country from being one of the most disorderly and violent into one of the most orderly and law-abiding (Shils and Young, 1953, p. 76).

In October 1950, Banton was appointed to the Department of Social Anthropology at the University of Edinburgh, and quickly established a reputation in the field of race relations. He was also at the forefront of 'the new tradition of sociological research' that favoured working with social anthropological methods that allowed researchers to get close to subjects in order to analyse interpersonal relations. His first book, *The Coloured Quarter: Negro Immigrants in an English City* (1955), was based on pioneering ethnographic doctoral research he had carried out on the impact of Commonwealth immigration in Stepney in the East End of London. As I shall show below, the urban ethnographic skills he gained in his research in the East End were to prove useful for the work he needed to carry out for *The Policeman in the Community*. Banton's next book, *The West African City: A study of Tribal Life in Freetown* (1957) looked at migration from the interior to, and the social life of migrants in, the capital city of Freetown, Sierra Leone. He subsequently undertook and published on research on race relations in Britain publishing *White and Coloured; the behaviour of British people towards Coloured Immigrants* in 1959. For family reasons Banton could not pursue further field research in Africa and he felt that research on race relations in Britain was difficult to conduct from Edinburgh. This led him to embark on the first sociological study of the British police.

Researching *The Policeman in the Community*

Banton's work on race relations had led him to conclude that British people could be both deeply prejudiced or very tolerant. Thus, for him, the interesting sociological questions were: 'in what situations were they one rather than the other? What factors in these various situations called forth the different kinds of behaviour' (1964a, p. viii). He detected signs of a similar difference of opinion about the state of police–public relations developing in Britain in the period leading up to appointment of the Willink Royal Commission in January 1960. There had been 'some much publicised stories of police brutality (one concerning a man called Podola and the other a civil servant) while on the other there had been much publicity about low levels of police pay. I thought it might be interesting to try to find out how different definitions of situations evoked different kinds of police conduct and the effect of this on police-public relations' (personal communication).

Banton was critical of the Royal Commission's reading of a social survey of the state of police–community relations in Britain which had, in his view, rushed to 'simple judgement about a complex and only partially analysed phenomenon' (Banton, 1964a, p. ix). The survey had made unverifiable claims about the British police being 'the best in the world'. He felt there was a pressing need to develop a sociological understanding of police–community relationships. In order to do so he would first of all have to learn more about 'the nature of the policeman's job and the pressures that bear upon him (Banton, 1964a, p. x). He also justified his research intervention on the grounds that: 'police officers have been too busy getting on with their job to philosophise about it at any length. I am going to try and do it for them' (1964a, p. 8). This provided him with the justification for initiating a discussion about what the policeman's role in society is and ought to be. His specific focus would be uniformed officers and their routine dealings with the ordinary public rather than the specialized work of detectives or the bureaucratic work of supervisors and senior officers.

Not surprisingly given his anthropological background, Banton's working premise was that policing was intimately connected to the quality of the order and density and texture of social relations that comprise a given social system. He wanted to pinpoint the sociological preconditions for what might commonly be described as 'organic policing'. He felt it was vital for the sociologist to analyse the police officer's role and status in a homogeneous society, in which the 'incidence of crime, social conflict and maladjustment' was low in order to 'see what happens when homogeneity gives way to heterogeneity and situations of tension' (1963a, p. 8). From the outset, Banton worked from a sociological truth 'that the police are only one among many agencies of social control' (1964a, p. 1). Law enforcement agencies, important though they are, 'appear puny compared with the extensiveness and intricacy of these other [informal] modes of regulating informal behaviour' (1964a, p. 2).

Research for the book began in Scotland in 1960 and was completed during 1963. Banton's stated aim was to collect basic descriptive information on the most visible and accessible parts of the police force to clarify what uniformed officers did most of the time and how they did it. Because patrol work was the principal activity of most police forces it was 'the problems of this kind of work and the attitudes to which it gives rise that most characterise the *culture of policework as an occupation*' (Banton, 1964a, p. 27). Banton's research would also produce one of the first sustained comparative sociological studies of UK and US policing. Indeed, he acknowledges that the book was only made possible because of the US research – the comparison allowed him to 'see Scottish police work in a new light' and highlight problems that were 'likely to grow in Britain if present trends continue' (1964a, p. 224).

The USA as an empirical reference point

There was a distinctive body of US literature that Banton was able to draw upon in formulating his research project. In addition to numerous histories of local US police departments, there was a rapidly developing administratively oriented police studies represented most obviously by O.W. Wilson's *Police Administration*. The first socio-legal articles on police discretion had also appeared in the US by the time Banton began his research, so he was able to pick up on the empirical significance of this issue (e.g., Goldstein, 1960; LaFave, 1962; Goldstein, 1963). Sociological studies were few and far between (Whyte, 1943). There was of course the pioneering sociological work of William Westley (1951, 1953), which Banton says, 'told me that you could do research on the police' (personal interview). In 1951 Westley had completed the first full-length sociological study of the police as a University of Chicago sociology doctoral student under the guidance of Joseph Lohman and Everett Hughes. Westley's controversial thesis did not appear in book form until 1970.

For Westley, the extremely influential police administration literature provided little in the way of information concerning the 'social characteristics, personal attitudes and community function' of the police (Westley, 1951, p. 7). His working hypothesis was that the police as an occupational group possessed distinctive group customs, attitudes and values and modes of socialization that influenced an officer's actions in a given situation. This was reflected in his methods. Similar to Banton's own in *The Coloured Quarter* (and later for *The Policeman in the Community*), he wanted to familiarize himself with the everyday realities of US policing. In the autumn of 1949 he started his research with intensive unstructured interviewing in the Chicago Police Department. He continued the bulk of his research in Gary, Indiana, a small Midwestern industrial city 'which had a very large slum area, a large Negro population with a history of friction with the population, a high crime rate, an organised political machine, and extensive vice and gambling [and] severe traffic problems' (1951, p. 26). Over four months he observed all types of police activities while 'walking the beat', cruising with officers, and observing raids, interrogations and training. He followed this with a further six months of intensive interviewing with over half of the police department and additional observation. Westley's study was extremely controversial because of his bleak rendition of police officers world view:

> The policeman's world is spawned of degradation, corruption and insecurity. He sees man as ill-willed, exploitative, mean and dirty; himself a victim of injustice, misunderstood and defiled. (Westley, 1951, p. ii).

> He tends to meet those portions of the public which are acting contrary to the law or using the law to further their own ends. He is exposed to public immorality. He becomes cynical. His is a society emphasizing the crooked, the weak and the unscrupulous. Accordingly his morality is one of expediency and his self conception one of a martyr. (Westley, 1951, p. 239)

And of course Westley argued that violence was a central part of routine police work. This underpinned his definition of the police as 'the portion of the state apparatus that maintains a monopoly on the legitimate means of violence' (1951, p. 5). Westley's was a remarkable study because it identified many of the key issues and dilemmas that would preoccupy Michael Banton and future generations of US sociologists researching the police. Banton felt that Westley's research findings could not stand as representative, being too extreme and pessimistic in terms of the politically corrupt policing environment he encountered and the brutal, cynical, lawless behaviour of the police officers (personal communication).

Accessing the police

In an initial conversation with the Chief Constable in charge of Edinburgh, the Chief Constable had asked Banton, 'Why do you want to study us? What are we doing wrong?'. In fact, despite (or perhaps because of) reading Wesley's work, Banton's research was premised on a very different view of the police. He explains this in the preface to the book:

> The tradition of research into social problems is now so firmly established that the public takes it for granted that sociologists study social institutions that are not working satisfactorily. *The idea that it can be instructive to analyse institutions that are working well in order to see if anything can be learned from their success has not yet taken hold* [italics added]. Yet obviously the science of social relations cannot be advanced very far unless people study all sorts of institutions to see how they function. (Banton, 1964a p. vii)

From his previous research experience in London, Banton was aware that access was likely to be the key issue in researching the police. His position as a member of staff at the University of Edinburgh obviously helped because of the proximity to Scottish policy makers. In 1958, he sought the advice of the relevant official at the Scottish Home Department, W. Kerr Fraser, afterwards permanent secretary, and subsequently principal of the University of Glasgow. Kerr Fraser was 'moderately encouraging and told me I would first need the consent of the three police associations: the chief officers, the superintendents, and the Federation' (personal communication). Kerr Fraser suggested to Banton that he begin by contacting the Scottish Police College in Kincardineshire. However, when he arrived for his meeting with the Chief Constable of Edinburgh, he was bemused by the reaction he received. Initially, he got the impression the Chief Constable was busy and that he might not allow Banton long. Banton notes that 'The prospects of his agreeing did not seem good'. However,

> To my surprise he spent half-an-hour explaining to me why I could not do such research; then a second half-hour telling me how interesting was the policeman's job; followed by a further twenty to twenty-five minutes saying what a

good job it was that I was going to do this research. It seemed as if the more
he thought about it the more he came to think the idea was harmless. (Ben
Whitaker, who started work in London on a book about the police a little later,
told me that when he went to see Sir Joseph Simpson, the Metropolitan
Commissioner, he had a similar reception.) At one stage it was suggested that
I might have to agree to be sworn in as a special constable; as my father had
been a 'special', the idea did not alarm me but it seemed quite unnecessary
and it was just as well that nothing came of this (Personal communication).

When Banton offered 'not to publish any information gained as a result of
their support, that had not been first agreed with them, they gave me every
assistance' (1964a, p. x). Banton comments that, when the book was eventually published, Kerr Fraser 'thought its content was less an achievement than
my having succeeded in carrying out the research in the first place' (personal
communication).

Banton was not able to use his ethnographic skills to the full in his study of
the Scottish police. In 1960 he was authorized to conduct eight group discussions with sergeants at the Scottish Police College to explore the differences
between policemen working in country districts and the city and to see what
effect these differences had upon their job satisfaction. Shedding light on this
problem was something that his police contacts indicated would be of interest
to them. Later in the year, he interviewed police recruits to get an insight into
what they expected of the job.

In early 1961, he began the final stage of the Scottish research. Officers of
'C' division of Edinburgh City Police agreed to keep a diary of two days' worth
of activities. In addition, Banton spent roughly 30 hours in total walking with
officers on the beat. This provided him with baseline descriptive information
about 'the great variety of tasks performed by policemen' as well as the organization and functioning of a police division and the bureaucratic rules and
regulations. He carried out no formal interviews with individual police officers either in Scotland (or indeed in the USA).

Banton extended his research to the USA after accepting an invitation
to take up a visiting post in African Studies at Massachusetts Institute of
Technology. The final and most substantial phase of the research took place
during 1962 with the study of one urban northern police department and two
urban southern American police departments. He also paid brief visits to several other police departments in the United States and Sweden. The Boston
Police Department would not give him permission to accompany officers on
patrol as they did see how it could benefit the department. The chair of the
political science section at MIT had thought it 'extraordinary that anyone from
Britain should have thought of possibly studying Boston's Irish Police
Department'. Everett Hughes helped Banton access the Massachusetts police
department. He found it difficult to get funding for extending his US research.
When he spoke to the research director of the International Association of

Chiefs of Police, he was told that a survey of funding foundations had shown that none would support police research. MIT funded him to spend 'four weeks with the police department of Charlotte, North Carolina, and two weeks with that of Atlanta, Georgia, under its enlightened chief, Herbert T. Jenkins' (personal communication).

He received considerably open-ended, relaxed co-operation from the three 'above-average' US police departments. As a result, the overwhelming majority of his observational research findings refer to the 200 hours spent with American police officers. Because he got the opportunity to ride the cruisers and mix informally with officers, he is able to use his ethnographic skills to provide readers with a more intimate insider description of what police officers routinely say and do as well as the demeanour, status and attitude of different members of the public officers come into contact with.

Michael Banton published his first thoughts on the police in *The Police Chief*, the journal of the International Association of Chiefs of Police, in April 1963. The origins of 'Social integration and the Police' (Banton, 1963a) lay in a conference paper he gave at the School of Criminology in University of California, Berkeley. This was followed up by a *New Society* article in August 1963 in which he expressly highlighted the issue of police discretion arguing that it is one of the most 'intractable problems' within the police (Banton, 1963a). In 1964 *The Policeman in the Community* was published as well as a short summary piece, 'A Policeman's Lot' in *The Listener* magazine. This is not the place to reproduce a detailed account of the research findings. Instead, it is more fruitful to concentrate on the distinctive sociological paradigm of police work articulated by Banton.

Policing British pre-modernity: the police constable's paradise

As was noted previously, Banton's working premise was that policing is strongly tied to the quality of the order and density and texture of social relations that comprise a given social system. In the course of the Berkeley lecture, he informed an audience of senior US police officers that he would tell them about 'a policeman's paradise' (1963b, p. 8). In doing so, he described the virtual absence of crime in the Scottish village where he lived and the relative lack of serious crime in nearby Edinburgh. This was because of the strength of the social order of the community, and 'not because the police are more efficient'. The distinguishing features of pre-modern Scottish village life – small scale, homogeneous, stability of the population, high levels of integration and interdependency and agreement on fundamental values – were conducive to social conformity. Because of these features, its members are folded into a 'popular morality': 'no one can afford to get out of line. People are dependent, morally, socially and economically, on their neighbour's good opinion and the sanction of gossip is a powerful one' (1963a, p. 9). In such an organic social order, the role of the 'Dixonian' police constable 'is to oil the machinery,

Figure 2.1   London East End bobby 1950s

not the motive power of law enforcement'. The constable is able to obtain co-operation and respect from the community because he is doing little more than guarding and administering established community norms. 'Consensual policing' was therefore embedded in the constitutive relationships of a naturally renewing organic social order.

The Policeman in the Community, developed this pre-modernity argument about policing in Britain further. He asserted that a stable community's ability to police itself 'provides the moral boundaries of police work and confers on police a significant moral authority' (1964a, p. 3). Crime, he notes, is not a primary concern in such a community. Instead, a great deal of police time is spent assisting citizens in distress and in most instances officers are being asked by members of the public to adjudicate on what are essentially moral matters. When a police constable responds to a call 'as often as not it is this reference to how someone ought to behave that he hears first. He is reminded what morality expects at the same time as he is told of an offence' (Banton,

1964a, p. 12). Even when dealing with incidents of crime the constable spends more time with complainants/victims/witnesses rather than with offenders.

Because the police mandate in society is clearly defined, widely understood and therefore predictable, even the youngest, newest constable on the beat knows that his uniform confers authority, status and respect across a wide range of public encounters. The constable 'often finds that he needs to do or say very little, the mere presence of the man in the blue uniform being sometimes sufficient to make people stop fighting, or to quiet down someone who was highly tensed' (1964a, p. 227).

Therefore, in the UK, many of the constable's actions derive from his moral involvement in and understanding of 'the community' rather than his law enforcement powers and constitutional obligations. Because the constable is working within a stable social order and shares the values and standards of his community, he is endowed with deep authority and legitimacy. Indeed, in many situations he depends on his 'judgements of the moral claims of the parties and the extent to which they acknowledge the moral claims of the officer' (1964a, p. 12). Police constables become involved in these cases as a human being as well as an agent of the law, and moral indignation can also determine an officer's course of action. A constables's moral authority is such that 'he can keep a lot of cases out of court by speaking to offenders and impressing them with the errors of their ways. He can do this because his office possesses authority as well as power' (1964a, p. 12).

This leads Banton to separate out a constable's authority from his legal powers in such a communal setting. While the public can in certain instances resent the exercise of police power, they are not offended by 'police authority because authority is conferred on the policeman by the community'. The constable's authority to require obedience is not disputed because members of the community 'consider it is morally right' (1964a, p. 12). The public also expects a predictable pattern of police behaviour. He notes that it is much easier for the British police constable to be predictable because in a highly integrated society there is greater consensus about what constitutes an appropriate response. Being fully aware of their dependence upon the effectiveness of broader communal mechanisms of control, constables prefer to work as 'peace officers' and to see their role in order maintenance terms. This is why there is considerable rank and file resistance to functional specialization of police work and to civilianization.

> Such developments strike at the conception of the police officer as personally committed to the people he protects, and substitutes a more technically conceived, limited liability kind of role. It is the officer on foot patrol who is regarded as the representative policeman. The tasks he performs are so varied that he has to be an all-rounder. The challenging variety of these tasks develops the capacities and understanding of the policeman in a way that few occupations at his socio-economic level could do, and police officers say that the variety of duties is one of the most satisfying features of the job. (1964a, p. 159)

Because they can count on public support, officers do not unquestionably stand by their colleagues and do not draw hard and fast distinctions between themselves and the public. There is less cause for them to close ranks against outsiders. Supervision is close and demanding with tight discipline and high standards and an organizational expectation that a constable's actions and decisions will conform closely to the rules of legal procedure.

If British police officers are socially isolated, it is because both the community and the police force require such high standards of conduct of officers that they are a 'race apart':

> The British policeman has an exemplary role ... The British policeman's uniform makes him highly 'visible': he stands out from the crowd. People are conscious of his presence and the policeman is unconsciously aware of this and the pressure makes him more inclined to act in an exemplary manner (1964a, pp. 123–4).

The police constable also occupies a complicated position in Britain's highly stratified social structure. He is supposed to be from as well as of the community but there is also a constitutional requirement for police officers to have an arm's length relationship with the community. As an officer of the Crown he is not allowed to engage in politics or to over-identify with a particular group or sectional interest. In order to carry out his work, the British police constable, like the priest or vicar, must be a 'classless' figure. Intuitive understanding of the well-established norms and values of different classes and indeed hierarchical class relationships, including deference, enables officers to maintain order and social control. The police and the British working class know each other and respond to each other in predictable ways. In working-class neighbourhoods constables operate as 'uniformed social workers as well as more active enforcers of the peace' (1964a, p. 181). In addition, the British criminal underworld recognizes the moral authority of the police when it does not interfere with their nefarious plans. Indeed, the police and criminals understand each other because despite their respective roles, they remain 'members of the community, sharing values and modes of communication' (1964a, p. 68). Interestingly, it is the middle classes who are more likely to challenge the authority of the constable and therefore need much more careful handling.

Because police constables are never off duty and because of the authority they exercise over others, members of the public may wish to keep a distance. The strict disciplinary code demands public respectability at all times and moral rectitude. Hence, the public role strictly governs all aspects of the life of the constable and takes precedence over the private obligations he has as a father, neighbour or friend. The community's ambivalent attitudes towards the police can also be problematic for their families, who may as a consequence of being cold shouldered find it hard to be accepted.

The rewards of being a British police constable are partly financial and partly psychological, in terms of the satisfaction they get from their work.

Constables would say that the psychological rewards are the sense of making an important contribution to the life of the community, being able to take pride in their occupation, the status and prestige that is accorded to being a recognized authority figure and representing the dominant popular morality.

In attempting to theorize rather than just describe the British police constable's organic role and status, all the above points ultimately converge on Banton's fundamental anthropological category of 'the sacred'.

> His role puts him forward as someone more moral than others, as someone slightly sacred and at the same time dangerous. Thus, the policeman's role has something of the quality of 'taboo' ... The more something is withdrawn from the ordinary mundane round of social and economic transactions, the more it is likely to have some special, sacred quality to it and it has been shown that policemen have to be withdrawn to some degree because of the power with which they are invested. (Banton, 1964a, p. 190)

In classic Durkheimian fashion, Banton defines the socially sacred as 'that which is set apart and that which is treated both as intrinsically good and dangerous' (Banton, 1964a, p. 237). He argues that certain customary procedures and core ways of doing things within bureaucracies may be described as 'sacred' and are therefore untouchable. As we noted earlier, following Shils and Young (1953) he argues that the same can be said about the venerated position of certain British cultural institutions. Because the monarchy, the church etc. epitomise fundamental social values they are isolated from secular evaluation. The same is true of the police (1964a, p. 236). However, it is not only the police as an institution that is sacred, 'but the British constable's role seems sacred compared with other occupational roles and compared with that of the patrolman across the Atlantic'(Banton, 1964a, p. 237). For Banton, the police constable is considered to be 'intrinsically good' because he symbolizes social order and 'dangerous' because of his guardianship powers. This is why 'many people – with or without justification – prefer to keep at a distance from policemen or feel slightly uneasy in their company' (Banton, 1964a, p. 237). In many core respects, the role of the constable is comparable to that of the priest: set apart and sacralized. But those who hold the office are also perceived by the faithful as human beings. And the faithful like to remark upon the human characteristics and failings of the sacralized to reassure themselves that they are not really different from anyone else (1964a, p. 237).

Banton does of course recognize that 'for a role to appear sacred in respect of certain of its duties does not blind people to the secular aspects of the role and of its incumbents' (1964a pp. 238–9). His contention about the core sacredness of the pre-modern British police stemmed largely from his comparative analysis. So what did Banton uncover in his travels through American modernity?

Policing American modernity: the patrol officer's nightmare

Banton's ability to undertake observational research in the USA provides us with a much more dynamic, multi-dimensional depiction of what uniformed officers actually *do* on patrol. In America Banton was re-energized as an anthropologist. It is while watching American officers working the street, sitting with them in cars and in diners, and listening to the locker-room chat that Banton formulates the key concepts that would be tested and elaborated upon in future sociological studies of the police.

The portrait painted by Banton demonstrates that despite the fact that it shares Britain's Anglo-Saxon constabulary tradition, the chaotic reality of US society is a police officer's nightmare. Officers are expected to work in conditions 'that are foreign to European circumstances' (1964a, p. 172). For Banton, the US is a relatively unintegrated and normless modernity marked by economic liberalism, rapid social change, geographical mobility, suburbanization, individualizm, depersonalization, affluence, pluralistic values, and complex ethnic divisions and racial segregation. The lower degree of social density and social control, lack of common culture, racial and ethnic differences and the secular mentality that are characteristic of US modernity directly affect the nature of police–community relations. The key difference for Banton is how social conflict and adversarial relationships structure all aspects of US police work and indeed the internal dynamics of the police organisation. It is worth keeping in mind that Banton arrived in the US in the midst of an economic boom and population growth as well of course as an intensifying struggle for civil rights. By the time he would return to Britain, the US would be rocked by the dramatic events unfolding: the Freedom Rides of 1961; televised police violence against civil rights marchers in Birmingham, Alabama in April and May 1963; the march on Washington in August 1963; and the assassination of President Kennedy in November 1963.

Banton does not use all the material he collected on how 'race' fundamentally complicates US police work in the book, with a much fuller analysis being provided in his article in *The Police Chief* (1963b). He makes the general point that police–racial minority relations cannot be addressed properly unless the force has the support of the courts, adequate resources and proper leadership. 'Race' complicates police work in the US at the time of his research in several ways. First, situations of racial friction are among the most difficult and dangerous that officers may encounter. Police officers who are ordered, for example, to carry out a de-segregation order can find themselves resisted by powerful local white groups. In stark contrast to Britain, this can put the police at odds with the dominant popular morality. He argues that if a police department has developed professional standards it will have a morality of its own that enables it to resist public unpopularity. However, such a policing requirement will cause serious trouble in an unprofessional police department.

Second, in contrast to the British 'paradise', many white police officers in the US spend their working lives in communities with which they have no real connection or identification. Discussing his time spent with southern police departments he noted that: 'at no time did I get the impression that white officers felt the same moral involvement in the colored areas as they did in the white' (1963b, p. 16). This has a serious effect on the quality of service offered to these communities. He was obviously intrigued by what black officers told him about how they approached policing in their own neighbourhoods. He notes that black police officers felt that they belonged in black communities and that in addition to an extra understanding, they had 'a moral involvement with its people'. He notes that a black officer 'claims moral authority as a policeman where the white officer relies upon legal power because rightly or wrongly – he rarely sees Negroes as subscribing to the moral norms acknowledged in his community' (1963b, p. 18). However, Banton notes that recruiting minority officers will not necessarily provide a complete solution to the 'race' problem. What is important is not the officer's colour but a willingness to sympathize with and understand the neighbourhood being policed. If officers, observe high standards of professional policework 'they will automatically have dealt with the race issue, for professional policing demands respect for all citizens and due consideration for the circumstances of every individual' (1963b, p. 16).

Third, the requirement to desegregate police departments had exposed the problem of the resistance of white officers. He concedes that this resistance could well be linked to individual racial prejudice but he also argues that it could be related to the culture of particular departments. Banton concludes that police departments that have developed a professional model of police work will be respected even in the most conflictual circumstances. He notes that the attitude of black officers is a good indication of general morale and professionalism of a police department.

This unpredictable and potentially dangerous policing environment fosters a workplace solidarity that is 'one of the principal values in the culture of the policeman' (1964a, p. 13). The demands for unquestioning in-group solidarity are strong and this is reinforced by the considerable informal socialising amongst officers. Consequently, in contrast to Britain, uniformed patrol officers take their cue not from their legal obligations or senior officers but from their immediate peer group. Public hostility and police solidarity are mutually reinforcing with officers 'closing rank' against the public and when necessary against supervisors and management. Because officers have little moral authority and do not identify themselves with the whole of the community, they depend on the threat of coercion to make people comply with their orders. Thus, like Westley, Banton confirms that the nightstick and revolver are used by officers to exact respect, to obtain information or punish particular categories of morally deviant offenders. The working environment and the prevalence of in-group solidarity is such that fellow officers will not condemn the use of violence by colleagues or report malpractice.

Figure 2.2   New York city cop 1950s

In contrast to Britain, Banton notes that there is nothing sacrosanct or sacred about the American police. First, there is a tendency for police departments to be seen as business organisations which must justify themselves in instrumental terms. Police departments operate in a highly politicized environment and among other things have to persuade local government to provide adequate funding. Second, there is the common assumption that corruption and malpractice are prevalent and the public do not expect or demand much from their police departments. Third, uniformed officers do not feel protected by the courts or supported by the public and politicians. They also work with the knowledge that many laws are unenforceable in certain neighbourhoods. The volume of calls officers have to react to, the volatility of police–public relations, intractable social problems, the emphasis on individual civil rights, the variety of improper political and communal pressures and the possibility of violence profoundly influence how police officers respond to members of the public and structure their relations with fellow officers. This produces a considerable degree of cynicism.

Although for American police officers, work is a central life interest and produces a strong occupational culture, they also view their work as just a job that has similarities with other municipal jobs. The clearly defined career structure and higher pay has greater symbolic value than in Britain. Officers are also much more integrated into the everyday life of the community and they have fewer restrictions on their personal lives. Their work does not seem to have an adverse effect on an officer's social and family lives. Officers are even permitted to take part-time employment and to undertake private security work while off duty. Class distinctions are not such an issue for American police officers because of the much more fluid, meritocratic social structure. As a result, in comparison to the situation in the UK, US police officers do not have to show deference to the middle or upper classes.

Policing British modernity: paradise lost?

As was noted in the Preface to this book Banton argued that it is important for sociologists to 'analyse institutions that are working well'. And as the 'policing paradise' section has indicated, Banton presented a very strong rendition of British policing and indeed British society as unsullied and unproblematic. This has led Reiner (2001, p. 213) to argue that the book was 'framed within a celebratory mode, and assumed a primarily harmonious view of British society'. This is reinforced by Banton's Reithian history of British policing that suggests that the pacification of the population and the gradual winning of consent led to increased acceptance and popularity. For Banton, the British police became more popular as they dealt with a wider range of classes and were no longer just seen as imposing order on the lower classes: 'A hundred years ago they must have been chiefly concerned with lower-class crime; as they have come to oversee more middle- and upper-class persons they must have been forced into a more classless, separate and 'sacred' position' (1964a, p. 240).

The popularity of the British police is based on an assumed relation between national character and the police model – self-control, self-restraint, reservation. The police are identified with a consensual society – and they are seen as both guarantors and symbols of that social order. Banton reflects on Gorer's (1955, p. 296) claims about the police as an 'ideal model of masculine strength and responsibility; as generations passed, aspects of this ideal figure became incorporated into the personality; and the English character became, to a very marked degree, "self-policing"'. He does call it an 'intriguing hypothesis' that will be difficult to accept until comparative studies are available. The vision of an idealized national character that Banton incorporates from the orthodox police historiography of policing consolidates a discourse of consent in which policing is seen as having a 'special symbolic character' and where the 'Dixonian' police force are a benign agency of social control and a representation of national unity. Marxist analyses of policing that would appear in the 1970s would render a very different story (Cohen, 1979; Brogden, 1982).

However, here are moments in the book when Banton, as a 'stranger returning to a strange land', expresses his concerns about the condition of the British police. Indeed, the tone of *The Policeman in the Community*'s conclusion is quite pessimistic: there is a powerful 'paradise lost' sentiment with Banton reflecting on a pre-modern sepia-shaded social order that is passing. Although these concerns are amplified in the conclusion, they have not really been commented on by reviewers. He acknowledges that he has idealized the set of social relations that characterize Scottish 'village society' and also cautions against assuming that meaningful levels of social consensus and popular morality cannot be a hallmark of urban modernity. However, he is concerned with the hurricane of American inspired modernization sweeping through Britain. In many respects 'our social organisation is coming to resemble that of the United States and many of the problems that have appeared there may be expected in Britain' (Banton, 1964a, p. 261). Increased social mobility, youth culture and the generation gap, occupational specialization, shifts in residential arrangements, individualism, secularisation, anonymity, acquisitiveness, and ethnic and racial pluralism (that were discussed in the previous chapter) will all throw a shadow over 'old' Britain.

Drawing upon his comparative research, he raises serious concerns about the ability of the British police to adapt to a post-traditional social order. Britain's transition from tradition to modernity will weaken traditional self-policing mechanisms and necessitate the strengthening of formal methods of social control. Banton was clearly impressed by the efforts of the top US police administrators, such as O.W. Wilson, William H. Parker and a generation of 'college cops', to construct a professional model of policing and forge a modern 'police science'. This indicated that US police departments were much more able to adjust to modern social circumstances and experiment with new styles of policing. His ambivalence about social change in Britain reflects both his fear of the social problems that will inevitably accompany the secularization of British culture and the instrumentalization of institutional practices. If social norms are to be transmitted, 'there will be greater reliance upon the internal controls deriving from early socialisation and schooling, and less reliance upon external controls such as punishment. Some social institutions will have to be overhauled to encourage citizen participation to a greater extent than they do at present' (1964a, p. 262). The police will have to adapt to these new realities and it is inevitable that they will be 'profaned' in the process.

A consequence will be that, whether they want to or not, the police will be asked to assume specialist responsibility for controlling crime, particularly with the inevitable trend to higher crime rates. This instrumentalization and the increasing emphasis of pragmatic results will have a dramatic impact on the role of the constable as a multi-functional peace officer. There will be increased professionalization of the core police functions with more resources going to detectives and specialist units. This will change the ethos and public image of the force from peace officers to law-enforcement officers and crime fighters. Banton suggests that in the future the British public might be more willing to question police authority and demand more scrutiny and accountability, particularly if the police fail to control crime and there is an increase in conflictual police–public encounters. Hence, police work in future would take place in a context of social, cultural and constitutional insecurity.

Banton believed that there was a danger that the British police would be increasingly dysfunctional because it was: 'a little too much of a special institution, a little too much apart from the general community', a little too much of a 'race apart' (1964a,b,c, p. 262). Their detachment, as exemplified by the sense of their own importance, the obsession with bureaucratic procedural rules, status and tradition was leaving them out of step with a rapidly changing society. He noted for example how sensitive the police response to the BBC's *Z-Cars* series had been: 'police officers objected to the series because they thought it would reduce public respect for the police. They were claiming that because of the importance of their occupation in society it should not be shown in an unfavourable light'. Other occupations and their practitioners could be presented 'as ordinary or profane because they do not touch on fundamental values' (1964a, p. 238).

Police forces were not only removed from the community but were remarkably insular and unaware or even suspicious of initiatives in other forces. He viewed the beat system as increasingly rigid and representing an inefficient use of scarce resources. Chief police officers operated in a secretive manner and denied the right of the public to have a say in important policy decisions. They were unwilling to admit errors and rejected any criticism of their force. The disciplinary control they exercised over the rank and file was repressive and arbitrary. The knock-on effect would be that it is impossible for a new generation of police officers to work out a satisfactory balance in their lives.

Banton also presented a modest reform agenda for the British police. He argued that forces will need to improve the quality of recruits and the training of probationers to handle new realities associated with their mandate. Human relations and race relations training would have to become a central part of policing as demands upon the constable's sense of judgement mount. The British police would also need to overhaul its management and should even think of appointing civilians to senior positions. Banton is concerned that increased public criticism of an increasingly 'out of touch', unresponsive police force will generate a US style defensive rank and file occupational culture and militant trade union mentality. This in turn could trigger a downward spiral of deteriorating police–community relations. The concluding tone of *The Policeman in the Community* is essentially pessimistic: radical social transformation meant that consensus or community policing might be moving beyond the reach of rapidly modernizing British society.

Evaluating *The Policeman in the Community*

As noted at the beginning of this chapter, Banton's work, sitting alongside William Westley's doctoral thesis, pre-dated the interest in sociological research into the police that was to take place in the 1960s and 1970s. As a result, because there was no body of sociological literature to compare it against, reviews in both the UK and USA found it difficult to characterize Banton's book. He was credited generally with not only the difficult task of accessing what was deemed to be a hitherto closed institution but producing a pioneering sociological understanding of the complicated 'life world' of the man behind the uniform. Banton had also highlighted the vital role that social context plays in defining policework. However, concerns were expressed about the representative nature of his research findings as well as its failure to address the realities of urban British policing. Banton does acknowledge that his research conclusions are based on data drawn from observation of police officers in a relatively law-abiding Scottish city and hinterland and in three 'above-average' American police departments. He had 'not been able to study what happens in situations where policemen are subject to strain and provocation, and can say little about the sorts of incident that attract newspaper attention ... My work provides no answer to questions whether police–public relations are good or bad, better or worse' (1964a, p. xii).

This is an issue that was taken up by reviewers on both sides of the Atlantic. British criminologists who reviewed the book were clearly not convinced by the Durkheimian 'sacralization of police' thesis. For Downes (1965) sociological research that should have been timely in fact offered little insight into pressing issues, such as: the police culture that had produced a Challenor case or a Sheffield Rhino whip scandal inquiry; questions of corruption; police attitudes towards crime, offenders and the criminal justice system; and differential community attitudes towards the police. For Mays (1965) the study was 'perhaps a bit too detached and impartial. Banton's knowledge of and regard for the officers he observed and his definition of the police as a sacred institution meant that 'there is little therefore to assist us to answer current questions about police–public relations in general at the level of moral evaluation, and this is a deficiency which for some readers may prove extremely frustrating' (Mays, 1965, p. 217). Although the book starts out with the intention of studying police–public relations, there is almost no public or 'policed' perspective in the study. The community where it appears is raised in terms of public attitudes to the police or in the somewhat nebulous terms that, by definition, regards the police as sacred or profane. Almost all of the empirical data is weighted heavily towards the perspective of police officers. Mays was also surprised that evidence on the ways in which the law was sometimes differentially enforced by the British police was not discussed. It was not difficult for reviewers to detect a tendency in the book to downplay or ignore allegations of malpractice. Indeed, the book can appear one-sided with officers subject to general pressure from the public; complaints without foundation; cheek and abuse from people 'which are so calculated that they are not quite serious enough to merit prosecution' (1965, xx); and unfair reporting by the mass media. (see also Mack, 1964).

US reviewers had little to say about Banton's portrait of the British police. However, Lennon (1967, p. 125) noted that 'the section on the alleged brutality by policemen, especially in the United States, seems to be based on rather dated sources and therefore sheds little light on the current situation'. Also commenting from a US perspective, Skolnick (1966) argued that the contrast between policing in the UK (consensus) and the USA (conflict) was so absolute because Banton did not include any discussion of organic police work in the small towns of 'middle America'. With its strong emphasis on family life, religious beliefs and civic mindedness 'the policeman is less reserved and even more approachable than in the city'. Interestingly, Skolnick's (1966, p. 62) seminal ethnographic research on detective work contains one of the first sustained engagements with Banton's work as part of his 'comparative glance' at the universality of police role and culture: 'Suppose ... we were to consider the "working personality" of police who constitute part of a relatively homogenous society, and who also enjoy an international reputation for honesty, efficiency, and legality'.

For Skolnick, Banton's study of the *Scottish* police could not be seen as representative of the British police in general. British police officers may not be so different from their American counterparts and British policing may not be superior to US policing. He reconsiders other information on British policing, such as the survey findings of the Royal Commission, newspaper reports and memoirs of British police officers. He concludes that 'the actual degree of difference often stated is open to serious question' noting, for example, that the Home Office 'spin' put on the Royal Commission social survey findings cannot disguise the fact that police relations with certain sections of the British public were 'clearly strained'. He concludes that the British police officer may well be more skilled than his American counterpart at appearing to conform with due process (Skolnick, 1966, p. 67).

He draws attention, as Downes did, to incidents of police-initiated violence that are not adequately discussed in the book and subsequent evidence of the existence of racial bias in the British police. Skolnick also reproduces a letter by the novelist Colin MacInnes to the *Partisan Review* in autumn 1963 indicating that the police were at odds with cultural change engulfing British society.

For McInnes 'it looks as if the hollowed myth that English coppers never use violence, perjury, framing of suspects – let alone participate in crimes – is at last being shattered in the public mind. Now, what has been foolish about this legend is not that coppers *do* these things – as all police forces do and must – but that national vanity led many to suppose that our coppers were far nicer men than any others' (cited in Skolnick, 1966, p. 69; see also McInnes 1957, 1963).

So, in many respects, even at the time of publication, Banton's pioneering sociological research was viewed by several reviewers as empirically limited in that it had little to offer by way of commentary on the heated debates that were engulfing urban British police forces. An interesting counter-perspective, penned by Tony Parker (1963), had already been published alongside Banton's *New Society* article. Parker noted in his interviews with professional criminals in London that police malpractice was viewed as 'part of ordinary life, omnipresent and accepted'. The occupational hazards associated with being a professional criminal included: being beaten up in police custody; having to offer bribes to officers; having evidence planted on them; and being fitted up for crimes they did not commit. Parker (1963) accepted that his disreputable informants were unlikely to be listened to by the authorities.

What is surprising is that none of the British reviewers drew attention to the fact that things were not well even within the pre-modern police officer's 'paradise'. Scottish newspapers during 1957 and 1958 carried reports of assaults on police officers, personnel shortages, disputes about pay and disciplinary charges and suspensions. And in April 1959 Lord Sorn's inquiry into the 'Thurso case' hit the national headlines. In order to safeguard his thesis, Banton had to downplay the significance of this incident. However, it prompted extensive discussion in Parliament, newspaper commentary and the establishment of an official inquiry. In conjunction with the other notorious incidents involving the police in the late 1950s and early 1960s, the 'Thurso Boy' case left many of the old certainties in tatters and sections of the British establishment in a state of doubt as regards to police practices and ethics (see Stevenson and Bottoms, 1989).

Conclusion

As was noted briefly at the beginning of this chapter, for all the limitations mentioned above, Michael Banton, in conjunction with William Westley, did create a 'knowledge structure' that would be tested and developed by the second wave of researchers attempting to construct a distinctive sociology of the police. The preferred methodological approach should be naturalistic rather than surveys or interviews and the micro-sociological focus should be on the cop 'working the beat'. A younger generation of sociologists collected observational on-the-ground data on: what patrol officers do when they are on duty; the formal and informal sources of the police officer's authority; how, why and with what effect officers use their discretionary powers; how officer/citizen interactions produce and shape policework; the defining features of the working personality of the police officer; and the characteristics and function of the rank and file occupational culture. An ongoing transatlantic conversation would also be necessary if police scholars were to find a comparative methodological filter through which to make sense of policing philosophies and practices. Police researchers would have to pay attention to ethical obligations. Because sociological research that attempts to get behind the 'blue curtain' is by definition sensitive and transgressive, it is not a place for armchair theorists who know nothing of the day in day out role conflicts that weigh heavily on police officers. Instead of making sensationalist claims or seeking, in the manner of the investigative journalist, to blow the whistle on malpractice, the professional sociologist should be the neutral chronicler who studiously avoids taking sides. The crucial task is accessing the police in the first place. Co-operation was only likely to be forthcoming if researchers framed their research proposals and findings in terms of policy relevance and if they were muted in their criticism of the organisation. Sociologists of the police also have an ethical obligation to ensure that they keep the door open for the next generation of researchers.

In terms of theoretical orientation, Banton conceives of the police as only one small component of a complex system for maintaining public order and regulating transgressive behaviour. Police constables should be conceived of not as crime fighters or law enforcers but as multi-tasked peace officers who are intimately connected to and highly dependent on informal social controls. In addition, routine policework should be conceptualized as a bundle of interconnected peacekeeping and order maintenance duties rather than law enforcement. Hence, Banton not only gave researchers the puzzle of working out the prerequisites for consensus policing but provided a Durkheimian inspired theory of community policing. The intriguing question was also posed by Banton as to what type of sociologically inspired discipline of police studies was likely to emerge (see Banton, 1971). Would this be a 'sociology of the police' that insisted on capturing the profane realities of police work in a dramatically changing society or a pure 'sociology of the police' that was continually attempting to re-run to a sacred pre-modern 'golden age' 'Dixonian' moment when the separation between the police and the community was unthinkable? And as we will discuss later in this book, there are crisis moments when the Anglo-American sociology of the police has taken a neo-Durkheimian 'sacralization of policing' turn insisting that policing must be public and communal in order to convey its full symbolic authority. The next generation of researchers would have to respond to Marxist analysis of the role of the police as the state on street patrol and government sponsorship of an applied police studies that would explicitly address management concerns about effectiveness, efficency and officer behaviour.

Police Studies: Traditional Perspectives

This chapter provides an overview of the main theoretical perspectives that constitute the backbone of Anglo-American police scholarship. As was noted in the previous chapter, the first book-length sociological study of the police by Michael Banton was not published until 1964. Hence, sociological analysis had a marginal presence in initial discussions about shifts and changes in initial post-war policing. However, the socio-economic, cultural and political transformations that convulsed Western democratic societies from the 1960s onwards created a fertile terrain for the development of a sociologically informed police scholarship (see, Sherman, 1974; Reiner, 1997a; Walker, 2004). The 1960s were marked by social and political unrest, urban riots, new social problems, the emergence of radical protest movements, political violence and the process of de-subordination. The police was the state institution that stood at the frontline of these transformations. Official reports from that time concluded that policing this 'restless society', characterized as it was by escalating crime, disorder and fear of crime, would require new methods of recruitment and training, organizational reform and the rethinking of operational philosophies and practice. Hence, the gateway was opened for a generation of researchers to interrogate the role of the police in contemporary Western society. In so doing they generated: ethnographic; Marxist; administrative and left realist perspectives on the police and policework. These are the approaches that this chapter will examine in detail.

Ethnographic perspectives: policing society

Symbolic interactionist perspectives were crucial for the development of police studies. They foregrounded the question of how deviance is produced by the defining agencies such as the police and how conformity to social rules and norms is secured by these agencies. They also helped to deconstruct dominant conceptualizations of the problem of crime by arguing that crime can never be an absolutely known 'fact' because its existence depends on a series of transactions between rule makers, rule enforcers and rule violators.

They also threw light on the core concept of 'deviance'. For instance, for one key interactionist, Howard Becker (1963, p. 14) deviance is not 'a quality that lies in behaviour itself, but in the *interactions* between the person who commits an act and those who respond to it'. The police are primary 'rule enforcers' in this moral enterprise who must justify their work and win the respect of those they deal with. In validating their work, the police are required to demonstrate that the rules have some meaning and that they can enforce them. They also have a vested interest in amplifying the significance of these problems. If necessary, police officers must coerce respect from the public. This means that an individual 'may be labelled as deviant not because he has actually broken a rule, but because he has shown disrespect to the enforcer of the rule' (Becker, 1963, p. 158). Officers must also decide what rules to enforce and who to label and frequently focus on those with the least power to respond.

The first wave of ethnographic Anglo-American police research, carried out by Bittner, Manning, Niederhoffer, van Maanen, Reiss, Muir, Wilson, Brown, and Rubenstein in the US, and Cain, Punch, Chatterton and Holdaway in the UK, represented part of the shift of the analytical focus from the offender to the agents of social control. This utilized observational methods to access the process of becoming a police officer, the 'inner realities of organizational life', the characteristics of the police work group and the determinants of officer interactions and relationships with citizens. The focus was on frontline urban patrol work because this was where all officers, irrespective of rank, served their apprenticeship and the majority would spend their working lives. Accessing the behind closed doors world of the patrol officer was deemed to be of vital importance because it would provide an understanding of the wider aspects of the police organization and its relationship with the criminal justice system. Westley and Banton had already established that police power is predicated on their role as 'gatekeepers' to the rest of the system.

Although there were differences in emphasis and actual methodological approach, this body of research established that only 'thick description' could 'tap that initial encounter on the streets, or in a private dwelling, with all its implications for the individual citizen concerned and for his or her potential passage through the criminal justice system' (Punch, 1979, p. 4; see also Van Maanen, 1973; Manning and Van Maanen, 1978, p. 1–10; Holdaway, 1983, pp. 15–16; Punch, 1993). The importance of recording, in an empathetic manner, the contradictory realities of 'round-the-clock' policework is accounted for by Punch vividly:

> Policemen work at the nerve-edge of society where control is exercised, where sanctions are applied, and where crises are resolved. They inhabit profane

areas of society, where good citizens fear to tread, and face situations where the buck can no longer be passed on. Encounters become instant morality plays with the abstract values of our civilization ... being daily redefined in unedifying and irresolute conflicts accompanied by blood, blasphemy and violence. The magic and the mundane, the sacred and the profane mingle in policework into a blend irresistible to the hackneyed plots of television serials and, less conspicuously, into rich and fruitful material for the study of social interaction. (1979, p. 17)

Researchers confirmed that, as with most public bureaucracies, police agencies are 'multiple reality' organizations. The formal organizational map characterizes the police department as a quasi-military hierarchical institution with standardized operational procedures and practices which is territorially structured and imposes discipline through strict regulations and ordinances. However, research indicated that the organizational form enclosing policework was in certain important respects a 'symbolic' or 'mock' bureaucracy. Manning (1978, p. 65) argued that the paramilitary command structure and 'the elaborate militarism of insignia and public rhetoric tend to mystify the basic fact that the control of policework lies in the hands of the lowest functionaries'. Organizational rules and regulations were in fact ambiguous and negotiable and there was little effective managerial control over the actual work practices of rank and file officers. Although police officers are formally required to do things 'by the book', researchers established that once they left the station there was considerable room for improvisation.

The production of street policing

Ethnographic research established that, from the officer's perspective, policework was a complicated activity because discretion has to be exercised as to whether in any given situation a criminal or disorderly act has taken, or is taking, place. In essence, the police must transform the precepts of criminal law into criminal law 'in action'. The low visibility of police work, with little direct supervision or monitoring by senior officers, means that patrol officers have considerable operational discretion regarding the 'when, how, where and who' to monitor, stop, search, arrest, charge or seize goods from and whether to use force. And of course the initial gate-keeping decision determines, to a significant degree, whether and how a member of the public will subsequently be processed by the criminal justice system. Equally importantly, formal action draws officers into a bureau-legal process that includes case construction and presentation, and organizational and judicial review.

Researchers noted how officers routinely ignored a substantial number of offences or potential offences or responded to situations informally. Petty legal infringements, crimes where the victim declines to make a formal complaint, and certain violations of the law where the officer suspects that there is insufficient evidence to guarantee a conviction may generate an action other than arrest. Although the widest exercise of discretion is more likely in routine street encounters involving relatively minor crimes and misdemeanours, serious criminal behaviour may also result in decisions not to make an arrest. Hence, as Wilson (1968, p. 203) noted, the police officer is the *source* of the criminal law and is required to decide 'which laws to enforce formally (by an arrest), which to enforce informally (by imposing a settlement on the spot or by punishing an offender without arresting him), and which not to enforce at all. This discretion is essential to the maintenance of a minimum of public respect for the police'.

For Wilson (1968) police discretion was an inescapable aspect of policing for four reasons.

- First, it is not possible for police officers to notice every infraction.
- Second, although the law lays down universal principles, *particular* situations and *specific* circumstances must be interpreted and defined by the police officer 'on the spot' before a principle can be enforced.
- Third, police officers can very often obtain information on serious crimes by overlooking minor infractions of the law.
- Finally, public opinion would not sanction the full enforcement of all laws all of the time.

Judicial rather than administrative in nature, the discovery of 'police discretion' gave rise to other concerns about officers abusing or exceeding their authority, using, for example, their stop, search and arrest powers on the basis of personal prejudice, moral indignation, loss of temper or to make the work more interesting. The discretionary nature of policework also provided an explanatory starting point for understanding the prevalence of police misconduct and corruption.

The multifaceted nature of policework

Thinking about the role of the police in crime control can conjure up images of officers on the beat, deterring criminals and reassuring the public; police vehicles rushing through city streets to stop crimes in progress, and of detectives investigating serious crimes, arresting offenders, and activating the criminal justice system. Despite the central position of this 'cops and robbers' model in both police culture and the public imagination, ethnographic researchers confirmed that the exact nature and scope of police activity is in fact difficult to define and, for the most part, unrelated to law enforcement and criminal detection. As Manning (1977, pp. 158–9) argues normal policework 'is boring, tiresome, sometimes dirty, sometimes technically demanding but it is rarely dangerous'. However, it is the infrequent hot pursuit, gun battle, drug bust, or dramatic arrest of a wanted criminal that has been 'seized upon by the police and played up by the public. The public's response has been to demand even more dramatic crook catching and crime prevention, and this demand for arrests has been converted into an index for measuring how well the police accomplish their tasks' (Manning, 1977, pp. 158–9).

Confirming Banton's findings, far more time is spent 'keeping the peace', maintaining order and regulating public conduct on the beat. Police officers are expected to handle a vast, complex range of problems and predicaments because no other means has been found to resolve them. Thus, the two defining characteristics of policework are that it is (a) not crime/law enforcement but social service related and (b) reactive, dealing with the crime after the fact, rather than proactive. It was this that originally led Punch to define the police as a secret round-the-clock social service expected to arrive 'when a crisis is happening' and the public requires a visible, authoritative intervention (Punch, 1979, p. 107). Bittner (1970, pp. 40–1) argued that members of the public 'call the cops', rather than other agencies because they are mandated by society to use force. Whatever tasks the police are called upon by citizens to undertake 'police intervention means above all making use of the capacity and authority to over-power resistance to an attempted solution in the natural habitat of the problem'. The involvement of police officers projects the message:

> ... that force may be, and may have to be, used to achieve a desired objective. Police procedure is defined by the feature that it may not be opposed in its course, and that force can be used if it is opposed. This is what the existence of the police makes available to society. Accordingly the question 'What are policemen supposed to do?' is almost completely identical with the question 'What kinds of situation require remedies that are non-negotiably coercive ... (Bittner, 1970, pp. 40–1)

Goldstein (1977) provided a succinct list of the policing tasks that require the potential application of 'non-negotiable force': regulating conduct that is threatening to life and property; aiding individuals who are in danger of physical harm; protecting the constitutional right to free speech and assembly and freedom of movement; assisting those in need of care and protection: conflict resolution and peacekeeping; and creating and maintaining public security. Researchers also noted that the ambivalence surrounding the police task in a liberal democracy needed to be formally acknowledged because it had implications for how policing should be organized, delivered and evaluated. One important way to realize this was through impression management strategies to 'dramatize the appearance of [police] control' (Manning, 1977).

Police culture

These early sociological police studies established that the rituals associated with putting on a blue uniform requires the recruit to cross the threshold and become part of a collective 'police culture'. For Manning, (1995, p. 472), this culture is defined as the 'accepted practices, rules and principles of conduct that are situationally applied and generalized rationales and beliefs'. Under the guidance of experienced officers, 'rookies' are moved from 'knowing how' to 'learning by doing' via the craft of policework, the territorial structures, working rules, pace of work and folklore of a particular force, division, and immediate peer group. Researchers noted how it was in the canteen and in the patrol car, in the locker room, in the quiet moments of the shift and during off-duty socializing that 'rookies' learn about the realities of 'the job', the street wise tricks of the trade, the 'easing' behaviour and the common-sense 'recipes' for dealing with and 'solving' highly problematic organizational and highly emotionally charged public situations. The 'togetherness' forged through this particularly strong version of occupational socialization produces a distinctive oppositional mentality with negative and defensive views common to majority of rank and file police officers. Gradually, officers become part of an institutionally sanctioned community of craft, tradition and memory (Manning, 1995).

Because of the ever-present possibility of being abused, threatened, provoked and physically attacked, police officers become hyper-sensitive to and suspicious of the routine aspects of daily life. The experienced, streetwise beat officer is alert to 'signals' that something might not be right. Police officers, made distrustful by experience, treat incidents and encounters with heightened vigilance. Skolnick also established that officers' highly developed sense of caution and suspicion worked to produce the notion of the 'symbolic assailant'. Officers, because their work requires them to be alert to the possibility of violence develop 'a perceptual shorthand to identify certain kinds of people as symbolic assailants, that is as persons whose gestures, language and attire that the policeman has come to recognise as a prelude to violence' (Skolnick, 1966, p. 266).

And as Westley (1951, 1953) had confirmed, many urban police officers, given the everyday realities of their 'dirty work' environment, develop a cynical perspective, losing faith in people, society, their senior officers and eventually the purpose of the job. According to Neiderhoffer (1967, p. 9), in their Hobbesian view, the world becomes 'a jungle' in which crime, corruption, complicities and brutality are normal features of the terrain. Added to this, the work of the police, as was mentioned above, frequently appears to be an illusory method of controlling crime. Officers have to cope with criminals who flaunt their protection from the criminal law and confront gangs of youths on housing estates and city centre streets who have no respect for the police. They also complain about being humiliated as a result of aggressive and unfair cross-examination by 'bent' or 'slick' lawyers and let down by incompetent prosecutors, gullible juries and out-of-touch judges (Graef, 1989; Young, 1991, 1993). 'Handcuffed' from doing policework by liberal politicians and anti-police pressure groups, the idea that they are enforcing criminal justice and upholding the rule of law becomes a joke. It is this that underpins the development of an authoritarian perspective on criminal justice and law and order.

Another important source of police officers' cynicism is the awareness that others may wish to manipulate or control their decision-making powers and authority. Officer views of 'the public' are influenced by contact not with the average law-abiding citizen but experience of 'heavy users' of police services (willingly or unwillingly). Wilson (1968) noted that when the police arrive 'to look for a prowler, examine a loss, or stop a fight, the victim and suspect are agitated, fearful, even impassioned'. However, experienced police officers 'have seen it all before and they have to distrust victim accounts (to say nothing of suspect explanations) of what happened. Instead of offering sympathy and immediately taking the victim's side, the police may seem cool, suspicious, or disinterested because they have learned that 'victims' often turn out not to have been victimized at all – the 'stolen' TV set never existed or was lost, loaned to a friend, or hidden because payments were overdue; the 'assault' was in fact a fight which the 'victim' started but was unable to finish' (Wilson, 1968, pp. 24–5).

Researchers also noted the hostile reaction of officers to those they believe to be defiant, disrespectful or questioning their authority. The individual who does not move away when ordered to do so, who asserts that she or he knows their rights, or who challenges a police officer physically is asking for trouble (Reiss, 1972, p. 58). When police officers speak of their authority, Wilson (1968) argues, they mean the right to ask questions, obtain a reply and have orders obeyed. When officers cannot exercise authority by their very presence or psychological advantage, they may decide to demonstrate who exactly is in control. For some, says Wilson, physical size and/or a confident attitude may suffice. However, other officers with an 'eye for an eye' mentality will resort to more coercive tactics. This explains why the discourse of violence is central to the institutional culture, even though it was rare for officers to experience actual violence. As Smith and Gray (1985, p. 369) noted, the defining meaning of policework for the majority of officers 'is the exercise of authority, and force (rather than knowledge or understanding) is for them the main *symbol* of authority and power, even if they actually impose their authority in other ways'.

Police officers also experience a process of social isolation and depersonalization. They expect to be viewed by many members of the public as uniforms rather than as individuals and to be routinely called 'pigs' and 'the filth' by some sections of society. In order to do their job, officers must in turn depersonalize the public, categorizing them into those deemed to be deserving of police help and the 'others', the 'toe-rags', 'slags', 'scrotes', 'scum' and 'animals'. Researchers argue that in certain important respects, these highly moralistic 'we and they' stereotypes drive the day-to-day nature and pattern of policework (see Smith and Gray, 1985; Young, 1991, 1993) and even structured views of supervisors and senior management. This stereotyping is directly related to the social/stratification or the racial/ethnic/religious divisions of a given society.

These cultural traits were found to have a critical role to play in understanding the 'invitational edges' of police deviance and malpractice. 'Blue coated crime' was not just an individual exceptional matter but intimately related to both the police mandate and the police culture. Manning (1977) found resistance to the internal rules to 'supervise, guide, sanction and alter behaviour'. Skolnick (1966) argued that the only way that police officers could 'resolve' the inevitable conflict between demands for high productivity and due process was by resorting to extra-legal practices. Because procedural violations can lead to criminal charges, civil actions, complaints investigations, reprimands, lost cases, demotion or dismissal, officers learn to watch their backs, say nothing and control the flow of information to supervisors. As a result, the strength of the culture is a consequence of the unique characteristics and conflicting pressures of policework.

The recusant culture also shields officers from questioning or investigating their decisions and actions. Trust and allegiance are 'not given to an abstracted set of legal norms, posited organizational structure or quasi-political and cynically defined 'professionalism', but to one's peers, those with whom the joy, drudgery, satisfactions and chaos of the streets are shared' (Manning, 1978, p. 65). When necessary, the rank and file had the power to erect a 'blue wall' of silence and resistance against both supervisory officers and outsiders – particularly those with the power to challenge their version of reality, voice criticism or advocate change. Secrecy shields the shared definition of situations. Group solidarity and an ever-alert 'grapevine' provides officers with the means to 'close ranks' against those officers who are deviant or different and therefore not to be trusted. Officers contemplating 'whistle blowing' on malpractice are aware that, if they are found out, they will face an isolated and vulnerable working life.

Ethnographic studies noted how the assertive features of police culture generates many pernicious problems for the organization. The negative attitudes of officers towards the public in general and particular social and ethnic groups are the source of many unnecessarily conflictual and counter-productive street encounters. The police culture also provides officers with the capacity to resist or 're-script' any 'top-down' modernization initiative that does not correspond to the 'lived realities' of policing, or to not 'action' policies that blur the distinction between 'real' policework ('feeling collars' and 'getting figures') and 'rubbish' or 'dead-end' community work (the rest) and/or expands organizational control over officers' operational autonomy. In its strongest version it might be more accurate to discuss a rank and file 'police ideology' rather than a 'police culture'.

Subsequent insider accounts that resulted from 'riding the cruisers' and 'walking the beat' deployed and developed the conceptual insights of the first generation of police researchers. As a result, we have been provided with increasingly sophisticated, nuanced, dynamic understandings of the ambiguous nature of the police mandate; how and why police officers and citizens encounter and interact with each other; when, why and with what effect do officers choose not to enforce the law; the degree to which policework is constrained by the organizational and territorial working environment; and the connection between officer attitudes and situational behaviour. In the process, the urban police officer has been further humanized as someone with an extremely complex job working in very difficult set of circumstances.

More recent research has deepened our understanding of the dynamics of occupational socialization and functioning of police culture. It affirms that there are cultural differences within the organization, which are most evident in the distinction between 'street cops' and 'management cops'; college graduates and old school cops; detective and uniformed officers; officers attached to specialist operational units and neighbourhood-based officers, etc. Researchers found that there is also space for officers to develop their own – progressive and reactionary – professional identity and policing style. Moreover, an understanding of virtually any aspect of police culture is limited to the extent that it does not work through how gender, race and sexuality define and structure police subjectivities and how each generation of officers both re-enacts police culture and renews it at the same time. A new concern is the new antagonistic 'copper versus copper' dynamics that are now playing out within police forces (for an overview see Chan, 1997; Waddington, 1999; Paoline, 2003; Crank, 2004). This is something we will return to in Chapter 6.

According to Chan (1997) further theoretical innovation is necessary to address the complexities that have engulfed the term 'police culture'. Using Bourdieu's concepts of 'field' and 'habitus', she argues that police practice should be understood 'in terms of the interaction between specific structural conditions of policework (the field) and the cultural knowledge accumulated by police officers which integrates past experiences (habitus)'. Her model 'emphasizes the active role played by police actors in developing, reinforcing, resisting or transforming cultural knowledge and institutionalized practice' (Chan, 1997, p. 225).

However, ethnographic studies have been subject to trenchant critique. For instance, Brogden et al. (1988, p. 45) noted that there are built-in methodological limitations. For them, the 'naturalistic' value of accessing the inside world of the police officer is offset by the fact that:

> Everything depends on how comprehensive that social world can be revealed by participation and observation alone. Two sorts of errors become possible: that resulting from participants successfully concealing aspects of their world from the researcher; and that resulting from the inability to take into account unobserved processes, beyond the immediate world under observation, that nevertheless affect the social world being studied.

The construction of the uniformed beat officer as the basis for sociological research and theoretical understanding of 'police culture' obscures 'how the law, formal organizational policy or senior officers impinge on this world' (Brogden et al., 1988, p. 45). In an early critique, Galliher (1971) argued that 'cop-sided' insider studies were unable to make the conceptual connections between policing and the structural features of advanced capitalist societies. The 'surrender' of the researchers to the police culture meant that they ignored or downplayed the variable of 'class' in their analysis of police culture and policework. If class was included, they would have to address the fact that the core function of the police is to control the poor and minority ethnic groups:

> ... in any way necessary while other citizens can continue to believe this is a free, democratic society and yet have their property protected at the same time. In fact, the dirty work of policing American slums is so well-hidden from the middle classes that even middle class sociologists fail to understand its meaning and function, the function being the maintenance of a highly economically stratified and racist society. (Galliher, 1971, p. 316)

He went on to question the research findings concerning police autonomy, arguing that 'it is incredible to think that social scientists would believe that a highly stratified society would allow lower class or marginally middle class people such as the police to control major social policy' (Galliher, 1971, p. 317). Allied to this was an inexplicable absence of research on police officer's position in the class structure and the role of the collective organizations that represent the material interests of police officers.

For reasons that will become apparent in the next chapter, Johnston (1992) provides us with another set of problems inherent in the ethnographic approach to policework. He argued that, despite the possibilities, the focus of police research was 'disappointingly narrow' due to the dominant influences that had 'distorted' the discipline's development. There was an inexplicable fetishization of 'the blue uniform' to the exclusion of a multitude of private security companies and voluntary agencies involved in 'policing' activities. And within this there was a tendency to concentrate on the activities and attitudes of front-line personnel. This 'eyes down' or 'street level' approach to police research 'addresses a field with a limited spatial range and, in consequence, generates more and more data with less and less scope' (Johnston, 1992, p. 186). The end result was to 'construct a sociology which, although producing an encyclopedic knowledge of the ins and outs of the patrol function, excludes other key areas of policing activity from serious consideration. In short, we come to know more and more about less and less' (Johnston, 1992, p. 186).

The first wave of ethnographic studies, with phenomenological tendencies, were unwelcome to police administrators because they de-mystified a number of problematic issues concerning policework, including the reality that police capacity to control crime is limited to symbolic gestures, police officers 'make' crime and deviance rather than control or suppress it; arrest is a selective process dependent on situational factors and suspect characteristics rather than the 'facts' of crime; crime statistics are an organizational construction; policing styles can amplify deviance; deviation from due process is integral to getting the job done; and the 'dial-a-cop' bureaucracy has limited control over the self-governing rank and file culture. In addition, because they empathized with the dilemmas of rank and file officers, researchers offered little in the way of practical help to: control street level policing practices; structure officer discretion; improve the effectiveness of police patrol activities; and/or develop positive relations between the police and the public. Consequently, the 'beyond bureaucracy' ethnographic research by the lone sociologist has been increasingly replaced by controlled observations by policy-oriented research teams recording the working practices of large samples of police officers and testing and surveying the psychological attitudes of police officers. These applied studies are harnessed to a 'what works' administrative police studies framework. As a result, some of the most 'realistic' contemporary insider accounts of policing from a rank and file perspective are now provided not by ethnographers but by investigative journalists, documentary makers, ex-police officers and of course police procedural novelists and television and film companies.

Marxist perspectives: policing capitalist society

Paul Chevigny's 1969 book, *Police Power: Police Abuses in New York City*, focused attention on 'the routine denials of due process of law' by false arrest, framing suspects, unlawful search and seizure, systematic harassment, violence and 'summary punishment' that were a routine feature of street encounters between police officers and citizens. Chevigny argued that police abuse was not just patterned and normal but political. For the powerful, the police are vital because they need an agency to keep society running smoothly and as a result are willing to turn a blind eye to police criminality. The police have been given the mandate to construct a criminal class and criminal threat that justifies the use of existing legislation and new legislation. However, police practices are also counterproductive creating contempt for authority. The criminal justice system within which the police work 'is evil, for the simplest of reasons: because it injures people and destroys their respect for the legal process. It is not for nothing that ghetto people have chosen police abuses as symbols of oppression; it is because they actually are acts of oppression' (Chevigny, 1969, p. 283). Following Chevigny, during the 1970s Marxist and critical Anglo-American criminologists sought to analyse the role of the police in advanced capitalist societies (Platt, 1971; Platt and Cooper, 1974; Takagi 1974, Bunyan, 1977; Cain, 1977, 1979; Quinney, 1977; Bowden, 1978; Hall et al., 1978; Ackroyd et al., 1980; Thompson, 1980). These studies were explicitly concerned with analysing the injustices of police–state–class relationships rather than 'the police' as such. This marked a radical departure from and challenge to ethnographic police perspectives.

In 1975 the Center for Research on Criminal Justice at Berkeley, University of California published *The Iron Fist and the Velvet Glove*. It expanded upon the Marxist theorizing laid out by Takagi and by Platt and Cooper et al. to combine historical studies of the origins and functions of the nineteenth-century police and the increasingly political role of the police in America in the 1960s and 1970s. A particular concern was the police role in the criminalization of political protest, for example, against anti-Vietnam demonstrators, the civil rights movement, the Black Panthers and the Weathermen. This indicated that in the 1970s the police would become 'a formidable and increasingly dangerous institution of oppression' and criminalization (1975, p. 184). As the USA moved rapidly from a liberal democratic state to what was defined as a 'garrison state', coercive policing would increasingly span both counter-insurgency work abroad and the pacification of the domestic ghettos. The demand for sophisticated public order weaponry and technologies and crowd control techniques would also generate a lucrative police-industrial marketplace.

This emerging Marxist perspective argued that critical criminologists would have to, as a matter of political urgency, theorize the precise nature of the relationship between the police and this new state formation. The starting point was the belief that underneath the illusion of consent the core function of the police was to enforce class, racial, cultural and sexual inequalities. Platt (1975, p. 12) pointed to the historical evidence that suggested that the police 'were not created to serve 'society' or the 'people', but to serve *some* parts of society and *some* people at the expense of others'. The 'social service' and 'peace keeping' functions ideologically mystified the true function of the police: this 'velvet glove' had been deliberately constructed to mask the construction of an 'iron fist'. As the economic and social crisis in the USA and other western societies deepened, we would witness the unmasking of a repressive, militarized policing apparatus and punitive control culture which would be used to regulate surplus populations, suppress cultural dissent, subdue political resistance and redefine citizenship rights.

The political police

In the UK, Marxist writers such as Bunyan, Bowden and Cain and State Research began to document the changing nature of British policing in a similar manner. The underlying premise was that the police are grounded in and structured by the state–class relations that encase them at particular historical moments. As British capitalism entered a period of crisis, the post-war democratic Keynsian consensus, and accompanying legitimating social welfare programmes, was breaking apart. This would have profound implications for the police as the core state agency mandated to maintain socio-economic and political order. The most apparent signs were the surfacing of the political police and security agencies and the politicization of the public policing. In so doing these writers created an understanding of the police and policing that was connected to the changing governmental capacities of the British state.

In 1977 Maureen Cain argued that ethnographic perspectives, with their focus on uniformed police work, were increasingly irrelevant to the task of understanding the changing nature of British policing. There was, most notably for Cain, no reference to those 'deep state' political police agencies that were mandated to protect national security interests:

> They have ignored them *theoretically* because they were constrained to ignore them empirically. Thus 'the police' have been presented as a more or less homogenous structure, divided internally only by dominant preoccupation with traffic, juveniles, criminal investigation or just plain patrolling. That would not matter if one could simply adds on other functions – internal intelligence gathering, control of overseas spy operations, counter revolutionary preparations and so on – but one cannot. For to add on these extra tasks transforms the equation. (Cain, 1977, p. 162)

Others, such as Bunyon (1977) and E.P. Thompson (1980), detailed how political policing and security agencies such as MI5 and MI6 'normally deeply concealed within the strategic centres of the state' along with chief police officers were increasingly intervening in the nation's political affairs. As with the US Marxists, there was the embryonic idea that, in an attempt to manage social conflict and dissent, authoritarian or law and order ideologies were taking hold *within* the core control agencies of the liberal democratic state.

Thompson (1980) noted the willingness of chief police officers to align themselves publicly with authoritarian political discourse. He argued that it is in the nature of the police to be attracted towards 'authoritarian and statist ideologies' and to press for more resources and powers. These tendencies and demands are normally checked by the constitutional requirements of the liberal democratic society. However, Thompson felt that the police and security services were increasingly pushing at an open door. For instance, in November 1973 Sir Robert Mark, the Commissioner of the Metropolitan Police, had used the high-profile BBC Dimbleby Lecture to make a sweeping attack on the ineffectiveness of the criminal justice system and the damaging effect that corrupt criminal lawyers were having on the criminal justice process and police credibility (see Mark, 1977, p. 118). He also declared that 'we who are the anvil on which society beats out its problems and abrasions of social inequality, racial prejudice, weak laws and ineffective legislation should not be inhibited from expressing our views, whether critical or not'. His forthright views on crooked criminal lawyers generated a news-media storm (see Mark, 1979; Chibnall, 1977). This lecture represented the first of a series of high profile interventions on 'law and order' issues by a generation of political police chiefs (see Reiner, 1991; McLaughlin, 1994; Wall, 1998; Savage et al. 2000; Loader and Mulcahy, 2003). For Thompson (1980, pp. 200–1) what was alarming about these developments was:

... the very powerful [police] public relations operation which disseminates these notions as an authorized, consensual view – an operation carried on out of our own taxes, which presses its spokesmen forward on every occasion upon the media, which lobbies inquiries and Royal Commissions constantly pressing for larger powers, which bullies weak Home Secretaries ... which reproves magistrates for lenient sentencing; which announces unashamedly that the police are in the regular practice of breaking judges rules when interrogating suspects; which slanders unnamed lawyers and lampoons libertarian organizations; which tells judges how they are to interpret the law and which justifies the invasion of the citizens' privacy and the accumulation of prejudicial and inaccurate records ... the notion that we should be instructed as to what value we are to put on freedom and democracy, and be instructed by the police. And that the police are to be seen as, somehow, for themselves, rather than as servants to us, so that we are to be instructed by the police as to what is to be our place.

Policing the crisis

The most comprehensive and influential elaboration of the 'authoritarian police' thesis can be found in Hall et al.'s (1978) *Policing the Crisis*. This complicated, wide-ranging book was the first cultural analysis of the relationship between crime, policing and the state in the context of the shift towards an authoritarian consensus. As many commentators have noted, *Policing the Crisis* is analytically constructed from concepts and ideas gleaned from new deviancy theory, news-making studies of 'moral panics' and 'crime waves' and a Marxist analysis of 'the state' derived from the work of Althusser, Poulantzas and Gramsci (see Sumner, 1981).

The empirical reference point for the book is how the 'moral panic' about 'mugging' came to define political debates about law and order in the 1970s. The intention of Hall et al., (1978, p. vii) was to go 'beyond the label to the contradictory social context which is mystifyingly reflected in it'. What was of particular interest was how from the very beginning news-media reportage of this particular crime was 'shadowed by the theme of race' and why this particular 'crime' rapidly acquired such powerful racial connotations in the official and public imagination. Everyone soon 'knew' that muggers were young black men and their victims were weak, vulnerable and white.

For Hall et al., the social and political reaction to 'mugging' was out of all proportion to the actual seriousness of the offence and the threat posed. They could find no reliable evidence to substantiate the 'mugging' crime wave claims made by police, judges, politicians, journalists and commentators. In order to understand the significance and importance of this particular moral panic it was, they argued, necessary to locate it within the convulsions engulfing British society in the 1970s. This crisis was not just economic but a deeper crisis of governance – what they termed a 'crisis of hegemony' – as the authority and legitimacy of the post-war social democratic welfare consensus collapsed. Manifestations of this crisis were to be found in the wave after wave of 'moral panics' that had engulfed Britain from the 1960s onwards. British society experienced major social dislocations through moral panics and in the 1970s the different concerns and panics began to weave a general image of Britain as an increasingly ungovernable society.

It is in this unsettled context that street crime and 'the mugger' achieved prominence. The moral panic about 'mugging' was not a rational well-founded reaction to an increase in violent crime but one of the most visible manifestations of the hegemonic crisis of the British state. As part of the reconstruction of the state, the ideological terrain was being re-shaped to manage the 'enemies within':

> The state itself had become mobilized – sensitized to the emergence of the enemy in any of his manifold disguises; the repressive response is at the ready, quick to move in, moving formally, through the law, the police, administrative regulation, public censure, and at a developing speed. This is what we mean by the slow 'shift to control', the move towards a kind of closure in the apparatuses of state control and repression. The decisive mechanisms in the management of hegemonic control are regularly and routinely based in the apparatuses of constraint. (Hall et al., 1978, p. 278)

Through the potency of 'moral panics', and the accompanying demands for 'something to be done', public consent was being gathered together behind an authoritarian set of policy responses. The image of the 'mugger' – young, lawless and black – in combination with increasing images of the British inner city as 'urban black colonies' came to serve as 'the articulator of the crisis, as its ideological conductor'. Black, male youth came to epitomize all the social problems of the inner city: racial conflict, generational conflict, poverty, degeneration, crime, and violence. This segment of British society was the ideal scapegoat or folk devil because of how they responded to the structural situation they found themselves in. With no chance of employment, their life chances limited by their class position and racial discrimination, this group of young people was deeply alienated from white society. Their response was to opt for a means of survival which included street criminality and petty hustling and subcultural resistance.

A 'law and order' crackdown on black youth overlapped with a crackdown on the poor, the unemployed, the disadvantaged and those living in areas ravished by the crisis. Hence, the task of policing black youth was 'for all practical purposes, synonymous with the wider problem of policing the crisis' (Hall et al., 1978, p. 332). The key themes of 'race-crime-youth' operated as a mechanism for 'the construction of an authoritarian consensus, a conservative backlash: what we call the build up towards a 'soft' law and order society' (Hall et al., 1978, p. viii).

One agency – the police – had a crucial role to play in the state's move from a social democratic to an authoritarian mode of governance because crises 'have to be remedied, their worst effects contained or mitigated. They also have to be controlled. To put it crudely, they have to be *policed*' (Hall et al., 1978, p. 339). Hall et al., argued that the role played by the police in the mugging panic went largely unquestioned because the dominant news-media image was of a beleaguered 'thin blue line' mandated to uphold law and order. The police because they are relatively autonomous from the state can play a pro-active and innovatory role in the construction of moral panics. The crime statistics are police property and this ownership, in conjunction with their professional expertise as 'crime fighters', ensures that their 'primary definitions' and pro-nouncements are newsworthy and presented as definitive by a news-media who are largely dependent on them for information and access. In certain instances, the 'police view' can stand in for 'public opinion' as the authorised, legitimate, consensual viewpoint on any given issue. Consequently, the police have a central role to play in the media's construction of moral panics because they are in a position to identify the nature and seriousness of the crime prob-lem, who the criminals are, who the victims are, and equally importantly *what should be done*. In essence, they are in possession of the 'raw material' required for the engineering of fully-fledged crime waves and moral panics and over-criminalization. The police are increasingly proactive in: (1) *defining* situations; (2) *selecting* targets; (3) *initiating* campaigns; (4) *signifying* their actions; and (5) *legitimating* their actions (Hall et al., 1978, p. 52).

It is of course open to the police to distance themselves from 'crime waves' and 'moral panics' about crime by issuing disclaimers to the news-media and calming public fears. However, the organizational temptation is to amplify pub-lic anxieties and manipulate 'moral panics' because the police can benefit from them in terms of resources, empowerment, legitimacy and status. Hence, in the case of mugging, key police officers actively pronounced not only on the extent and nature of the problem but also on the solutions. The question is why?

Hall et al., argue that the police-society relationship was changing as a result of the policing task becoming more difficult. A combination of conflicting demands, the emergence of alternative cultural value systems, low morale, a sense of not being valued, de-subordination in the form of increased ques-tioning of their authority resulted in the growth of 'a particular "mood" within the police, a mood characterized by a growing impatience, frustration and anger' (1978, p. 50). Police officers and their representative organizations were increasingly allying themselves with right-wing political forces in British soci-ety by pronouncing Britain to be on the edge of anarchy and demanding the resources and mandate to launch a decisive 'war against crime'.

At a mundane routine level, it was day-to-day relationships with black com-munities which was a source of increasing frustration and discontent. The police had responsibility for 'controlling and containing the widespread disaffection among the black population, attempting to confine it to black areas, and had 'heightened sensitivity to, and expectation of, black involvement in trouble, and by extension, "crime"' (Hall et al., 1978, p. 45). This locked rank and file officers into a conflictual set of relationships because there had developed a 'deep and complex culture of resistance' in black communities. The resistance ranged from community campaigns against racist crime and controversial policing actions to threats of 'war in the ghetto' by more radical black groupings such as the Black Panthers. By the early 1970s the nature of the response to casual police harassment was changing: 'sharper, quicker, tougher – above all more organized' (1978, p. 331). The result was that without recourse to tough public order tactics, the police were in danger of losing control of certain neighbour-hoods in the major conurbations.

For Hall et al. (1978) the mugging panic cannot be understood outside of the police belief that black youth were a potent threat not just to law and order but to *social* order. The police needed more autonomy and powers to deal with this problem population and the fact that they were actively engaged in a 'frightening' new strain of violent street crime provided the necessary pretext. The state let the police 'slip the leash' of constitutional control by mandating this agency to define the social and political problems of the inner cities as essentially criminal matters requiring a forceful response.

The outcome of this significant shift in police practices and philosophy was not just the over-racialization of street crime (and criminal victimization) but the over criminalization of a whole section of society. In addition, this com-munity was defined as being undeserving of police protection with regard to criminal victimization. And, crucially, given that anyone who questioned the policing of black neighbourhoods was automatically condemned and labelled as anti-police, it was left to the police and black communities to fight out this intensifying war of attrition.

Published in 1978, *Policing the Crisis* warned of a very specific set of con-flictual police–community outcomes if the state's authoritarian lurch contin-ued. The moment of the 'authoritarian state' moved decidedly closer with the election of a 'free market, strong state' New Right government in 1979 with a mandate to restore law and order and dismantle the institutional framework of post-war social democratic Britain. The Thatcher government committed itself to enhancing the role of the police in order to do both. When the most serious anti-police riots for a century broke out in 1981 it looked as if the warnings of Hall et al., had been fulfilled. The after-shocks of the riots rever-berated through police scholarship in the UK. Howard Becker's question of 'who's side are we on' took on a new relevance and the different answers resulted in a fundamental and irrevocable split between Marxist criminolo-gists and other police scholars in relation to how to conceptualize the distur-bances and the police and formulate a response. Marxist criminologists rejected the dominant idea that these were mindless, criminal riots. They were political 'uprisings', 'rebellions', 'insurrections' – black people had risen up in order to defend their communities against a racist and oppressive army of occupation. The mask of consensual Dixonian policing had finally dropped and the police had willingly taken on the role of being the Praetorian guard of the New Right. Hall argued (1980, p. 6) that the police were 'willing and able, indeed anxious to impose the neglect of the state on the people ... and to provide the disciplinary means by which the poor and working people are made to bear the brunt of Mrs Thatcher's tough medicine.'

The 'iron fist in the velvet glove'

Marxist police scholars viewed post-riot 'community policing' proposals by Lord Scarman (1981) as the authoritarian state's latest attempt to conceal the shift to normalised paramilitary policing. 'Community policing' was defined as a complementary part of a 'totalising policing' initiative geared towards: persuading people to allow a seemingly benign police presence back into their communities; gathering community information on extremists and trouble-makers; and co-opting other social agencies into the policing function because the police had lost their legitimacy. The attempted synchronization of social services, education, housing and the probation service in a corporatist policing exercise was necessary because whole communities and neighbourhoods rather than just individuals and individual offences now needed to be policed. Multi-agency initiatives would result in welfare agencies being reorganized to carry out territorially/community-based crime control functions under the direction of the police. Hence, a concerted effort was being made to construct an authoritarian local state, one in which social welfare and civil functions and their respective knowledge bases would be integrated in an overarching attempt to re-establish control over crisis-ridden neighbourhoods (Bridges, 1983).

As far as Marxist scholars (Christian, 1983; Gilroy and Sim, 1985; Hall, 1985; Scraton, 1985,) were concerned, the only possible response to these developments was to recognize that for certain communities the police themselves were the problem and therefore to support:

- campaigns to bring the police under democratic control in order that their autonomy could be curbed and discretionary powers restricted;
- community-based monitoring initiatives which could provide an authentic picture of local policing practices and defence groups which could provide legal support for those victimised by the police;
- unmasking the realities of community policing initiatives and the futility of trying to reform a fatally flawed policing system;
- people regulating their own community space and protecting their lives and property without lapsing into vigilantism;
- the right of communities to resist the authoritarian state and its coercive agencies.

The Marxist thesis about the real role of authoritarian policing was further confirmed by the unveiling of new paramilitary tactics and strategies to suppress industrial conflict and further inner city riots and counter-terrorism policing in Northern Ireland. During the 1980s, Marxist police scholarship on the 'authoritarian state' generated innovative research on police powers and accountability; police–community conflict; police corruption and criminality; police complaints system; police–news-media relationships; police interventions in the political process; police racism and sexism; the paramiltarization of police practices and culture; the deployment of criminalization strategies; the development of new urban policing intelligence and surveillance methodologies; and the use of deadly force (see Scraton, 2002). There were also attempts to analyse the developing relationship between political or 'high' and conventional or 'low' policework (see Brodeur, 1983), the 'Fortress Europe' securitization of policing, and more recently the post 9/11 'national security state'. Marxist researchers also developed a range of 'police watching' methodologies to research state–police relationships including community rather than police based ethnographic methods; sustained analysis of police policy documentation and investigative case studies and crisis moments (see StateWatch website).

However, the 'authoritarian state' thesis that underpinned this research suffered a heavy critique from those who argued that it had been constructed out of highly selective evidence (Sumner, 1981; Downes and Rock 1983; Waddington, 1986). In addition they were accused of being overly political in their analysis and unable to provide any practical response to the increasing levels of criminality and disorder engulfing dramatically changing working class inner city neighbourhoods. However, more significantly, Left Realist perspectives emerged to counter what they viewed as Marxism's political dead end reading of policing developments in the UK. For them, the self-fulfilling logic of the 'authoritarian state' thesis did not allow for and therefore could not conceptualize the possibility of contradictory developments outside of a base line 'crime as conspiratorial moral panic' framework.

Administrative perspectives: the police and crime control

At the same time that ethnographic and Marxist perspectives were establishing themselves, a significant number of applied research studies were conducted with the intention of improving the effectiveness of police administration and management of resources, professional practice and generating expert knowledge. Patrol work, as we have seen previously, has always been presented as the backbone of the Anglo-American police and in most forces, the majority of officers were formally assigned to this work. However, applied research studies verified a number of key policing facts, including: increasing the numbers of police officers would not necessarily reduce crime rates, nor would it raise the proportion of crimes solved; random preventative patrol would not have a marked effect upon crime levels or raise the proportion of solved crimes; intensifying patrol coverage and/or improving the speed with which patrol cars respond to calls from the public would not necessarily impact on the crime rate; and follow-up investigations were of little use without witness or victim.

In addition, these strategies were insufficiently preventative in focus and were incapable of addressing the circumstances that generated crime and disorder. And of course, this was in a context where the police come to learn about only a small percentage of all committed crime and most of the crimes they do come to learn about are reported to them by the public rather than uncovered through their own efforts. As numerous reports testified, a primary police role was managing the crime statistics in a politically acceptable manner.

However, in the course of 1980s, US policing underwent a remarkable renaissance as a result of a pragmatic 'what works' shift in thinking by administrative – police scholars working in a variety of forums (see Sherman et al., 1997; Sherman and Eck, 2002; Skogan and Frydal, 2004). Some even went so far as to talk about a 'blue revolution' in the policing of crime. There seems to have been a determination to ensure that the US police would not be gripped by the 'nothing works' policy paralysis that had seized the rest of the criminal justice system (see Skolnick and Bayley, 1986).

A detailed analysis of 'what works in policing' movement would discuss its connections with various innovative post-war policing initiatives. For the purposes of this chapter, I will focus on Herman Goldstein's 'problem-oriented policing' and James Q. Wilson and George Kelling's work on 'broken windows' and 'order-maintenance' policing. These authors provided the police with both new operational strategies and a core operational philosophy. Ideologically, Wilson and Kelling were important because their writings drew a distinction between policework as *is* with policework as it *could be*. In the process, they re-motivated the police to face up to their professional responsibilities with regard to controlling crime and social disorder, reducing fear of crime and neighbourhood protection.

Problem-oriented policing

Herman Goldstein articulated the concept of 'problem-oriented policing' in a seminal 1979 article and developed it in his 1990 book. He critiqued the key assumptions of the technocratic policing model, namely that continuous administrative and personnel improvements would produce more effective policework. The drive for professional status, organizational effectiveness and procedural propriety had produced a conservative mindset that was amplifying rather than resolving the practical dilemmas facing the police. First, a corporate police mentality had foregrounded managerial processes to the exclusion of concern about the outcomes of responding to persistent problems.

Second, the police continued to devote most of their resources to responding to ever increasing numbers of calls from citizens. The dominant 'dial-a-cop' model meant that there was very little time available to the organization to act on its own initiative to prevent or reduce crime. Third, the community was a major resource for reducing the number and magnitude of problems that were becoming the responsibility of the police. Fourth, within the organization, police managers had readily available to them another resource: rank and file officers whose time and talent was not being used productively. Finally, reforms to improve policing were failing because they were not adequately connected to the complexity of the police mandate (Goldstein, 1990, pp. 14–15).

For Goldstein (1979, p. 236), the reform focus had to shift from an obsession with bureaucracy towards specifying the end results of policework. This would require separating out the 'unrelated, ill-defined and often inseparable jobs the police are expected to handle'. Police departments exist to deal with a wide range of behavioural and social problems, that is 'the incredibly broad range of troublesome situations that prompt citizens to turn to the police, such as street robberies, residential burglaries, battered wives, vandalism, speeding cars, runaway children, accidents, acts of terrorism, even fear. These and other similar problems are the essence of policework. *They are the reason for having a police agency* ... [italics added] (Goldstein, 1990, p. 243). 'Incidents' that come to the attention of the police are rarely random: officers return to the same places to deal with the same individuals or groups. And yet the dominant model of policing requires officers to respond to an 'incident', whether citizen or police initiated, as a de-contextualised event with neither a history or future.

Goldstein argued that the 'the problem' in all its complexity should be the basic unit of policework. And he noted that categorizations such as 'crime', 'case', 'call', 'incident', 'disorder' and 'violence' were problematic because they were not accurate enough descriptors. Understanding 'problems' meant analysing precisely and accurately the core of the problem. There must also be the capacity to review why existing police responses to particular problems have failed as well as exploring possible alternatives to traditional law-enforcement practices. A large part of the predicament of professional policing is that the police have become unduly reliant on arrest, prosecution and imprisonment as 'solutions' to complex 'problems'. Hence, police chiefs would have to countenance the 'de-policing' of complex problems.

He cautioned against alternatives that sought to remove 'chronic' problems from the police. This has obvious attractions for police chiefs but Goldstein warned that in all likelihood – irrespective of governmental re-designation of responsibility – they would remain problems that the police would be eventually called on to deal with. Many problems become the responsibility of the police 'because no other agency has been found to solve them. They are the residual problems of society'. Consequently, 'expecting the police to solve or eliminate them is expecting too much. It is more realistic to aim at *reducing* the volume, *preventing* repetition, *alleviating* suffering, and *minimising* the other adverse effects they produce [italics added] (Goldstein, 1979, p. 242).

Goldstein argued that the police needed to shift to a decentralized, flexible teamwork system that would allow officers to develop the local knowledge and interpersonal skills to deal creatively with non-criminal matters. Dealing with neglected problems, necessitated the mobilization of different govern-ment agencies with the police, if required, acting as 'community ombudsman' making the connections happen and creating new community justice forums. Increased regulation and tightening up on what is expected from shop owners, residents, local authorities etc, could to prevent crime. City ordinances could be used to resolve non-criminal matters and zoning could be deployed to deal with neighbourhood problems and disputes. 'Problem-oriented policing' requires police officers to take greater initiative in attempting to deal with problems rather than resign themselves to living with them. Focusing on con-crete problems would be attractive to both rank and file officers and citizens. The benefits for the police would be developing new expertise and proactive relationships.

He also noted that police departments had already been forced to re-think more creatively about how to respond to specific crime victims where the traditional response had manifestly failed. The development of new spe-cialisms around child abuse, sexual assault and domestic violence had required new working methodologies and approaches. These initiatives 'sub-ordinate the customary priorities of police reform, such as staffing, manage-ment and equipment, to a common concern about a specific problem and the police response to it'. The overall outcome of shifting to problem-oriented polic-ing would be to amplify the operational capacity of the police and enhance organizational effectiveness. Thus, Goldstein argued that:

- policing consists of dealing with a wide range of criminal and non-criminal problems;
- police should work to *prevent* problems rather than simply responding to an end-less number of incidents;
- developing an effective response to a problem requires prior analysis rather than simply a customary response;
- each problem requires a tailormade response;
- the criminal law is only one means of responding to a problem;
- the police should be willing to act as facilitators, enabling and encouraging the community to maintain its norms governing behaviour.

A practical 'problem solving' tool is SARA: *scanning* for recurring problems and prioritizing in terms of seriousness, frequency and impact and connections; *analysis* to develop a sharper understanding of the causes and extent of 'the problem'; *response* via widening the range of appropriate tactics that police might adopt as well as stakeholders who need to be involved; and *assessment* to measure the effectiveness of the analysis and whether the problem solving plans (see Eck and Spelman, 1987). SARA was intended to enable officers to formulate not just more precise answers but sharper initial questions. The crucial point about SARA is that it was supposed to be iterative in nature with analysis going back and forth between the different stages. The critical analytical task is to identify those issues that can be practically transformed or influenced.

Goldstein's 'problem-oriented policing' was also strengthened through connecting it with rational choice/actuarial criminologies. Marcus Felson's (1998) routine-activities approach provided the police with a method for thinking about how to tackle mundane crime and disorder problems. The routine activity approach is premised on the belief that when a crime occurs, three things happen at the same time and in the same space: a likely and motivated offender is present, a suitable target (person, object or place) is available and there is the absence of capable guardian whose presence would prevent crime. A target's suitability for victimization is determined by *value, inertia, visibility* and *accessibility*. It is the offender's rational assessment of the situation which determines whether a crime will take place. The convergence is made possible by the routine structures of everyday life. Although the routine activity approach began with predatory street crime, it was subsequently expanded to include fights, illegal sales, and illegal consumption.

Offenders can be controlled by 'handlers', targets and victims can be protected by 'guardians' and places can be controlled by 'managers'. Thus, effective problem solving requires understanding of how offenders and their targets/victims come together in specific places and times, and understanding how those offenders, targets/victims/places are or are not effectively controlled. 'Problems' that the police are called upon to handle routinely cluster around behaviour, that is, place, persons and time. Crime and disorder are not evenly distributed across time, place or people and police need to recognise clusters of: repeat offenders attacking different targets at different places; repeat victims repeatedly attacked by different offenders at different places; and repeat places or 'hot spots' involving different offenders and different targets interacting at the same place (Sherman et al., 1997; Sherman and Eck, 2002).

While routine activity theory helped police officers to analyse and map problems, Ron Clarke's situational crime prevention approaches provided a framework for practical intervention (see Clarke, 1980). Situational crime prevention takes offenders' propensities or motives as given and works from what might be defined as a 'good enough' account of criminal behaviour. Crime is best understood as 'rational action performed by fairly ordinary people acting under particular pressures and exposed to specific opportunities and situational inducements' (Hough et al. 1980, p. 5). Hence, much 'commonplace' crime can be prevented, reduced or displaced by police manipulation of opportunities and inducements. Proceeding from an analysis of the immediate circumstances giving rise to particular 'criminal events', it introduces specific changes to influence the offender's initial decisions or ability to commit these crimes at particular places and times. Thus, it seeks to make criminal actions more difficult, more risky and less rewarding for offenders rather than relying on detection, punishments or attempting to reducing criminality through social policies. According to its proponents, situational crime prevention can be applied to any environment, product or service. Changing the immediate crime situation in these different ways involves: increasing the efforts associated with crime; increasing the risk of detection; reducing the anticipated rewards of crime; and/or removing the excuses for crime.

Effective situational crime prevention requires the police to undertake comprehensive problem-solving and risk analysis. The intention behind problem-oriented policing was to encourage a new generation of reform-minded chief police officers to: re-conceptualize the police mandate to include, crime prevention, fear reduction, community tranquillity and to be imaginative about the operational methods and identify evidence-based decision-making techniques that might be used to realize departmental goals. However, evaluations of problem-oriented policing found that the police were concentrating on easy problems. There was also a lack of long-term organizational commitment to mainstream problem-oriented policing; ongoing cultural resistance to a move from traditional law-enforcement methods; a lack of skills to analyse problems and evaluate strategies; police workloads ruling out anything other than superficial analysis of poor quality data; and an unwillingness to involve the community or partner agencies (see Eck, 2004).

In the United States, the problem-oriented policing philosophy has also been compromised by being absorbed into broader Community Oriented Policing (COP) initiatives. Bayley (1988, p. 225) provided one of the most sustained critiques of COP, noting that COP was being used as an umbrella term to cover a variety of 'feel-good' intiatives: 'public relations campaigns, shop-fronts and mini-stations, rescaled patrol beats, liaison with ethnic groups, permission for rank-and-file to speak to the press, Neighbourhood Watch, foot patrols, patrol-detective teams, and door-to-door visits by police officers. Community policing on the ground often seems less a programme than a set of aspirations wrapped in slogans'. He warned that an undue focus on general community issues was diverting police attention away from the task they are uniquely authorized and trained to do, i.e., maintaining order and enforcing the law. (see also Klockars, 1988; Scott, 2000)

Policing and the 'signs of crime'

In the same period as Goldstein was formulating his concept of problem-oriented policing, James Q. Wilson was producing a body of work that stressed that policing philosophy and strategies needed to relate directly to the crime problems afflicting increasingly disorderly Western societies. Wilson had been writing about policing and crime for several decades before the publication of

'Broken windows' in 1982, arguably the most influential article published in contemporary police studies. In the early 1960s he had questioned whether the technocratic model of policing was beneficial or indeed effective especially with regard to the needs of lower class urban neighbourhoods. The old 'order–maintenance' or 'watchman' model of policing had historically served some useful social functions in such neighbourhood settings, especially in terms of officers' knowledge of the populace and their ability to use their powers to suit what he viewed as 'the conditions of the jungle' (Wilson, 1963, p. 216).

In a series of publications Wilson (1968, 1969, 1975) reiterated that although the police could do very little about serious crime, in an era of rapid social change and changing crime patterns they needed to act and talk 'as if they *were* able to control crime'. To do so meant a return to neighbourhood policing and a focus on the overriding responsibility to protect communities from predatory street crime. This form of crime was increasingly impacting on the quality of metropolitan neighbourhood life, impeding 'the formation and maintenance of community ... disrupting the delicate nexus of ties, formal and informal, by which we are linked with our neighbourhoods ... [it] atomizes society and makes of its members mere individual calculators estimating, their own advantage, especially their own chances for survival amidst their fellows (Wilson, 1975, p. 23).

For Wilson, policing needed to 're-localize' in focus because it was the breakdown of informal neighbourhood controls and 'standards of right and seemly conduct' that gives rise to a 'sense of urban unease' and anxiety about being in public places. It is in the neighbourhood where people's 'sense of security, self-esteem, and propriety is either reassured or jeopardized by the people and events we encounter (1975, pp. 26–7). Wilson noted that fear of crime derives from many sources other than direct or indirect experience of victimization and generates serious problems. He warned that if the police did not pay attention to visible signs of deterioration of quality of everyday life and public civility, respectable residents would move out, leaving neighbourhoods to a predatory underclass who would undermine anti-poverty and regeneration programmes. He also cautioned liberal America that 'broken promises' on combatting street crime was capable of being transformed by conservative politicians into a potent electoral issue that would generate demands for punitive law and order measures.

Fixing broken windows

In conjunction with George L. Kelling, Wilson elaborated upon the original 'order-maintenance' thesis in 'broken windows' (1982), presenting a thought-provoking thesis regarding both the role de-policing played in neighbourhood de-civilization and the role re-policing could play in protecting neighbourhoods from such de-civilization.

'Broken windows' emerged, in part, from the findings of the Newark experiment of the late 1970s, which evaluated the effect of foot patrol on crime and public perception. The activities of foot patrol were obtained from a daily log maintained by officers. Officers reported that they made few arrests and filed few reports but did issue summonses, primarily for traffic violations. One of their main activities was not reported: the amount of time spent talking to residents and visiting local businesses. The study found that while foot patrol did not actually reduce crime, it did increase public order. Foot patrol officers kept an eye on strangers, and also helped to keep 'disreputable' elements under control. As a result, people's fear of being bothered by 'disorderly people' decreased, and their perceptions of public safety increased, despite the fact that crime levels had not actually gone down. Wilson and Kelling noted that the positive response of citizens to officers on foot patrol suggested the need to rethink what concerns and what reassures people in public places. This was reinforced by the fact that officers involved in the experiment 'had higher morale, greater job satisfaction, and a more favourable attitude toward citizens in their neighbourhoods than did officers assigned to patrol cars' (Wilson and Kelling, 1982, p. 29; see also Bahn, 1974).

The police priority had been on combatting the 'real' source of public fear generated by potential violent assault by the nameless, faceless stranger. However, the police needed to also pay attention to the much more multifaceted public fear being generated by a combination of environmental dilapidation and 'worrisome' encounters with 'disorderly' people. Not violent criminals but 'disreputable, obstreperous or unpredictable people: panhandlers, drunks, addicts, rowdy teenagers, prostitutes, loiterers; and the mentally disturbed' (Wilson and Kelling, 1982, p. 30). Environmental and behavioural disorder and crime were inextricably linked in a developmental sequence:

> If a window in a building is broken and is left unrepaired, all the rest of the windows will soon be broken. This is as true in nice neighbourhoods as in rundown ones. Window breaking does not necessarily occur on a large scale because some areas are inhabited by determined window breakers whereas others are populated by window lovers; rather, one unrepaired broken window is a signal [italics added] that no one cares and so breaking more windows costs nothing. (It has always been fun). (Wilson and Kelling, 1982 p. 31)

Neighbourhoods can be de-stabilized by 'actions that seem to signal that no-one cares' (Wilson and Kelling, 1982, p. 31). Residents no longer take care of their homes, look out for and, if necessary, correct one another's children, and deal with unwanted intruders. When property is abandoned, windows broken, buildings graffitied, lighting smashed, litter uncollected, weeds allowed to grow, etc., control over the public realm is lost. When teenagers are allowed to congregate on streets in a disruptive fashion, low level, sub-criminal misconduct will trigger more serious criminal behaviour which, in turn, increases the potential for 'criminal invasion' (Wilson and Kelling, 1982, pp. 32–4). The only people not concerned by the amalgam of disorder, deterioration and criminality are the people who are oblivious to or benefit from such an anarchic environment, e.g., drug dealers, street criminals, prostitutes and the homeless.

Wilson and Kelling note that in the 'old days' if there were signs that matters were getting out of hand, respectable residents had a vested interest in re-affirming control over the disorderly elements. And police officers had a vital role to play in the re-establishment of neighbourhood authority: 'Young toughs were roughed up, people were arrested "on suspicion" or for vagrancy, and prostitutes and petty thieves were routed. "Rights" were something enjoyed by decent folk, and perhaps also by the professional criminal, who avoided violence and could afford a lawyer' (p. 34).

In the contemporary city respectable residents leave the neighbourhood at the first signs of social disorder and environmental dilapidation. In addition, police officers had been trained out of understanding the very obvious connections between order-maintenance and crime control. Wilson and Kelling noted that much serious crime is opportunistic rather than the result of 'inexorable social forces or personal failings'. It exists because of a criminogenic local context:

> The link is similar to the process whereby one broken window becomes many. The citizen who fears the ill-smelling drunk, the rowdy teenager, or the importuning beggar is not merely expressing his distaste for unseemly behaviour; he is also giving voice to a bit of folk wisdom that happens to be a correct generalisation – namely, that serious street crime flourishes in areas in which disorderly behaviour goes unchecked.

> The unchecked panhandler is, in effect, the first broken window. Muggers and robbers, whether opportunistic or professional, believe they reduce their chances of being caught or even identified if they operate on streets where potential victims are already intimidated by prevailing conditions. If the neighbourhood cannot keep a bothersome panhandler from annoying passersby, the thief may reason, it is even less likely to call the police to identify a potential mugger or to interfere if the mugging actually takes place. (Wilson and Kelling 1982, p. 34)

Patrol officers have been dissuaded from intervening as a result of an individual rights culture, the bureaucratization of policing, the de-criminalization of petty crime and anti-social behaviour, the assumption that certain crimes are 'victimless', the de-institutionalization of the mentally ill and the erosion of legal authority for controlling disorder. As police indifference to their order–maintainance role grew, disorder had engulfed vulnerable neighbourhoods.

For Wilson and Kelling, the primary police role must be neighbourhood protection. Crime statistics and victimization surveys measure individual but not communal losses. The priority must be maintaining, 'communities without broken windows' and arresting window breakers. This necessitated a highly visible uniformed police presence and beat officers working with respectable residents to take back their communities to make them hostile to criminals.

In addition, policing had to be morally re-dramatized. Wilson and Kelling provided the example of the old style Irish cop, 'Officer Kelly' who (like PC George Dixon) kept an eye on strangers and required disreputable elements to observe informal baseline community norms:

> Drunks and addicts could sit on the stoops but could not lie down. People could drink on side streets, but not at the main intersection. Bottles had to be in paper bags. Talking to, bothering, or begging from people waiting at the bus stop was strictly forbidden. If a dispute erupted between a businessman and a customer, the businessman was assumed to be right, especially if the customer was a stranger. If a stranger loitered, Kelly would ask him if he had any means of support and what his business was; if he gave an unsatisfactory answer, he was sent on his way. Persons who broke the informal rules, especially those who bothered people at bus stops were arrested for vagrancy. Noisy teenagers were told to keep quiet. (Wilson and Kelling 1982, p. 30)

For Wilson and Kelling, effective order–maintenance policing reconnects police and community, strengthens the dynamics of informal social regulation and amplifies feelings of safety and social order. Ideally, municipal authorities would allocate the resources to put more police officers back on the beat.

> The police officer's uniform singles him out as a person who must accept responsibility if asked … A private security guard may deter crime or misconduct by his presence, but he may well not intervene – that is, control or drive away – someone who is challenging community standards. Being a sworn officer – a 'real' cop – seems to give one the confidence, the sense of duty, and the aura of authority necessary to perform this difficult task. (Wilson and Kelling, 1982, p. 38)

If not, the police would need to think more systematically about the nature of neighbourhood and community dynamics. To allocate patrol effectively and to cultivate a proactive 'guardianship' role, police departments would be required to decide where the deployment of additional officers would make the greatest difference. There was little point in expending scarce resources on either 'demoralized and crime ridden' or 'stable and serene' localities. The police should concentrate resources on 'thickening' the informal community control mechanisms in 'tipping point' neighbourhoods: where 'the public order is deteriorating but not unreclaimable, where the streets are used frequently but by apprehensive people, where a window is likely to be broken at any time, and must quickly be fixed if all are not be shattered'.

Wilson and Kelling conceded that order–maintenance policing was not easily reconciled with adherence to due process, equal treatment and a 'rights culture'. It could not be subjected to the same legal and organizational strictures as serious crime work. Police activity should be shaped by clearly articulated and accepted community (particularistic) rather than state (universal) standards. To ensure that officers do not become 'agents of neighbourhood bigotry' it needs to be emphasized that the police exist to 'help regulate behaviour, not to maintain the racial and ethnic purity of a neighbourhood'. Redefining the police mission would require radical organizational change. Authority over patrol officers would have to be decentralized, so that they had the freedom to manage their time. This implies giving them a broad range of responsibilities: to identify and understand the problems that create disorder and crime, and to deal with other public and private agencies that can help cope with these problems. It would mean committing officers to a neighbourhood for an extended period of time and providing departmental support and resources.

In addition to addressing 'quality of life' problems, order-maintenance policing can have a significant impact on serious crime. Responding proactively to disorder and low level offenders both informs the police about and puts them in regular contact with those who commit serious crime and persistent offenders. High visibility police actions and the concentration of police in disorderly neighbourhoods protects the decent and law abiding and sends a message to potential offenders that their actions will not be tolerated. Citizens regain the confidence to assert control over their lives and property and help the police to identify and prosecute offenders. As the problem of crime and disorder becomes a community responsibility more 'weed and seed' resources can be mobilized against specific forms of crime and disorder.

The ideological impact of the 'broken windows' thesis, unlike problem-oriented policing and situational crime prevention approaches, on not just police thinking but governments cannot be overstated. The thesis became a central reference point in an unfolding public debate about the role robust policing could play in the re-establishment of municipal political authority. The most obvious point of – 'the smallest details speak the loudest' – influence, as we shall see in Chapter 5 was the 'zero tolerance' or 'quality of life' policing experiment that was implemented when Mayor Rudolph Giuliani appointed William Bratton as Commissioner of the New York Police Department in 1994 (see Kelling and Coles, 1996; Bratton, 1995; 1996; 1998; Maple, 1999; Giuliani, 2002).

However, despite or perhaps of its popularity and influence, the 'broken windows' thesis has also been subject to serious critique. Some criminologists have questioned the connection Wilson and Kelling make about: the 'grime to crime' relationship; the career trajectory of petty criminals; and the relationship between *feeling* and actually being safe. In policy making terms, the thesis was extremely light on empirical data. There has also been concern that 'broken windows' would divert scarce resources from the policing of serious violent and organised crime. Others have argued that there was an empirical need to separate out 'broken windows' as a signalling theory as distinct from 'broken windows' as a theoretical formulation of the relationship between minor disorder and predatory criminality.

Walker (2000, p. 336) has argued that the thesis is based on a 'false and heavily romanticised view of the past'. Wilson and Kelling had exaggerated the flaws of the professional model and the historic capacity of the police to control crime. He also questioned the implicit assumption that old style policing enjoyed political legitimacy and expressed concern about the scope for both summary justice and corruption. Walker warned: 'such a revitalised form of policing would represent something entirely new in the history of the American police. There is no older tradition worthy of restoration' (p. 336).

Critics also contextualized the seemingly benign 'broken windows' thesis within the broader ideological framework of right-realist criminology. Wilson and Kelling have been vocal critics of a liberal rights culture and Wilson has been at the forefront of campaigns to return to a rational choice based criminal justice system consisting of swift and certain justice; proactive street policing; and incarceration. Wilson's advocacy of a 'punitive turn' also required the abandonment of the search for the 'root causes' of crime. He himself commented that:

> Though intellectually rewarding, from a practical point of view it is a mistake to think about crime in terms of its causes and then to search for ways of alleviating those causes. We must think instead of what it is feasible for a government or a community to do … Wicked people exist. Nothing avails except to set them apart from innocent people. And many people, neither wicked nor innocent, but watchful, dissembling and calculating of their opportunities, ponder our reaction to wickedness as a cue to what they might profitably do. We have trifled with the wicked, made sport of the innocent, and encouraged the calculators. Justice suffers and so do we all. (Wilson, 1977, pp. 235–6; see also Wilson and Herrnstein, 1985)

Kelling's strong affinity with Etzioni's communitarianism reinforces his insistence that the police should realize that they are in the business of defining and enforcing public morality. Hence, policework should be oriented towards strengthening the crime resistant capacities of primary social control institutions, namely the family and the community. Although beyond the reach of the present discussion, it should be noted that Wilson and Kelling's concern with policing 'street barbarism' and 'predators' and communal de-civilization connects across to Charles Murray's (1995: 2000) highly influential 'underclass' thesis. Murray insisted that the underclass, or the 'New Rabble', was the result not of poverty or material inequalities but of behaviour, characterized by drug abuse, casual violence, criminality, anti-social behaviour, illegitimacy, child neglect, work avoidance and welfare dependency.

For Murray, the anti-social value system of a rationally calculating underclass threatens all notions of liberal civilization. Consequently, he has repeatedly argued that restoring public civility, respect for social institutions and lawful behaviour will require radical welfare reform, public condemnation and stigmatisation and re-imposing the punitive capacities of the criminal justice system. Seen in this context, a combination of 'broken windows' and problem oriented policing combined with situational crime prevention techniques constitute the perfect hard edged right realist crime control model for sweeping the disadvantaged, dispossessed and dysfunctional into the 'underclass' neighbourhoods that they are quite content to abandon to criminal depredation.

Left-realist perspectives: the police and community safety

In 1975 Paul Hirst berated Marxist and critical criminologists for their politically irresponsible posturing on policing, crime control and social order:

> All societies outlaw certain categories of acts and punish them. The operation of law or custom, however much it may be associated in some societies with injustice and oppression, is a necessary condition of existence of any social formation. Whether the social formation has a State or not, whether it is communist or not, it will control and coerce in certain ways the acts of its members. The police force in our own country is not *merely* an instrument of oppression, or of the maintenance of the capitalist economic system, but also a condition of a civilised existence under the present political-economic relations ... One cannot imagine the absence of the control of traffic or the absence of the suppression of theft and murder, nor can one consider these controls as purely oppressive. (Hirst, 1975, p. 240)

This was supported by, among others, Maureen Cain (1977) who argued that Marxists 'must go further than identifying the police as agents of state coercion. Socialists do not face a lumpen, monolithic, and therefore invincible state structure; they face a political situation' (see also Marenin, 1983; Kettle, 1984).

Taking policing seriously

During the 1980s Jock Young and colleagues went on to develop a grounded 'left realism' as an alternative to Marxism's 'idealistic' position on crime and policing and the superficial solutions of administrative and right realist criminologists. The fundamental principle of left realism is that crime is an endemic product of the class and patriarchal structure of advanced capitalist societies. This is why it must be taken seriously by radical criminologists:

> This involves a rejection of the tendencies to romanticise crime or to pathologise it, to analyse solely from the point of view of the administration of crime or the criminal actor, or to exaggerate it. And our understanding of methodology, our interpretation of the statistics, our notions of aetiology follow from this. Most importantly, it is realism which informs our notion of practice: in answering what can be done about the problems of crime and social control. (Young, 1986, p. 21)

Criminal victimization is a real and increasing problem for the most vulnerable sections of society because it is driven not just by relative economic deprivation but by individualistic attitudes. The concentration of new forms of predatory criminality and anti-social behaviour in urban working-class communities was destroying the quality of life for residents:

> Crime is the endpoint of a continuum of disorder. It is not separate from other forms of aggravation and breakdown. It is the rundown council estate where music blares out of the windows early in the morning; it is the graffiti on the walls; it is aggression in the shops; it is bins that are never emptied; oil stains across the street; it is kids that show no respect; it is large trucks racing through your streets; it is streets you do not dare walk down at night; it is always being careful; it is a symbol of a world falling apart. It is lack of respect for humanity and fundamental human decency ... It is items like this that rebuff those commentators who maintain that because most crime is minor it is unimportant. (Lea and Young, 1983, pp. 55–8)

Escalating fear of crime and disorder had disorganizing and de-civilizing social effects: undermining social relationships, valorizing individualistic and acquisitive values; destroying the quality of life associated with public spaces; and generating 'populist punitive' demands for law and order policies. As part of taking the lived realities of crime and disorder seriously, democratic socialists needed to affirm that the police have a vital role to play in protecting the quality of life of the poorest and most vulnerable sections of the population from criminality and anti-social behaviour.

For left realists the class interests represented by the police in a liberal democratic polity are neither obvious nor ideologically pre-determined. Hence, the major deficiency of Marxist analysis was 'the over-emphasis on the coherence of the police as an institution and their interconnection with all other agencies of the state'. This neglected both the degree of conflict within the police and the nature of the autonomy the police had carved out from the state. As a result, Marxist analysis ruled out the existence of political space for progressive police reform (Baldwin and Kinsey, 1982; Cowell et al., 1982; Kinsey et al., 1986).

The relative autonomy of the police

Left realists argued that there was a need to come to terms with the fact that the police were a relatively autonomous institution. Chief police officers are 'operationally independent' from the formal political process and police constables are law officers not employees of the state. Consequently, all sections of the police enjoy guaranteed autonomy from the realm of formal politics. This provides them with the critical organizational leverage to mediate state interests. Organizational autonomy is amplified as a result of the discretionary powers of the rank and file. In addition, public demands and expectations regarding policing mean that the police cannot just represent the interests of the state or the bourgeoisie in a straightforward manner.

Furthermore, the police are not solely dependent on the state for their ideological legitimacy. The ever-present symbolism of the unarmed PC George Dixon-style 'bobby on the beat' – the citizen in uniform who is drawn from the people and acting on behalf of the common good – constitutes a distinctive and powerful ideology that bestows public legitimacy on the police. This also acts as a powerful counter against moves to a state-controlled police force. Rank and file police officers spend their working lives, for the most part, among the working class. As a consequence, they may be disliked by the poorest, youngest and criminogenic sections of the working class but they are 'viewed with a contradictory mixture of respect and suspicion by the majority – and in particular by those sections of the working class from which they themselves are recruited, and in whose interests they see themselves, in the vast majority of interests to be acting'. The police in short are 'the organized super ego of the respectable working class' (Kinsey et al., 1986, p. 172).

The conditions for consensus policing

In a liberal democratic society the obviously paramilitary role of the police in suppressing urban riots and industrial conflict remains exceptional rather than the norm for the following reasons. First, routine crime control constitutes real policework for the majority of police officers. Second, consensual policing has been the aspirational norm for post-war liberal democracies. In the immediate aftermath of the Second World War socialists recognized that the police had an important role to play in securing a just and equitable social democratic society. In this period, according to Taylor, the police had a paternalistic relationship with the working class. The 'bobby on the beat' was 'a court of appeal in cases of domestic and neighbourhood dispute, a firm hand in cases of trouble between local youths, and a helping hand for the elderly or the indisposed. He was also a useful resource in dealing with drunks' (Taylor, 1981, p. 69).

Beat officers apprehended juvenile delinquents who were in need of care and protection and would hand them over to the professionals of the welfare state. They also attempted to combat fraud offences which were exploitative of the working class. Hence, the beat officer according to Taylor was 'the hard working defender of the new social democratic community, burrowing away in pursuit of the predatory crimes of the powerful' (1981, p. 70). This 'public service' policing, because it corresponded to community needs and priorities, constituted the basis for a consensual relationship between the police and the working class. The Dixonian police force was successful at catching criminals and controlling crime in this time period because of the strong communal social controls and active community support and information.

Third, the shift to paramilitary policing styles has not been a dominant feature in all forces or for that matter in all areas covered by a particular force. Indeed, it has no presence in the policing of respectable working-class and middle-class neighbourhoods or rural areas. Finally, paramilitary policing strategies cannot be sustained and the urgent political task is to determine the alternative policing styles that are capable of enlisting the active support of local communities in crime control. For the left realists, consensus policing collapsed in Britain's inner cities as a result of the dramatic changes of the 1960s and the 1970s. Established urban working-class communities were physically and morally destabilized by constant development. At the same moment, new Commonwealth immigrant communities were established with different value systems and this contributed to the sense of fragmentation and cultural dislocation. Finally, structural unemployment and increasing deprivation produced soaring crime rates. Thus, it was major social changes, new social divisions, rising crime rates and the emergence of a distinctive criminal youth subculture that undermined the conditions for consensual policing. The respectable working class demanded a much tougher police response to the young black men they held to be responsible for this social crisis.

The police in responding to these concerns 'were not responding simply to figments of their imagination' (Lea and Young, 1984, p. 166). Because of their position in British society, black communities enjoyed an uneasy relationship with all agencies of the British state, including the police. However, once the police began to respond to the rising crime rate, the alienation of the black community increased dramatically. Because information was not forthcoming about specific incidents and criminals there was no alternative but to police whole communities and neighbourhoods. Information was prised from the community through the cultivation of informers and intensive stop and search operations which were also intended to act as a general deterrence. Such an aggressive policing style inevitably led to allegations of harassment and discrimination and the crucial distinction between the innocent/non-offender and the law-breaker/non-offender quickly blurred. The attitude of the wider community also changed towards offenders and as confidence in the police collapsed they were more willing to intervene to halt arrests. Alienation undermined the other social institutions in the community that have a direct role to play in controlling crime, especially the family and schools. The harassment of children led to the harassment of the parents because of the raids on homes. Police raids in youth clubs alienated youth and community workers whose work was crucial to keeping children out of trouble.

The police came to expect collective resistance in certain neighbourhoods and responded by mounting paramilitary operations that did not need community support or acceptance. This generated 'a vicious circle in which moves in the direction of military policing undermine whatever elements of consensus policing may remain, and lay the conditions for further moves in the direction of further military policing'. The police came to view the population in these areas as criminogenic (Lea and Young, 1984, p. 175). It is this conflictual street policing dynamic that fuelled rank and file racism rather than any notion of institutionalized racism.

Even though they rejected the Marxist 'authoritarian state' thesis, left realists were also highly critical of police controlled community policing initiatives. Community or multi-agency policing must be seen as the official response to the crisis in urban crime control rather than as a conspiratorial attempt by the police to penetrate and control civil society. These approaches reflect a shift away from a concern with crime detection and deterrence to 'situational crime prevention' and 'problem-oriented policing' and the sharing-out of responsibility for the fight against crime. Community policing approaches are also inherently undemocratic because the police define 'the parameters of debate for the other agencies' and the community is conceptualised as just another resource to be used in the officially defined fight against crime. Such strategies would create new difficulties if the police attempted to harness them to paramilitary crime control strategies. Social welfare agencies cannot work with the police in such circumstances because it would damage their credibility and effectiveness.

Minimal policing philosophy

In terms of effective policing, left realists argued that it was necessary for policy makers to commit themselves to social crime prevention strategies. Young noted:

> It is not the 'Thin Blue Line', but the social bricks and mortar of civil society which are the major bulwarks against crime. Good jobs with a discernible future, housing estates that tenants can be proud of, community facilities which enhance a sense of cohesion and belonging, a reduction in unfair inequalities, all create a society which is more cohesive and less criminogenic. (Young, 1992, p. 45)

Resources must be concentrated in the deprived crime and disorder torn neighbourhoods that Wilson and Kelling would write off as beyond redemption. A new set of relationships must be constructed between the police, the public and local government departments in order to ensure that policing policies are constructed out of and manifestly address community concerns and anxieties. Elected representatives should have the lead role in developing localized policing strategies. In order to do so, they would have to research local crime problems to identify real community needs and priorities and formulate appropriate policies and practices. In order to ensure maximum public access to the police decision making, communities would be directly involved in neighbourhood panels. Elected representatives, police officers and the community would be required to work on neighbourhood priorities. Such arrangements would open up the dialogue deemed crucial to re-establishing consensual forms of local policing. They would also break down the barriers between police officers and the community and encourage different groups to join the police. This in turn would make the police more representative of the communities they served.

Left realists argued that 'consensual policing' and active community participation would shift towards what was defined as a 'minimal policing' philosophy. Maximum public initiation of police action would ensure that information and evidence was freely brought forward to the police by witnesses and victims of crime. Left realists accepted that the police have an inevitable and legitimate coercive role to play in society and they are entitled to use reasonable force in conflictual situations. However, these coercive powers should be tightly defined and monitored:

> Minimal policing, with the emphasis on public initiation, thus presents a radical form of policing by consent. The public are not being asked to place blind faith in 'police expertise', nor are they 'obliged to cooperate' for fear of the consequences. Minimal policing entails a strict limit on police powers, working from the premise that it is for the police to cooperate with and respond to the demands of the public, rather than vice versa. (Kinsey et al., 1986, p. 192)

In order to ensure that the 'minimal policing' crime control model is established as the core function of policework there needs to be internal change. First, all other non-core roles presently carried out by police officers should be jettisoned. Second, all police officers, not just specialist units, would be responsible for active criminal investigation. This would ensure that all members of the police force were brought into constructive relationships with members of the public when their help is requested. This would also cut down on the number of hours spent on unproductive random patrol. It would also mean that specialist or elitist 'troubleshooting' units could be abolished. Such an overall framework would undermine the negative value system underpinning the occupational culture. Finally, there should be co-ordinated multi-agency interventions to deal with

1   the structural causes of crime;
2   the moral breakdown of communities;
3   the situational aspects of criminality and disorder;
4   effective crime detection;
5   offender rehabilitation; and
6   victim support.

Left realism represented a significant policy intervention in policing debates, not least because it placed emphasis on prioritizing the safety and security needs of deprived communities and vulnerable groups. Through it local crime victimization surveys played a major role in orienting Labour controlled local authorities towards a more proactive stance on crime prevention and community safety. And it also attempted to construct a democratic dialogue between police and community that could halt the drift into paramiltary policing of Britain's inner cities. Left realism also laid the foundation for the emergence of New Labour's 'tough on crime, tough on the causes of crime' and anti-social behaviour policy shift. However, its critics argued that it under-estimated the role that race was playing in constituting urban policework; idealized the police–working-class community nexus; under-theorized the changing nature of the state-police relationship; tacitly accepted the tough policing and criminalization of the disreputable and disorderly; did not research the drift to paramilitary and highly political policing forms; and had effectively anchored themselves to US right realist 'broken windows' conceptualizations of the supposed links between disorder, anti-social behaviour and serious criminality.

Conclusion

In 1993 Maureen Cain in a review of the latest batch of police books, noted that police scholarship had 'come of age' in the 1980s as 'a mature, steady sub-discipline, not easily shocked, much slower to anger, and with a solid base of ethnographic, historical, comparative, and theoretical work to draw upon' (Cain, 1993, p. 67). She noted that the 'first generation' sense of excitement at going behind the 'blue curtain' to access the realities of policework had gone. However, also gone was:

> that touch of voyeurism which made the Policeman as the Other so much larger than life. The officers emerge at least in some of the texts, as thoughtful, differentiated, concerned about politics, careers, religion, families and organizational change rather than puppets of a locker room culture. The authors are allowed to appear too, although reflexive history has not yet touched this branch of the subject. Women officers remain sadly off stage. (Cain, 1993: 63.)

For Maureen Cain, the parameters of police scholarship on police officer–society; police–state; and police–community relationships had been set. However, there were signs that all was not well within the emergent sub-discipline of police studies. It became increasingly clear that as a result of funding decisions, that policy-oriented methodologies were being used to colonize the soul of police studies. This was driven in the United States by the Police Foundation, the Police Executive Research Forum and National Institute of Justice and in the UK by the Police Research Group at the Home Office. The consequences for academic police scholarship was two-fold. First, there was a notable drying up of ethnographically based in-depth research monographs and research papers. Research funders seem to have concluded that there was nothing 'relevant' or 'useful' to be gained by supporting sociological research that continued to foreground disgruntled rank and file perspectives on their job and reached the ('nothing works') conclusion that policework had little effect on crime rates and it was almost impossible to measure police effectiveness. What was advocated instead was systematic observation and recording of police officers 'on the job' using quantification procedures that would allow for replication and comparison. The purpose of this research would be to produce the 'what works' paradigm necessary for both the managerialization of police practice and scientific crime control. Second, Marxist scholars left the field, some because they were disillusioned with the institutionalization of police studies and others because they realized that the theoretical registers they had been working with were inadequate to the task of explaining the new forms of policing, crime control and security surveillance that were emerging. This in turn left policing to researchers who were more than willing to deploy 'cut and paste' evaluative methodologies to address management and government agendas about the effectiveness of new initiatives. In the process, the independence and intellectual rigour of police studies have been seriously compromised.

Police Studies: New Perspectives

The rationale for this chapter is not to provide a comprehensive summary of current developments in policing studies. Rather, this chapter identifies the innovative scholarship that has transformed our understanding not only of the defining characteristics of contemporary policing but also its theoretical approaches and methodologies. At various moments since the 1990s there has been a recognition of the urgent need to rethink the assumptions and registers on which police scholarship have been based. There has been an increasing acknowledgement that the starting point for any contemporary analysis of policing must be the recognition that economic and cultural globalization, dematerialization of production processes, new information and telecommunication technologies and networks, commodification and mass consumerism, and profound and rapid social complexity have all worked to alter the institutional configuration of Western society. These fundamental 'runaway world' transformations in economy, social structure, culture and identity have constituted the coming of postmodernity (see Bauman, 2001; Jameson and Miyoshi, 1988; Baudrillard, 1990, 1994; Giddens,1999; Harvey, 1991; Sennett, 2006). Since the 1990s, the term postmodern has dominated many aspects of Western academic and cultural debate. The degree of controversy and contestation the term has generated across many disciplines 'signals that a sufficient number of people with conflicting interests and opinions feel that there is something sufficiently important at stake here to be worth struggling and arguing over' (Hebdige, 1988, p. 182).

A quick survey of the vast literature tells us there is no possibility of constructing clear-cut definitions of the terms, not only because of its interdisciplinary utilization but also owing to its disparate origins. Prominent practitioners of 'post-theorizing' exhibit considerable differences in the nature and scope of their enquiries, as well as their particular emphases. For the purpose of this chapter, it is not necessary to rehearse these complex distinctions. However, there is a consensus that two simultaneous dislocating processes delineate post-modernity: *hyper-differentiation* in the form of fragmented, fissured and fractured social relations and *de-differentiation* in which traditional boundaries between institutional and cultural spheres conflictually erode:

> In its total acceptance of … ephemerality, fragmentation, discontinuity and the chaotic … postmodernism responds to that fact in a very particular way. It does not try to transcend it, counteract it or even to define 'the eternal and immutable' elements that lie within it. Postmodernism swims, even wallows, in the fragmentary and the chaotic currents of change as if that is all there is. (Harvey, 1990, p. 395)

Suffice to say that among police scholars, there is a heightened sense that alongside radically different forms of risk, uncertainty and instability and the way they are perceived, an incisive re-ordering of the techniques and logics of policing, security and social control is under way. In the case of the UK, these can be categorized under the inter-linked cross-cutting thematic trends of policing as both security governance and cultural disintegration. After providing an analytical overview of these different trends, the final sections of the chapter elaborate on the ways I believe that postmodern analysis can be used to produce a culturally textured understanding of the intensely fractured state of contemporary policing.

Security governance: the pluralization of policing

The implicit assumption across police studies has been that 'the police' represent the institutional 'high point' of the sovereign nation state. Fukuyama (2005, p. 163) reminds us that 'what only states and states alone are able to do is aggregate and purposefully deploy legitimate power. This power is necessary to enforce a rule of law domestically and it is necessary to preserve world order internationally'. The modern police force is the most obvious institutional expression of the state's monopoly of power within its territorial boundaries. And as we have seen in Chapter 3, Marxist police scholars anticipated that the 'authoritarian state' would seek to centralize and paramilitarize all policing activity. As a result, 'policing' has been automatically associated with the organizational structures, activities, perspectives and methodologies and personnel of 'the police'. In 'state-centred' understandings of 'the police', very little attention had been given to less visible, seemingly peripheral, forms of policing, most notably those associated with the commercial security sector. The dominant perspective was that private security was limited to the 'stop-gap' protection of private interests while the public police represented the ever-expanding public interest. It was unimaginable that frontline police duties might be subjected to a reverse process of re-commodification. Consequently, with one or two notable exceptions, the private security industry was not taken seriously as a discrete theoretical or empirical issue. Nonetheless, some researchers did point to the importance of commodified policing. For instance, in a brief overview of US developments in 1971, Scott and Macpherson (1971, p. 285) noted that the surreptitious expansion of private security resulted from 'the nationally based, heavily capitalised firms that are able to utilise equipment and methods not usually available to the public police agencies'. The rebirth was the result of increased use of security personnel employed by firms engaged in commercial or industrial activity (see also Becker, 1974). Moreover, at two criminology seminars held in Britain in 1971, researchers were also advised to pay much closer attention to developments in the private security sector (see Banton, 1971; McClintock and Wiles, 1972). By this time, as Radzinowicz observed, the sector's accelerating growth was already well underway:

> Fifteen years ago the private security industry had barely gained a foothold in Britain. To most people crime prevention was a matter for the police and there was no reason to look any further. Now it is openly admitted that the police are overstretched, that there may be areas and aspects, in business, in commerce, even in the protection of people's homes, which they cannot cover adequately – and which it may not be appropriate for them to cover at all. And here, as in other industrial countries throughout the world, a second, private and commercial, line of defence is being thrown up with quite phenomenal speed. Perhaps, therefore, we ought to start by asking a few fundamental questions about this new hybrid, apparently half business, half police. (Radzinowicz, 1971, p. 13)

In 1977 Spitzer and Scull developed what turned out to be a highly significant Marxist thesis concerning the role being played by profit-driven policing at different stages of capitalist development. They highlighted the vital 'big-stick' function fulfilled by private policing agencies 'in industrial capitalism's struggle against working class militancy' (Spitzer and Scull, 1977, p. 22). For Spitzer and Scull, state-organized policing subsequently developed as the dominant modality of law enforcement and crime control because corporate capitalist interests realized this was a more efficient use of resources. They also related this seemingly decisive shift from private to public policing to corporate capitalism's deployment of more subtle managerial controls over the labour force and trade unions. In the process, public order was defined as a collective good and the private sector was marginalized.

However, for Spitzer and Scull three key tendencies were likely to drive the re-commodification of policing in the 1980s. First, there were fiscal limits to the number of public police officers that could be employed and deployed. As a result, the 'thinning blue line' would not be able to meet the baseline security needs of the private sector. Second, capitalist corporations had a range of specialist security requirements that were creating a niche market for new forms of expertise and knowledge. Finally, private security agencies offered a range of 'service not authority' benefits to corporate clients to keep customers satisfied: responsiveness to confidential interests – such as the need for discretion – in their approach to problem solving; flexibility and adaptability because they were attuned to market conditions; the deployment of sophisticated technologies; minimal legal bureau-legal constraints; and the ability to access and call upon the public police resources if required. Consequently, there was every possibility that corporate capitalism would start to invest heavily in private security services.

The twilight of the sovereign nation-state

Shearing and Stenning (1980; 1981; 1983) argued that it was imperative to elevate private security from the margins to the centre of theoretical analysis. Looking to the writings of Foucault, Cohen and later Rose to consider the future of policing, they shifted the analytical focus from the state police to 'policing', 'security' and 'governance'. They confirmed that in the North American context at least, the shift to a postmodern consumer society was driving the growth and influence of the private security sector. They noted that the emergence of 'mass private property' (in the form of commercial districts, residential estates, and shopping and entertainment complexes) was unmaking traditional understandings of the post-war 'public/private' distinction. Corporations were increasingly in charge of significant expanses of both private property and 'public' spaces. As a result, they were quietly developing 'an extensive security apparatus, of which uniformed security personnel are only the supervisory tip of the iceberg ... control is at once pervasive and minute: it takes the form of small, seemingly insignificant observations and remedies that take place everywhere' (Shearing and Stenning, 1981, p. 503).

For Shearing and Stenning, therefore, the systematic privatization of property relations in North America potentially signalled a shift from 'state' to 'corporate' sovereignty. This posed fundamental questions about the accuracy of Marxist claims that the increasingly authoritarian state was becoming more dominant in capitalist societies. On the contrary, 'the evidence of direct control by capital over important aspects of policing points to the necessity of a thorough re-examination of conventional theoretical statements – be they instrumentalist or structural about the relationship between the state and police under modern capitalism (Shearing and Stenning, 1981, p. 504).

The public police did not have the resources or inclination to inhabit the proliferating corporate spaces of these 'proxy states' and business and industry preferred to use private security services for the reasons laid out by Spitzer and Scull. As a consequence with the emergence of 'mass private property', private security was 'encroaching upon the traditional 'beat' of the public police. In so doing, it has brought areas of public life that were formerly under state control under the control of private corporations (Shearing and Stenning, 1981, p. 497).

Not only was private enterprise in a position to perform a significant number of policing tasks but it had its own distinctive risk-based methodologies that challenged the conventional policework paradigm. For example, the status of the private security sector as designated agents of 'mass private property' allowed it to exercise a range of pro-active surveillance and investigative powers within its operating territories that exceeded those of the public police. As Shearing and Stenning (1981, p. 497) note:

> While modern private security guards enjoy few or no exceptional law enforcement powers, their status as agents of property allows them to exercise a degree of legal authority which in practice far exceeds that of their counterparts in the public police. They may insist that person's submit to random searches of their property or persons as a condition of entry to, or exit from, the premises. They may even require clients to surrender their property while remaining on the premises, and during this time they may lawfully keep them under more or less visual or electronic surveillance. Before allowing clients to use the premises (or property such as a credit card) they may insist that clients provide detailed information about themselves, and authorise them to seek personal information on others with whom they have dealings. Private security may use such information for any purpose, and even pass it on, or sell it to others.

'Security' could be institutionalized across a variety of functions, tasks and responsibilities and thought processes. 'Crime' is only one concern for the private security sector: actuarial and future oriented in nature, the focus of private security was 'what works' in preventing loss. The protection of client property, data and personnel and profit interests was achieved through anticipating and designing out criminal opportunities, risk management, target-hardening strategies and loss adjustment. Continuous surveillance ensured that not only were individuals profiled but also categorized into groups who posed risks or were deemed 'suspect' or 'undesirable'. Sanctions were primarily geared towards compliance and exclusion rather than punishment and moral censure. This meant that many offences were dealt with by private means rather than the public criminal justice system. Equally significantly, one of the vital tasks of private security was to create secure, controlled environments that could 'informally' reinforce conformity, facilitate compliance and promote self-regulation.

Moreover, the private security industry is in a position to exercise its own discretion as to whether to involve the public police and criminal justice process. The neo-liberal project of constructing the 'entrepreneurial state' was conducive to the private sector transforming 'policing' and 'security' into products that could be sold in the marketplace. This could lead to the privatization of routine public policing functions and the emergence of new providers of additional or supplementary policing services. The state police would be left with the order-maintenance responsibilities that could not stand market testing. It was also possible that a totalizing policing environment could be created as a result of a negotiated 'contracting-out–contracting-in' settlement between the two sectors over resources and capabilities. In later papers Shearing (in conjunction with Bayley, Johnston and Stenning) expanded upon the original thesis arguing that the materialization of private security was emblematic of a shift to postmodern governance, providing 'a dark glass through which we may be able to catch glimpses of the shape of the world we are tumbling toward'. The emerging society one in which governance and security will not be monopolized by the state. Instead, 'a 'Brave New World' of unseen, embedded and pervasive control that eliminates autonomy and privacy may well become an everyday reality. The net will be widened and thinned, but those fishing will not be exclusively state officials' (Shearing 1992, p. 427).

As the 1980s progressed, it became clear across a variety of jurisdictions that neo-liberal governments were determined to privatize core state assets, contractualizing key functions and responsibilities, and defining the state's role as purchaser of services from a free market of competing providers. The terms 'the contract state' or the 'market state' have been used to describe the thrust and direction of the neo-liberal reform process. As a result of this process, a defining moment had been reached in crime control and law enforcement and future generations would 'look back on our era as a time when one system of policing ended and another took its place' (Bayley and Shearing, 1996, p. 585). Basic assumptions about the role and purpose of 'the state' and 'governance' were shifting. The legitimacy of the post-war Western state system was premised upon the notion of a coherent nation promising effective defence against external attack and a high degree of internal stability and communal security. This stability was based on the principles of Keynsian macro-economic policy, collective welfare provision and social security. However, there is evidence of the consolidation of neo-liberal forms of 'beyond the state', 'at a distance' or managerial/contract governance through a network of responsibilized agencies, communities and individuals (Rose, 1996; 1999; 2000; Dean, 1999).

In a post-Keynesian or indeed post-social context, terms such as 'privatization', 'decentralization', 'devolution' and 'delegation' are not adequate to explain what was unfolding. 'Policing' – the process whereby societies designate and authorise representatives to create and preserve public tranquillity and safety – is pluralizing and dispersing, and security is multilateralizing. The emergence of a diversity of clients (state, private, community, individual) for – and providers of – policing means that 'public' and 'private' are 'being combined in new ways, ways that sometimes make it difficult to separate public from private' (Shearing 2001, p. 15). According to Shearing, these developments offer the intriguing possibility of a 'complex network of governing auspices and sites of capacity that play different and varied roles, in different governmental spaces ... to contribute to both the steering and rowing of governance'. This amalgam 'of intersectional sensibilities, institutions, technologies, and governmental activities' constituted 'an emergent nodal governance' where citizens as they moved 'through different spaces (both real and virtual) they are governed by different sets of state and non-state agencies according to the rules and standards that are set by both state and non-state auspices' (Shearing, 2001, p. 17).

The future configuration of public policing?

The 'security governance' thesis has generated a heated debate about the practical and normative implications of ever greater private and voluntary sector involvement in public policing around issues of state responsibilities; the uneven distribution of safety and security across different social groups; and issues of human rights and democratic citizenship. The insistence by Shearing et al., that the traditional conflation of policing with 'the police' is now inhibiting our ability to comprehend contemporary developments has required police scholars to think in a much more sophisticated way about the nature of governance and security. In so doing they have had to grapple with the possible 'de-throning' of state-centred policing and the state.

This has generated scholarship on: the goods and services that are constitutive of the new security market; the defining features of the multiplicity of state, non-state and quasi-state agencies who carry out policing and security functions; the roles and responsibilities of, and unfolding division of labour between, the different sectors and their varying practices, techniques and mentalities; the regulatory regimes that encompass each sector; the implications of the proliferation of electronic surveillance security and data collation technologies; the consumers of various security services; and the future shape of the global market in security expertise and products (see Button, 2002; Wakefield, 2003; Sarre, 2005). There have also been attempts to work through the consequences for the organization and delivery of public-sector policing services in an emergent 'security market'. For Shearing et al., the rationales, contractual status, regulatory structure, organizational and managerial systems and associated technologies, sources of legitimacy and modes of accountability that are constitutive of private security are likely to have a noteworthy impact on the public police. Arising from this, the following futures for public policing have been identified:

1 nodalization
2 residualization
3 managerialization
4 re-sovereignization and
5 global securitization.

Nodalization

Throughout their analyses, Shearing and his colleagues have been extremely careful not to register approval or disapproval of the emergence of neo-liberal forms of 'security governance', arguing that advantages and disadvantages depended on social conditions, combinations of auspices and providers, the nature of criminal threats and the feasibility of alternatives. However, they have been criticized for suggesting that (a) the state police should not be privileged analytically; (b) private-sector accountability mechanisms such as marketplace competition and consumer pressure could be applied to the public police; (c) communities might prefer to employ private security if they had a choice; and (d) the private security sector should not be regulated and legalised through the state.

They recognized that pluralization could result in a drift towards fragmentation and a widening gap between the 'security rich' who would live their lives in overlapping 'security bubbles' and the poor who would be fated to insecurity. However, as far as Shearing et al. are concerned, there is little point in yearning nostalgically for welfare statist modes of governance or wasting time formulating radical socialist alternatives. For them, it is not politically viable to produce security through 'the state' for several reasons. First, expanding neo-liberalization means that the state is no longer a stable locus of governance. Second, emergent post-state modes of governance are relational, contingent, overlapping and multi-sited. They are the property of 'networks' rather than a product of any single centre of governmental action. According to Shearing, the urgent practical task is to construct a strategy 'that moves beyond a dismissal of anything that bears a family resemblance to neo-liberal thinking, to a more nuanced analysis that accepts the value of some neo-liberal premises while proposing alternative arrangements for realizing them, including (but not limited to) the reconstitution of market mechanisms' (Shearing, 2001, p. 270; see also Bayley and Shearing, 2001; Johnston and Shearing, 2003; Shearing and Woods, 2003; Kempa and Johnston, 2005; Shearing, 2006)

The aim must be to maximize the benefits of neo-liberal 'nodal governance' arrangements and minimize the 'security deficits'. Disadvantaged communities can be empowered to participate – like the 'private governments' that are constitutive of the corporate sector – in 'security markets' through the allocation of a 'security' rather than 'police' budget that can be used to maximise the flow of resources. The ideal is an 'optimal-security' model, which satisfies requirements of accountability, effectiveness and justice. The 'block grant' allows for a 'levelling up' of access to security and 'the furtherance of democracy, empowerment, justice and security':

> Nodes are identified as locations of knowledge, capacity and resources that can be deployed to both authorize and provide governance. Nodes may or may not form governing assemblages, and they may or may not develop networks

that traffic in information and other goods to enhance their efficiency. (Shearing, 2001, p. 6)

It also allows 'security governance' to become integrated into broader 'problem-solving' programmes producing new forms of 'indigenous' sovereignty. There is the intriguing possibility within Shearing et al.'s analysis that state organized policing as it has been traditionally conceived and organized could be communalized into more sophisticated forms of legitimate governance.

Residualization

The fear of residualization relates to worries about the deeper long term consequences of the postmodernization of both social relations and policing. What concerns scholars such as Reiner (1992 a,b; 1995; 1997a) and Taylor (1999, p. 218) is that neo-liberalization means policing and security will be subject to uncontrollable free-market hyper-pluralization. Taylor (1999) argues, for example, that the private sector's primary concern with maximizing its return on investment requires it to liberate itself from the constraints of the state, and of the obligations to public institutions such as the police and the criminal justice system. This raises the possibility of a 'switch back' to pre-modern or 'New Feudalism' forms of 'without the state' policing.

Reiner (1997) believes that this unfettered free-market dynamic is moving us forward to the restless, ungovernable *Bladerunner* society depicted in Ridley Scott's film, or the 'Fortress LA' scenario described so vividly by Mike Davis (1993; 1994). Davis had detailed how postmodern architectural design, was and would be increasingly deployed to secure the financial, commercial and governmental quarters of Los Angeles from a variety of internal threats. This also involved the surveillance and regulation of the public space surrounding these power-laden, heavily-fortified corporate edifices. Equally significantly, the mall was fast becoming the dominant face of corporate retailing, replacing traditional commercial thoroughfares drawing business offices, leisure facilities and retail outlets into privately controlled environments. Accompanying the neo-corporatization of security were new overlapping forms of residential securitization resultant from an ever-increasing number of urban neighbourhoods which were opting for voluntary ghettoization through walling, gating and blocking (see also Blakely and Snider 1997; Caldiera, 2000). What disturbs Reiner et al., is the very real possibility that wealthy elites will increasingly take refuge in inter-locking 'defensible locales' protected by space, architecture, technology, transport and customer-friendly private guards, whilst the 'underclass' is consigned to the 'dreadful enclosures' of the lawless, predatory urban ghettoes.

Reiner (1995) is keenly aware that time cannot be turned back to a mythical 'golden age' of social-democratic 'Dixonian' state policing. As a result, a strong sense of loss and fear is woven into the heart of his analysis. At the beginning of

a new century, he sees that the once 'sacred' expressive institution originally identified by Michael Banton (1964a) has been thoroughly profaned. The 'blue lamp'
will 'fade to grey' with the painful but inevitable passing of the social-democratic
welfare state. In this dystopian scenario the public police are fated to manage their
own privatization by taking on the non-profitable 'no frills' role of patrolling the
frontlines between these two worlds. In carrying out this role they will also be
symbolically acting as the 'sandwich boards' for the postmodern values of fragmentation, division and intolerance (Reiner, 1995, p. 3). Reiner predicts:

> The police will be replaced by a more varied assortment of bodies with polic-
> ing functions, and a more diffuse array of policing processes: 'pick-n-mix' polic-
> ing for a postmodern age. Police officers can no longer be totems symbolising
> a cohesive social order which no longer exists. They will have to perform spe-
> cific pragmatic functions of crime management and emergency peace-keeping
> in an effective and just way, or forfeit popular and political support. (Reiner,
> 1997a, p. 1039)

There is a strong sense in Reiner's analysis that postmodern 'citadel culture'
is condemned to live within its most fearful shadows because its extremely
volatile exclusionary and punitive dynamics are irreversible. Consequently,
there is no long term future for state organized policing as it has been traditionally understood.

Managerialization

McLaughlin and Murji (1995, 1996, 1997, 2001) developed this perspective to
analyse how the public police were becoming increasingly subject to the
intensive managerialization that had been deployed across the public sector.
Intellectual and political proponents of a new public management paradigm
on both sides of the Atlantic sought to mediate the trend towards neo-
liberalization by reinventing notions of the public sector at the end of the
twentieth century. The task was not to uncritically defend the public sector
but to develop a model of public service that demonstrated the efficiency and
responsiveness of non-market solutions. Relations of power within public-
sector organizations would have to be radically realigned in order to transform
the structures and reorganize the processes for the delivery of 'public'
services. In a 'market state' era of service competition and entrepreneurial
government, a variety of mechanisms and techniques would be used to drive
the managerialization of all aspects of the formulation and delivery of policing
services. This would be done in several ways, for instance in the:

- creation or appointment of professional managers who are required to extract
  maximum value from specified resources;
- setting of measurable standards and targets;

- explicit costing of all activities;
- development of performance indicators to enable the measurement and evaluation of efficiency;
- publication of tables showing comparative performance against these indicators;
- increased emphasis on outputs and results rather than processes;
- rationalization of the purpose, range and scope of organizations through the consolidation of core competencies and the outsourcing of peripheral activities;
- adaptation to a competitive environment characterized by full or quasi-market relations, service contracts, and agency status;
- separation of finance from provision, a split between providers and purchasers of services, and client–contractor relationships;
- reconfiguration of the recipients and beneficiaries of policing services as 'customers' and 'consumer-citizens';
- overhauling of the work culture to improve productivity, accountability and representativeness.

Taken together, these steps represented the means through which public sector institutions would be reconstructed as 'business-like', that is, customer focused, performance-oriented and responsive to market conditions. The pressure for continuous reform in order to mimic the private sector as closely as possible would be relentless because, no matter how effective public policing is, it is unlikely to have a major impact on the demands for private security. A modern slimmed-down 'entrepreneurial police' could have the role of (a) accrediting and managing a consumer-driven 'mixed economy' of security and policing services; (b) developing specialist 'products' to 'trade' on the national and international security market; (c) professionalizing core competencies in criminal investigation, prosecution; and forensics and/or (d) co-ordinating confidential information flows between a range of private and public institutions (see also, Ericson and Haggarty, 1997).

Re-sovereignization

Loader and Walker (2001; 2004; 2005), have provided one of the most sustained critiques of the 'security governance' thesis, particularly the core principle that the 'least worse' option is to work within the private–public security logics and techniques of neo-liberal governance. Like Reiner and Taylor, Loader and Walker's starting point is that the central ambition of unregulated neo-liberalism is to downsize the state to facilitate the further commodification of social relations and public institutions. Free-market values are therefore fundamentally at odds with not-for-profit public values and proposed private–public alliances will compound existing and produce new inequalities and instabilities. Reliance on the 'hidden hand' of the market to deliver security should be resisted because there is a fundamental conflict of interest: profitability and market expansion necessitates feeding public fear of crime and steering clear of high risk/bad risk situations and locations. Zedner (2006, p. 92) also makes this point succintly:

> Although the practice of state policing never fulfilled its collectivist preten-sions, it did profess, at least, to provide a public service available to all. To the extent that it failed to fulfil this idea, as fail it did, its failing could be mea-sured, criticized and sanctioned. Private providers make no such claim but avowedly seek to protect the partisan interests (whether individual, communal or commercial) of those who pay. No surprise here: it is central to the logic of market societies that goods be distributed not according to need, but to the ability of the consumer to pay. (Zedner, 2006, p. 92)

For Loader (1997a, p. 155), meaningful security is connected 'with the quality of human association; referring to the degree of social cohesion, the 'thick-ness' of the social bond depends upon, and is the product of a richly textured and inclusive set of social relations'. In addition, à la Banton, state-constituted policing embodies a complex of interlocking 'sacred' qualities – monopoly of legitimate coercion, delivery of civic governance, guarantor of equitable pro-vision and social cohesion and symbolising not just the state but the nation. Because of their instrumental orientation, commercial policing and security they not only cannot replicate or generate such 'paleo-symbolic' virtues, they undermine them. Therefore, theycannot have a central role to play in security governance. Private security guard officers lack '"the symbolic aura" of the public police. They possess – "copycat" uniforms aside – few of the icons, rit-uals and warm associations with "Englishness" that enable the police to spread among many such a gratifying sensation of order and security' (Loader, 1997a, p. 154; also Loader 1997b; 1999).

Loader and Walker (2004; 2005) also argue that the death of the state, and indeed the social, has been hugely overstated by Shearing et al. Irrespective of its exact form, the state's sovereign status will continue to have a central role to play within any pluralised network of 'security governance' because it has 'ultimate authority over who may resort to coercion, if not to other non-coercive "dispos-als"', as well as the capacity to determine their regulatory provisions. Thus, it is the state that structures 'the security network both in its presence and in its absence, both in its explicit directions and in its implicit permissions. No other site within the security network may or does make that claim' (pp. 224–5).

Only the 'solidarity-nourishing' authority and legitimate sovereignty of democratic statecraft can guarantee notions of 'security' and 'safety' as collective or public goods and prevent social balkanization or what they describe as 'levelled-up tribalism' that will accompany free-market driven policing. Hence, they stress the continuing importance of the democratic state remaining as the key 'power-container' and 'norm-enforcer' in the promotion of a public or collective good of security model rather than more restricted and exclusive 'club' goods or nodal governance/'security bubble' models.

For Loader and Walker the urgent task must be to argue the case for the de-marketization of policing and the re-establishment of clear boundaries between the public and private so that there is no confusion about who is and who is not authorized to use force and deprive people of their liberty. This retrofitting will necessitate a systematic broadening of the role of the universal constabulary. Manning (1999, p. 51) has also amplified Banton's 'sacralisation of policing' thesis to suggest that the sovereign character of the public police can be re-asserted through culturally revalidating and deepening rather than thinning 'constabulary blue'. This is seen as being necessary because public policing 'cues' to deeper cultural connections:

> While it could be argued that police are dramaturgical figures, engaged in a massive theatrical attempt to sustain the illusion or allusion of order and ordering – it is perhaps more accurate to argue that the police engage in a form of magic ... it draws on the collective, the emotive basis of display, marking and deference. It evokes feeling and yet it also uses them for ends, purposes other than and apart from the emotional state of the collective. In that sense, then it is a form of magic, or a practice that mimics or simulates religion but stands apart from it. (Manning, 2004, p. 6)

Other commentators have developed a more pragmatic perspective, noting that the state and its policing apparatus will continue to be required to intervene in order to: close 'security gaps' that threaten the broader social order; maintain an effective communications and technological security/policing/control infrastructure; and monitor, evaluate and respond to high-level security threats and risks. They argue that this requires stronger rather than weaker forms of governance and 'hard' rather than 'soft' state formations (see Button, 2002; Jones and Newburn, 2002; Rigakos, 2002; Newburn, 2003; Crawford, 2005).

Global securitization

Re-affirmation of the role of the state police also comes from those scholars who argue that we need to pay close attention to the thickening of 'high policing' that is taking place beyond the territorial borders of the nation state. As the hitherto fixed boundaries of nation states and law enforcement fracture under globalisation, this historical correlation between 'state' and 'police' is inevitably called into question. Sheptycki (1998, p. 498) argues that police organizations around the world 'have had nation states as their nesting sites' and that 'character of the nation state system is currently undergoing significant transformations that is both visible in changing forms of policing and constitutive of these new forms'. He acknowledges that transnationalization per se is not necessarily new and that there are also tendencies towards the localization of certain policing functions. However, 'local' crime control matters are not driving or directing the new transnational policing agenda.

Sheptycki (1998; 2000) identifies several parallel 'stretching' processes at work. The first process includes the marketization of insecurity and the decline of state control which could produce either a marginalized state police force that is dwarfed by a much larger corporate private sector or a hybrid model might emerge in which there is an uneasy alliance between the two sectors. The second process under way is the transnationalization of policing. A 'global crime village' has been spawned by the spread of neo-liberal free market ideologies, as well as by time–space convergence as a consequence of globalization. Both reduce the ability of a national government to shape regulatory systems and policing itself is increasingly pulled into the transnational realm in attempt to deal with these particular organized crime problems. This is reflected in the growth of international criminal law instruments and policing treaties between governments. For Sheptycki the new policing order will consist of (a) transnational and local private sector security corporations and specialists; (b) political or high policing agencies; and (c) public police forces who are increasingly networked in complex ways to secure the postmodern global social order. The amplification of perceived 'crime threats', securities and risks will result in the extension of reach of the operational reach of transnational policing agencies to 'top-end' crime: organized crime, drugs, terrorism, illegal immigration and human trafficking.

If we follow the 'offshore' logic of global security scholarship we will witness four main trends. First, there will be an institutionalization and rationalization of relationships between different national police and law-enforcement, immigration, and customs agencies. This corresponds to the development of a post-'9/11' 'national security' or 'homeland security' state. Second, there will be the interconnection of 'policing' and 'security' rationales that had previously remained constitutionally separate and the creation of new transnational 'security fields' and relatively autonomous supra-regional 'policing archipelagos'. Third, specialists will emerge who will transfer policy expertise, technical assistance and hardware within the newly emergent transnational policing regime. As part of this, certain 'branded' police forces such as the NYPD, LAPD, FBI and the DEA can run global merchandizing operations. This will, in turn, generate new capacity-building policy circuits and ideological configurations that have the USA as their centre. Finally, there will be a shift from 'territorialized' control to the at-a-distance identification, monitoring, management and regulation of 'suspect populations' and security 'hot spots'. The crucial research question for those working in this field will be identifying how, where and with what effects do the 'transnational' and 'local' interact.

Accelerating transnational dynamics are capable of generating a globalized policing and security paradigm. Nation-states and their institutional manifestations are becoming more fragmentary and de-centralized, as they try to respond effectively to increasingly global forms of disorder. 'State', 'nation' and 'police' and 'security' are being reconfigured in unprecedented ways. Police researchers also need to be aware of the implications of shifts towards what has been described as 'a police with no state' and 'beyond nation state forms of policing'. Certain conceptualizations and modalities of 'policing' can no longer be considered, for example, except within the unfolding European superstate framework in which it is being nurtured. And Europeanization is replete with possibilities for 'spill-over' into as yet unidentified new policing domains.

However, the work on transnational policing developments is being further complicated by the post-9/11 'war on terrorism' awareness of the increasing governmental role being played by private military companies in international security coalitions. The most obvious example to date is the strategic positioning of Private Military Corporations (PMCs) in the reconstruction of Iraq. In 2005 an estimated 100 PMCs with 30,000 personnel were operating in Iraq offering protection to government ministries, oil pipelines, building sites, power stations, hotels, etc. PMCs such as Blackwater and ISI are also lobbying the United Nations to use them for 'policing actions'. At the same time, there are strong indications that the private sector will be increasingly contracted in to deliver the training, logistics and supply operations for military forces. This has produced speculative research on the privatization of twenty-first century warfare, peacekeeping and 'state-making' and the further securitization of conventional policing. (see Singer, 2003; Eagar, 2004; Duffield, 2005)

Cultural disintegration: the broken 'spectacle' of policing

As was indicated in the introduction, most of the thinking for this chapter has grown out of an effort to move between the free flow of ideas that debates concerning the postmodern condition has unlocked. It is to the cultural spaces of postmodern theorizing that the next section of this chapter seeks to reflect upon in order to understand developments in contemporary police–media relations. While this theorizing cannot be reduced to any one writer, it is Baudrillard who has pushed it to its limits, coining soundbites that are endlessly parroted (Baudrillard, 1990, 1994, 1995). A radical fissure has occurred and the resulting postmodern era is constituted through new media technologies and forms of consumption. He sketches out a 'history of signification' in which signs have become increasingly detached from their referents until today we inhabit a hyper-real universe made up entirely of surfaces, signs and images proliferating and circulating with no reference to any 'real' world outside of themselves.

Hyper-reality points to the blurring of the distinction between the 'real' and the 'unreal'. When the 'real' is no longer straightforward or obvious, but is artificially reproduced as 'real' it becomes, as Best and Kellner (1991, p. 119.) point out, 'not unreal or surreal but realer than real – a real retouched and refurbished in "a hallucinatory resemblance" with itself'. With the advent of hyper-reality, which results from the fusion of the virtual and the real into a third order of reality, representations are devoured and simulations can come to constitute reality itself. We do not need to concur with everything that Baudrillard writes to realize that his thesis can be seen most clearly in emergent multi-media-scapes where the boundaries between fact and fiction, information and entertainment have imploded. They are simulacra, simulations that do not conceal reality, but instead the disappearance of reality.

What does this have to do with our discussion of contemporary policing? Very little for the majority of police scholarship we have just discussed. However, once upon a time, when the world was 'real', the police could rely, as we discussed in Chapter 1, upon relatively stable deferential media representations of an idealized 'police self', as personified by PC George Dixon. However, in the late 1970s Manning (1978) argued that the police were facing a permanent crisis because they had laid claim to an 'impossible mandate' of promising society that they could control crime. As a result, they had no choice but to resort to 'the manipulation of appearances'. There was every possibility that the police would attempt to use the media to insulate the public from the realities that could not be tolerated. Because society had lost the ability or desire to live in a world of intractable social problems – such as crime – we have contrived an alternative mediaized reality in which these problems can be resolved in a fantastical manner.

Thus, we are observing the displacement of dominant factual and fictional media images of the police with fragmentary, contradictory and ambiguous ones that inter-penetrate fiction and reality. The hurried circulation of hybrid, hyper-real and 'counterfeit' images of policing in proliferating media spaces means that old distinctions between the 'real' and the 'fictional' are rapidly collapsing into a police–entertainment simulacrum. Media representations of policing are flickering at such an intense rate on the television and movie screens that 'real' policing is in danger of 'disappearing'. The 'real' police find themselves increasingly networked into a set of high-risk potentially chaotic media contradictions that have the potential to trigger an uncontrollable crisis of the hyper-real. Ratings-driven media representations 'without guarantees' or deference have the potential to undercut, stand in for and/or replace the foundational narratives of the 'real' police. A combination of audience demands for crime news, police dramas, an over-flow of media spaces to be filled and the consequent over-production of 'fly on the wall' programmes generates pressure on the police for ever greater media access. Ironically, as we shall see, the police are having to invest ever more resources in public relations and the management of new 24/7 mass media spaces at a moment when they are increasingly trapped within a disintegrating 'representational regime'.

Factual disintergration

The body of work on the police and the media cited by Manning (2003) and Reiner (2003) reminds us that policing, is a matter of symbolism as much as substance, and the media constitute the most prominent arena in which different conceptions of policing have been articulated. Reiner's work detects a foundational theme of 'police fetishism' across both the factual and fictional media in a variety of jurisdictions. By this, he means the unassailable media assumption that the police are 'a functional pre-requisite of social order, so that, without a police force there would be chaos and uncontrolled war of all against all' (Reiner, 2003, p. 259). What is effectively blocked out by 'police fetishism' is 'the variety of other forms of policing that have and do and could exist. Even more importantly, it obscures the fundamental significance of other aspects of social structure and culture for the maintenance and reproduction of order and security' (Reiner, 1997b, pp. 259–60).

A substantial body of research has demonstrated how positive news-media representations of the police result from: journalistic conceptions of what counts as a newsworthy crime story; a dominant crime-control discourse and police communication strategies (see Leishman and Mason, 2003). Ericson (1989) argued that we need to understand the police at two interrelated levels. First, we need to look at them in material and physical terms where they have the responsibility for enforcing the law, preventing crime, managing problem populations and exercising the legitimate use of force. Moreover, the public and government expects to see the police doing these things. However, at a second level, the police also 'patrol the facts' of policework in order to produce various 'symbolic orders'. For Ericson, police officers are 'information workers' projecting, shielding and glossing over the key aspects of policework at rank-and-file and senior-management levels. Policing is a matter of the heart as well as the head playing on dominant cultural themes. Consequently, the police have enjoyed a dominant place culturally and therefore socially and politically. Although many criminal justice professionals and pressure groups can provide expert commentary on the problem of crime, it is only the police 'who proclaim a professional expertise in the "war against crime", based on daily personal experience' (Hall et al., 1978, p. 68). Hence the police as 'primary definers', have been able to 'traffic' in images of the 'thin blue line' standing between order and chaos (see also Doyle and Ericson, 2003).

Media-conscious senior police officers have acknowledged the crucial influence that media representations can exercise upon the public perception of the legitimacy, mandate and authority of policework (see Mawby, 2003). Increasing awareness of the damaging consequences of adverse or contradictory newsmedia coverage is an important reason why police forces have invested extensively in media and public relations work. Forces have well-resourced press or corporate communications offices staffed by civilian personnel with experience in journalism, public relations and/or market research to ensure that brand image and message are accurately and positively represented to key stakeholder audiences. What we might define as 'promo-policing' attempts to proactively manage relations with the news-media in terms of:

- responding to routine news-media inquiries both in terms of basic information and 'what happened' in a given criminal incident;
- framing news stories by writing press statements, press releases, setting up press conferences, briefings and interviews, release of crime statistics, etc.;
- managing news-media interest if there is a high-profile crime, outbreak of disorder or any incident involving the police;
- co-ordinating news-media publicity for special police actions concerning terrorism, international and organized crime, serious crime;
- organizing access, cultivating reporters, editors, commentators and programme makers;
- employing specialist PR firms to 'brand' and represent the force or chief officers and to co-ordinate damage limitation and crisis-management activities;
- running advertising campaigns re. particular target groups or issues;
- co-producing, in the form of initiating or supporting factual television documentaries on specialist police units, operations and crime reconstruction shows.

This professionalization process has created an awareness among senior police officers that they can project a powerful organizational image through multi-layered communication and promotional strategies and actively construct a supportive public constituency. This is particularly the case when it comes to news media coverage of high-profile violent or serious crimes, the role that the police play on public occasions and in national security emergencies and the death of an on-duty police officer. However, the ability of the 'promo-police' to manage the newsmedia is increasingly circumscribed by a highly competitive 24/7 instantaneous tabloid news-media culture with a multitude of news gatherers and commentators looking for a distinctive angle and not necessarily tied to responding to or privileging a police perspective. This can lead to struggles over broadcast material, photographs, and reporters' notes. The 'promo-police' are also increasingly meshed in a complex web of proliferating internal and external stakeholders and publics with different agendas and needs who are willing and able to use the newsmedia to further their interests. Consequently, there is the increased possibility of highly damaging images and destabilizing representations of policing proliferating in the newsmedia (Lawrence, 2000; Ross, 2000; McLaughlin, 2005; Greer and McLaughlin, 2006).

Fictional disintegration

For Brunsdon (2000) the fictional police series has become a key ideological site for working through broader social anxieties and traumas. As was discussed in Chapter 1, it is not surprising that there has been an historic concern among police officers and politicians about the impact of popular cultural representations of the police upon both reputation and community relations. Fictional representations are deemed to 'stand in' for the real police. Ideally, the police will be portrayed in a manner which exemplifies their symbolic status within society, that is, as the disciplined 'thin blue line' that stands between order and chaos. And as numerous authors have noted, fictional representations are deemed to be crucial in terms of securing a degree of public legitimacy and respect for uniformed authority. The 'fictional fuzz' can become a key reference point in public conversations about the 'real' police and tutor the popular imagination about the type of policing to come. This 'cycle of perceptual influence' can also frame police–public/public–police interactions, affect recruitment as well as the morale and self-esteem of police officers (Perlmutter, 2000).

Television drama has always been enthralled by the dramatic visuality of the police and, for programme makers, shows that foreground the spectacle of wailing sirens and flashing blue lamps guarantee high ratings. As was discussed in Chapter 1, certain police dramas also attain cultural significance, becoming cult viewing or part of the collective 'coptalk' of the nation. Reiner (2003) has periodized British police dramas as a 'dialectical development'. In its highly formalized valorization of post-war consensus policing, *Dixon of Dock Green* denotes the original 'thesis' of British police dramas. In the early 1960s a transitional moment was reached with the screening of *Z Cars,* widely recognized as the first 'authentic' British police show. Its 'real-life' feel was strengthened by its insistence that policework was not glamorous and police officers were not paragons of virtue (see, Sydney-Smith, 2002). For Reiner, the 'anti-thesis' of 'Dixonian' policing was fully realized when the fast-paced *The Sweeney,* the quintessential police series of the 1970s, hit the television screen. The programme was one the first British police dramas to have cinematic production values and to be shot on location. The action was structured around hardboiled 'thief takers' Detective Inspector Jack Regan and Detective Sergeant Carter. As members of the Metropolitan Police 'Flying Squad' they had responsibility for outwitting London's organized criminal fraternity and keeping them in check by any means necessary. Because key storylines were based on real events, the show was able to capture the hard-hitting, fast paced, testosterone-fuelled 'you're nicked' fantasy of urban detective work (Paterson, 1980). The post-*Sweeney* antithesis was reinforced by G.F. Newman's path-breaking four-part serial *Law and Order* which tackled systemic police corruption and malpractice. In these representations the police have no illusions about criminal justice and the rule of law. For Reiner (2000), ITV's primetime cop show *The Bill* represents an attempted 'synthesis' of the 'heroic' *Dixon of Dock Green* and 'anti-heroic' *Sweeney.*

In 1984 the first eleven-part series of *The Bill* was made. Following *Z Cars* and the US *Hill Street Blues*, it used a 'fly on the wall' documentary style of using hand-held cameras, natural lighting and everyday speech patterns. The action centred on 'Sun Hill' police station, tentatively based in the East End of London. The onus was on illustrating the importance of teamwork. The programme prided itself from the outset on a 'mundane documentary style realism' that was a result of paying meticulous attention to the details of real-life policing, operational pressures and police culture. The foundational principle was that events should be shown from the police perspective so that every scene had to include a police officer. Viewers seldom saw a crime being committed and 'criminals' had fixed identities. Each episode consisted of self-contained storylines, which highlighted the diversity of policework and crimes which were always resolved. In its adherence to police procedures, *The Bill* was to resemble a dramatized version of a workplace documentary, without voyeuristic interludes highlighting the protagonist's personal lives (*The Guardian*, 27 October 1997, p. 11). The programme makers were advised on storylines and procedures by retired police officers and given considerable assistance by the Metropolitan Police. The original pre-watershed storylines emphasized policing as a 24-hour social service and that crime did not pay. A producer of *The Bill*, Michael Chapman noted:

> We are story tellers – we have no real ambition beyond that. We exist to enter-tain, but we are able to incorporate all kinds of other elements. Occasionally we tell a story about a bent copper, but we are not denigrating the Metropolitan Police as a whole. In any case we are not PR agents for the Met, but we do behave responsibly, in portraying them and there is an educative element in our work. The subject matter is usually small scale, we trade in small coinage, not in big currency notes. (*Guardian*, 10 October 1994, p. 14)

However, ratings driven programme makers recognize that cultural shifts in public attitude must also be taken into account when it comes to both the development of new police dramas and the 're-vamping' of well-established shows. As a consequence, de-constructive critical narratives which could not be previously be represented are included. These range from unflattering or ambivalent fictional representations which 'play' with layers of moral ambi-guity and foreground images of ethical disorientation and organizational lawlessness, through to highlighting miscarriages of justice and police mal-practice. Stuart Cosgrove (1996) noted that a radical transformation of the police drama was under way not just from benign to adrenalin-driven scan-dalizing plots 'but also in ideology from the Reithian authority of the 1950s BBC to a more aggressive modernity'. The police officer was moving 'from being a lawman to a flawed, impulsive and para-criminal character who is pro-foundly damaged by society as well as guarding it' (Cosgrove, 1996, p. 12).

This post-synthesis shift in perspective is reflected in the hyper-dramatisation of relatively conventional police dramas. There is little doubt that this is con-nected to the sophistication and complexity of a new generation of US cop shows such as *Big Apple*, *Boomtown*, *The Shield* and *The Wire*. For example, *The Bill* – even though it remains the stable media reference point for uniformed British policing – engages increasingly in multiple contortions in attempts to cope with the burden of representing the 'reality' of both the problem of policing London and police culture in the first decade of the twenty first century. Episodes inscribe and subvert, assert and deny the generic narratives, conventions and stereotypes of fictional policework. The programme has increasingly dealt with controversial policing issues, such as officer criminality, racism, sexism and homophobia; includes storylines that foreground emotionally-charged personal lives; and has more of a 'real' crime focus.

As with all primetime competitive dramas, there have to be re-launches to retain, win back, and/or gain new audiences. In October 1998 ITV's *The Bill* was challenged directly by Tony Garnett's new BBC 2 series *The Cops*. This was previewed at the Edinburgh Festival as part of a special discussion on Tony Garnett's track record as the producer of *Law and Order* and *Between the Lines*. The gritty real-life promotional adverts for *The Cops* looked like trailers for a real documentary about the depressing realities of contemporary urban policing. Lurching hand-held cameras followed officers around 'Stanton', a fictional northern English town, observing them interact and clash aggressively with the residents of the local white 'underclass' 'Skeetsmoor' housing estate. *The Cops*, according to Garnett, consciously set out to subvert the defining characteristics of the British police television series. Filmed in an ethnographic style, with a 'it's never a fair cop' theme there are no heroes. The authenticity was heightened by the use of unknown and non-actors.

The opening scene of the first episode shows a young blonde woman – Mel – rushing into a packed nightclub toilet to snort a line of speed with her friend. This, of course, would normally be used to mark out the 'drug-trance' state-of-the-nation territory of the cop show. As the dance music pounds, Mel suddenly realises that it is 5.30 a.m. and that she has exactly half an hour to get to work. Her friend tells her to call in sick. Instead, she rushes from the club and in the back of a taxi removes her mascara and nose and belly-button studs. As she enters a crowded locker room and quickly changes into a police uniform we become aware that the young clubber is rookie WPC Mel Draper. She is surrounded by young male and female constables swapping stories about the previous night's escapades. As the episode unfolds we see the hungover, sleep-deprived WPC Draper attempting to cope with the grim realities, sharp banter and cruel humour of routine policework. She needs to take another line of speed to stay awake while on duty; vomits violently as she has to deal with a badly decomposed body; fends off the advances of male colleagues; and explains to her friends why she wants to be a cop. The first episode ends with an emotionally distraught Mel on the mobile to her friend insisting that she cannot go clubbing in Manchester. The sound of a distant siren accompanies Mel as she walks away from the police station.

As the series unfolds, we see the corrupting nature of 'the job'. Officers are portrayed as flawed, individualistic, sexually predatory and frequently brutal as they pursue personal vendettas, bitter generational and rank rivalries, dole out their own brand of street justice, and do anything to avoid being grounded in the station filling out paperwork. One officer complains that he joined the job for the camaraderie 'but no fucker likes me'. The rank-and-file are dealing with life at the sharpest end of policing, fighting a losing battle to maintain any semblance of law and order in a poverty-ridden, criminogenic residual sink estate. They spend most of their time threatening, humiliating and winding up the 'scrotes' and returning to the same problem estates and family households day after day. There is squalor, hopelessness and vulnerabilities among the members of the public who take up most of their time. Highly politicized senior management are viewed as part of the problem espousing the mantra of modernization and reform. The new sergeant is informed that the establishment of 'client responsive, intelligence led, proactive' ethnically sensitive, community-policing style will necessitate getting rid of 'change resistant' officers. The 'bollocks of community policing' is viewed by the rank-and-file as preventing them getting on with the job of making sure the anti-social 'scrotes' do not get the upper hand. The attitude of Skeetsmoor residents to the police is made clear in episode 1. Two officers stand by freshly painted graffiti 'SKEETS 1 PIGS 0' which has been scrawled on a wall. This is the place where Sergeant Pulley recently died of a heart attack whilst chasing an unidentified suspect.

> PC Danny: Could be anyone on this estate. You know they all hate us up here.
> PC Roy: Look at 'em. Breeding like rabbits'. 'I'm sick of 'em all. The dirty, thieving, lying scumbags'. I'm sick of 'em.

As Tony Garnett made clear, *The Cops*, in its representation of policework and police culture, was a very distant relative of *Dixon of Dock Green* or indeed *The Bill*:

> Doing this I thought we could avoid this fiction where there is a big crime, this 'murder a week' business. In our show most of the crime isn't very serious and most of it isn't solved. I also felt that if we kept it low key we'd have a chance of getting behind the uniform and getting to know these people as human beings. And they are human beings, just like us and they are under particular pressures. But they also have the power over other human beings that most of us don't have. There are very few shows that go out into life in Britain as it's really lived by so many people, and I felt there might be a way of making a cop show where the cops took us to parts of Britain and to the experiences of people that you usually don't see on television. (*Radio Times*, 24 October 1998, p. 27)

The relentlessly grim ' ... So Fucking What?' model of policework represented in *The Cops* did not find favour with the police forces who had originally co-operated with the production company in its filming around Bolton and Preston. Greater Manchester and Lancashire police forces both made complaints about what they viewed as a gross misrepresentation of professional policing. For the police, this was an irresponsible unbalanced, sensationalist almost too realistic representation of frontline policing and officers that had the potential to under-mine police–community relations. This evoked memories of the Lancashire police force's furious reaction to the first episode of *Z Cars* in 1962.

The Cops gave permission to *The Bill*, in turn, to court further controversy and scandal for ratings purposes. For instance, in April 2002 six police officers were murdered when Sun Hill station erupted in a ball of flames as a result of a fire-bomb attack. The first gay kiss between police officers was screened in August 2002 between Sergeant Craig Gilmore and PC Luke Ashton. This was followed by a lesbian kiss in August 2003 between bisexual DC Juliet Becker and DS Debbie McAllister. The two women comfort each other and start kissing when DC Becker confesses to her lesbian tendencies and DC McAllister reveals she was raped by a colleague when she was pregnant. In December 2003 the series featured an incest storyline involving two of the main characters, Sergeant June Ackland and PC Gabriel Kent. This turn of events led one of Britain's leading cultural critics Brian Sewell to puzzle on the complexity of the post-*Dixon of Dock Green* contemporary police culture conveyed by *The Bill* as follows:

> Long ago in the dim and distant past, it may have seemed a lineal descendent of 'Dixon of Dock Green', but now no friendly constable boxes the ears of pre-pubescents or rescues a timorous kitten from a tree, nor does any constable ride a bone-shaking bicycle and wave cheerily to the worried mothers of young criminals 'who are really not so bad'.
>
> Instead we have the domestic, sexual and amatory problems of the policemen and women themselves, their drug taking, their alcoholism and their delusions ... We could of course look at *The Bill* as some sort of existentialist reinterpreta-tion of Dante's inferno, or at Sun Hill police station as Sartre's *Huis-Clos* – a closed circle of Hell in which the cast inevitably climbs into bed with a disas-trous partner, man with boy, girl with woman, alcoholic with alcoholic and drug addict with pure soul. All human life is concentrated here, all human sins are introduced, even perjury and murder, and the ingenuity scriptwriters knows no bounds as they replace the theatre of realism with sordid fantasy. (Sewell, 2003, p. 11)

This criminogenic theme was picked up by a *Guardian* review (25 June 2005) of the increasingly 'demented' nature of *The Bill*: 'with its cast of murderers, psychopaths, child molesters and arsonists all of them in police uniforms and all emotionally interlocked with each other. New arrivals at Sun Hill station are ruthlessly asset-stripped of whatever weaknesses they try to hide and then discarded. Emotion rules rather than reason'. It is notable that recent press 'Real Crime, Real Close' and 'Join *The Bill*' adverts for *The Bill* suggest that it aspires to further feats of 'no holds barred' realism.

These deconstructive shifts are also reflected in a new generation of 'Brit-Grit' detective dramas. In November 2000 an audience of thirteen million tuned in to watch 'The Remorseful Day', in which Chief Inspector Endeavour Morse collapsed with a suspected heart attack on the quad of Exeter College, Oxford. Detective Sergeant Lewis, his faithful sidekick, was ordered by Morse on his deathbed to stop the prime suspect in their final murder case from boarding a plane. This meant that it was Morse's superior officer Chief Superintendent Strange who was with him when he died. Lewis hears of the death of his boss on his mobile. When he comes to pay his respect at the mortuary he uncovers the Chief Inspector's face, kisses his forehead and says 'Goodbye, Sir' before walking away.

His carefully choreographed death brought to an end the most praised detective series ever produced in Britain. First broadcast in 1985 and based on the Colin Dexter novels, *Inspector Morse* represented a conscious effort to reinvent and revalue the 'intelligent detective' genre. John Thaw, of *The Sweeney* fame, played the character as an idiosyncratic, reclusive, moody, world-weary Wagner lover, with an Oxford education in Classics, who drove a burgandy 1963 Mark II 2.4 Jaguar, was fond of crossword puzzles and was attracted to 'a certain type of woman' (Brunsdon, 2000, p. 230). For Brunsdon, Morse's commitment to solving crime and misdemeanours through deductive logic and experience and the Oxfordshire setting enabled each series to connect across with the cultural sensitivities of the 'golden age' detective novel and indeed Sir Arthur Conan Doyle's *Sherlock Holmes*. The consciously bourgeois cultural value system underpinning the programme deepened and extended its cross-over appeal.

With each series, the cerebral Morse was shown as being increasingly distant from and dismayed by the rise of management speak within the police force. Nostalgia for both policing as craftwork and more comprehensible, crime-free times infuses the series. Not surprisingly, given Morse's popularity, 'The Remorseful Day' generated comment across all sections of the news media. John Humphrys (2000), the BBC Radio 4 news presenter, summed up 'Middle England's' sense of loss with the on-screen death of the 'last detective':

> It is Morse's humanity that makes him a great character. He is, himself, a tortured soul. He seeks solace in Wagner or Mozart rather than the jukebox of a crowded police-club bar. He is capable of falling in love, assuming the woman is both beautiful and intelligent, but is often disappointed. It does not help that the woman you are attracted to turns out to be the murderer you end up

arresting. His taste is refined – his car a classic Jaguar, his home exquisitely furnished – but he prefers a good pint of bitter to a fine claret at High Table.

There is an air of mystery about his past, but it is clear that he has been deeply wounded and the scars remain. It is that vulnerability, I suspect that makes him irresistible to so many women. But part of the appeal of Morse is what he is not. He does not threaten us, as modern television policemen so often do. In our heads we know that policemen reflect modern society and are, if anything, more brutal and ruthless than most of us. They have to be. They must swim in the same waters as the dregs of society. To outwit a criminal you must try to think like him … But Morse represents what we really want our detectives to be.

Humphrey notes that Morse 'oozes integrity' and he does not enact violence:

Occasionally we might see a victim fall down stairs or scream as she walks through the door, but we do not see the knife slide in or the fist crunch on the bone. And we welcome that. We welcome, too, the fact that it is not the sort of violence we must fear in real life: random assaults by savage thugs against whom we have no defence. These are intricately plotted, carefully crafted murders. We frequently end up feeling almost sorry for the perpetrator. Murder in Morse is as civilised as it gets. That's what really sums up Morse: he is a civilised man in civilised surroundings. Yes there is murder – but murder to the strains of Mozart and the backdrop of the most elegant buildings in Christendom. (Humphrys, 2000)

John Thaw's death in February 2002 occasioned one final goodbye to Morse with David Blunkett, the then Home Secretary, declaring that the Inspector had been a perfect role model for the police. In a letter to the *Daily Telegraph*, Chief Inspector Rachel Green disagreed saying that 'a cantankerous alcoholic, whose psychological dys-functionality inhibited the formation of any personal and meaningful relationship is certainly not my idea of a role model' (*Daily Telegraph*, 26 February 2002). However, this was challenged by another reader who argued that the nation would rather have more 'thief-takers' like Morse rather than 'teetotal, happily partnered officers who say the politically correct things and get their forms completed on time' (*Daily Telegraph*, 27 February 2002). Morse's national treasure status was completed by the decision to feature him as one of a set of Royal Mail stamps celebrating 50 years of ITV.

The remarkable international success of the *Inspector Morse* series spawned a generation of detective shows frantically trying to capture the 'Morse factor'. The stock feature was that they featured white, middle-aged, heterosexual, male detectives, married to the job, who delighted in exasperating their desk-bound managers and younger colleagues by ignoring the paperwork and bending the rules to get results. Crompton (2002, p. 10) argues that 'Morse-like' detectives are popular because:

They make order out of chaos on our behalf; they bring moral certainty to the messiness of life. But if we are to love them truly, they must be truly loveable. They can't be too perfect, yet they must be kind. They have, at some unconscious level, to represent both the best and worst qualities of the audience that watches them. And that, I suspect is what makes them so difficult to write.

However, the television detective drama is developing in diverse, transgressive and 'unloveable' directions. Sitting along the 'fading memories' representation of the classic detective represented by Morse et al., is a new generation of twenty-first century US influenced forensic, psychological, 'investigative techno-chic', and conspiratorial national security visualizations. Realms of difference and otherness articulated through gender, race, ethnicity and sexuality have been used to complicate the characterizations, plots and settings. And uncertain shifts in social values and moral climate also inflect the highly-charged, even deviant off-duty lives. In the cutting edge post-Morse vice-without-virtue detective series, the tendency is for chiaroscuro lighting to be much harsher, grainier images, disturbing 'shades among the shadows' plots, and snappy dialogue. The tangled nature of the hardcore narratives of *Messiah*, *The Vice*, *Wire in the Blood* for example, produce a sense of ominous, oppressive threat as they show detectives having to track down psychopaths who enact stomach-churning incidents of homicidal violence and brutality. There is a discernible American-inspired shift to the 'spectacularization' of the bodily violence; the 'clinicalization' of the crime scene investigation and the 'psycho-dramatization' of motive. The main police protagonists in these signature dramas are psychologically disturbed and morally corrupted by the unbearable nature of the post-social Luciferean society they are dealing with. Because they have discarded narrative and genre conventions, there is no consoling sense of moral or indeed social order to be automatically restored at the end of these dramas. The detective is doomed to live with the increasingly sadistic sins of post-society.

The only escape, until recently, open to viewers from this merciless cop world was to flick over to light hearted 'out-of-time' re-productions of the 'golden age' whodunnits or endless repeats of Morse et al., on 'classic gold' satellite and cable stations. However, in 2006, a new much praised BBC1 detective series, *Life on Mars,* provided viewers with another 'out-of-time' escape route. Politically correct DCI Sam Tyler is hit by a car while hunting a serial killer who has abducted his girlfriend. He wakes up in 1973 where his detective unit is run by 'old school' DCI Gene Hunt. In the course of the first series Tyler must adjust to a parallel world without mobile phones, computers, intelligence-led detective work and any semblance of an ethical approach to policing. This part thriller, part ironic comedy and part nightmare series can also be read as a desperate retro-yearning by police and society for both a *Sweeney*-style police series and a form of pre-politically correct policing that concentrated on no-nonsense thief-taking.

Conclusion

No one can be in any doubt that a significant reshaping of police and policing is under way and there is enough evidence drawn from across different juris-dictions to argue that the changes outlined in this chapter are so fundamental in implication that they amount to a paradigmatic revolution. This chapter first of all analysed trends in policing and security governance. And what has become abundantly clear is that there is no reason why a society's need for social order requires the establishment and/or maintenance of a public police force. 'Policing' is a socially necessary function but a state-structured police bureaucracy is not. The formation of a state police was contingent on a polit-ical élite's vision of what an orderly, disciplined society might look like. Policing regimes have always had to struggle to establish the legitimacy to operate in the local framework of public, communal and private social con-trols. New modalities of policing have to be negotiated with different audi-ences, and multiple versions of policing have been produced, each with particular symbolic and instrumental meanings for specific social groups. Furthermore, societies have re-organized or even discarded previously hege-monic police bureaucracies once they have outlived their political usefulness or as a result of public disenchantment.

A postmodern political and cultural environment is highly unstable and unpredictable. It is characterized by fragmentation and diversity – of organi-zational formations, governing rhetorics and cultural identities. 'Traditional' boundaries and sources of authority and legitimization are questioned, or even disappear. There are no guarantees that any 'old' order can be recreated (except as nostalgic or ironic pastiche) or that there will be a 'return' to sta-bility and predictability. There is no necessary state of organizational being 'beyond' fragments – there are only the fragments themselves. A postmodern 'bricolage' of tattered incoherent images and conflicting discourses defies attempts that claim to make sense of the whole via an over-arching logic. This constitutes the root of the police's crisis of cultural representation, a position from which there can be no modernist resolution. Figuratively, there is no doubt that the police organization is being 'hollowed out'. Haunted by the ter-ror of its own demise it is having to negotiate being turned inside out and out-side in, fast-forwarded and re-pasted through multi-mediated, simultaneous but non-aligned looped 'futures' that 'might have been', namely, nodalization, residualization, managerialization, re-sovereignization and post 9/11, post 7/7 global securitization. Moreover, the macro-structural futures currently trans-forming policing are supplemented by 'broken spectacle' popular cultural images of the police and policework. The difficulty for the 'promo-police' in a

24/7 multi-media saturated environment is that the boundaries of the 'real' have become heavily blurred and, to some extent, erased. This means, among other things, that attempts to retro-fit sovereignty to 'the police' to make it 'real' again will necessitate conciliation with multiple popular cultural images that profane and/or fantasize a once sacred icon of national security and social order.

Policing Crime and Disorder

5

Even the most poetic representations of the contemporary city acknowledge that the intensity of the urban experience is capable of also producing disorientating, disconcerting and painful lived realities. History provides us with fearful angst-ridden representations of the city, in different locations and times, as a breeding ground for exploitation, crime, disease, and disorder. Contemporary celluloid representations of the metropolis as a chilling crimescape in the grip of the 'dangerous stranger' often seem anything but products of the paranoid imagination of science fiction authors. Such dystopian visions of the city as a place of multi-layered fears insecurities and merciless pressures need, however, to be continually juxtaposed against the perennial attractions of the city as a place of heightened stimulation, excitement, experimentation, anticipation, empowerment and fulfilment. The intention in this chapter is to explore how contemporary perceptions of the metropolis as fractured, polarized 'noir ruination' have generated demands for both the re-imposition of order and stability and produced new 'born in the USA' high-definition 'sovereign policing' that both complicates and contradicts several of the 'no futures' for Anglo-American public police discussed in the previous chapter.

The insecurities of the metropolis

With the 'passing' of the twentieth century the global market economy is generating chaotic, postmodern urbanization processes representing according to Soja: 'something less than a total transformation, a complete urban revolution, an unequivocal break with the past; but also to something more than continuous piecemeal reform without significant redirection. As such, there is not only change but continuity as well, a persistence of past trends and established forms of (modern) urbanism amidst an increasing intrusion of post-modernization'. In postmodernity, 'the modern city has not disappeared. Its presence may be diminished, but it continues to articulate with both older and newer forms of urbanization and maintain its own dynamic of change making the normal adjustments and reformations of the modern city and the distinctive processes of postmodern restructuring difficult to disentangle' (Soja, 1995, p. 126; see also Soja, 2000).

For Soja the following characteristics define contemporary cities. First, they have consumer/culture oriented economies shaped by post-Fordist production technologies and global communication/information systems and a new international division of labour. In key sites, production, commodification and consumption are brought together in ways that confirm the city's status as nodes of the networked global market economy. In fact such cities have more in common with each other than with their suburban and rural hinterlands. Second, they undergo a radical rescaling and restructuring of the traditional urban form. The 'immaterial' city' is ensnared in an endless regeneration/degeneration/assembling/disassembling dynamic as it attempts to orient itself towards new global economic and cultural shifts. Third, in terms of 'within-ness' these cities are multi-social, multi-cultural, multi-national and multi-ethnic in nature. Fourth, there is a hyper-reality to the everyday life associated with all facets of the urban experience.

Finally, the primary objective of contemporary urban governance is to fashion a 'cultural city' by restructuring the economy towards the arts, design and 'high end' consumption. Glossy brochures and advertorials for the prosperous 24-hour metropolis show us thoroughfares of bustling sidewalks, arcades, parades, and courtyards, crowded market places, boutiques, cafes, restaurants, bars, music venues, clubs, hotels, etc. We see cultural institutions such as arts and crafts galleries, festival halls, museums, libraries, theatres, parks, gardens, plazas, fountains, waterside promenades as well as ethnic 'villages', 'Old Town' heritage quarters and off-beat 'bohemian' districts. Ideally, the key arteries of the stylized, neon-lit contemporary city will be showcased by spectacular skyline views. These cities have also invested in landmark architectural projects and artistic events that further authenticate the sensation of the contemporary city as cultural spectacle and excitement. Culture itself should be able to act as the primary civilizing process in the thriving street life of the regenerated city (see also Hubbard and Hall, 1998; Clarke, 2003).

Attempts to govern such volatile cityscapes are dramatically re-shaping the spatial patterning and policing of the heart and environs of many cities. As was noted in the last chapter, the private-minded middle and upper classes in an ever increasing number of global contexts, are opting to work, shop and live in increasingly securitized, privately guarded fortified enclaves or 'security bubbles' and moving along 'safety corridors', exemplifying Shearing and Stenning's (1983) original 'mass private property' thesis. However, as indicated previously, the regulation of the contemporary city has also required the public police to develop and deploy base-line disciplinary and civilizational strategies that network with the new configurations of spatial securitization and regulation.

The bright 'blue lamp': the New York policing model

The image of New York as the ultimate 'Fear City' to come has been powerfully established in the popular cultural imagination with a variety of Hollywood films – *Warriors, Taxi Driver, Escape from New York, Bonfire of the Vanities,* etc. portraying the city, present and future in the grip of the violent, criminal and insane. Damaging news media coverage such as the *Sunday Times* 'The Big Apple turns Sour' (McCrystal, 1989) and the *Time* article 'The Decline of New York' (Attinger, 1990) noted that the negative aspects of living in New York had been always more than compensated for by the material opportunities and cultural excitement of living in the world's greatest city. Traditionally, liberal middle-class New Yorkers had not viewed crime as a pressing social problem because it did not impact unduly on their neighbourhoods or lifestyles, or viewed street crime as one of the unavoidable hazards in living in a multi-cultural city (Siegel, 1995; Zukin, 1997).

Throughout the 1980s a visit to New York suggested that it was in increasing danger of replicating the hyper-pathologies of third world cities, due to a surge of drug fuelled violent crime that the police and municipal authorities seemed to be unwilling or unable to combat. Equally significant, victimization moved out of the ghettoes and spread across all neighbourhoods and classes. A rash of murders in the summer of 1990 generated panic news headlines that the city's gangs were determined to turn Manhatten into a killing ground. In addition, the homeless, drug addicts, and the mentally ill were making the neighbourhoods of central New York seem increasingly disorderly. Everescalating fear of crime and a host of unregulated social problems were driving away tourists, businesses, potential investors and middle-class residents. The populist New York news media ran 'enough is enough' editorials and commentary pieces about the threatening, disorderly, uncivil nature of the 'feral city'. The sources of this crime panic are deep and diverse but a particular focus was on the presence of increasing numbers of what were defined as 'aggressive beggars'. As a result of a hardening of public attitudes and 'compassion fatigue', it was agreed that beggars were becoming more insistent and menacing and feeding a broader public culture of fear, insecurity and disorder. This generated a potent 'politics of behaviour'.

The city declared that it would not tolerate activities that impacted negatively on the 'quality of life' in the city. In doing so the NYPD popularized not just Wilson and Kelling's 'broken windows' thesis internationally but also an urban policing philosophy of 'zero tolerance'. The change occurred with the election of Rudolph W. Giuliani, a former prosecutor, as mayor of the city in November 1993. Giuliani's electoral campaign promised to 'reinvent the city of New York' by implementing measures to reassure residents, workers and visitors that they were safe (Barrett, 2000; Giuliani, 2002). Given the scale of the crime problem instead of adhering to the dominant 'COP' rhetoric he instructed William Bratton, the new NYPD commissioner, to re-police the sidewalks, squares, parks and neighbourhoods of New York.

In 1990 Bratton had been appointed head of the crisis-ridden New York Transit Police. He drew upon his experience with the Boston police and his familiarity with both problem-oriented policing and 'broken windows' which he had encountered when he attended an executive seminar on policing at Harvard's Kennedy School of Government. Bratton argued that highly visible minor crime was of strategic significance because it was an everyday rather than exceptional experience in certain location. Public complaints about increasing low level crime and disorder should be an early warning sign to the police that an environment is experiencing stress and how the police could make a difference to quality of urban life. So while the NYPD tested its 'Officer Friendly' COP initiative, Bratton, drawing on the advice of George Kelling, rolled out 'broken windows' based anti-crime initiatives to 'win back' the transit system for law abiding commuters. The state of the New York subway system had been a source of concern for years. Lack of enforcement and widespread perception that the transport authorities would not intervene had, according to Bratton, encouraged petty criminals to push at the limits of acceptable behaviour (Bratton, 1998; see also, Glazer, 1979).

In order to transform the perception of public safety on the New York subway, Bratton set out to re-motivate transit officers under his command by re-establishing their police identity and investing in new uniforms and state of the art equipment, including new weaponry. An enforcement policy consisting of sweeps, targetting and harassment of offenders and collating street level intelligence for crime mapping purposes was the order of the day. The stations, platforms and trains were 'unclogged' as a result of cracking down on petty criminals, fare evaders, violators of transit regulations, panhandlers, the homeless, drug addicts, illegal vendors, vandals, graffiti artists, etc.

In the process, Bratton (1998) claimed he had evidenced Wilson and Kelling's 'broken windows' thesis that cracking down on low-level lawlessness, petty criminality and disorder would deliver results in terms of tackling serious offending. The crackdown was intended to send out the message that the primary role of the transit police was to defend the public space that the subway represented. Equally importantly, the 'turnaround' boosted rank and file morale because Bratton and his team established that petty criminality was also a verifiable 'gateway' to serious criminality. Finally the robust policing style was intended to re-establish public respect for transit ordinances and regulations.

According to Bratton, when he was appointed Commissioner of the NYPD in 1994, he inherited a highly centralized, over-specialized police department that was preoccupied with HQ and municipal politics and power games. A generation of senior NYPD officers had been socialized into a mentality of avoiding public scandal and controversy. The result was that the NYPD seemed to withdraw from controlling the streets of New York and conditions deterioriated.

He argued that the police had also been ideologically 'handcuffed' by the research findings of criminologists and police scholars who insisted that: 'nothing works' in the policing of escalating crime rates and that meaningful organizational reform was impossible. Hence, changes in policing strategy or extra resourcing would have little or no meaningful impact on the city's crime rate. Rank and file officers were thoroughly demoralized having been reduced to 'de-policing' crimes in an effort to keep the crime statistics politically manageable and to avoid enflaming tensions in black and Latino neighbourhoods. Officers had lost the 'will to police' and were effectively presiding over a process of de-civilization of the streets (Bratton, 1998).

Mayor David Dinkins responded in 1991 by hiring 7,000 additional officers to support the largest community policing initiative in the country (see, Silverman,1999). According to Giuliani and Bratton, this had only compounded the NYPD's problems. The news media had reported how 'community policing' – the most promising trend in urban law enforcement – would see a new generation of problem-solving beat officers working closely with communities and neighbourhoods. In practice it was marked by classic implementation mistakes: inadequate training, high turnover of personnel, poor co-ordination with other municipal agencies, inadequate management and the failure to address the highly cynical culture of the NYPD. The community policing initiative had made the beat cop the central 'agent of change' figure in co-ordinating and managing the police–community interface. However, 'Officer Friendly' beat cops were simply not experienced enough to deal with the city's problems of race, crime and disorder (Bratton, 1998, p. 35) nor did they have the organizational authority to fulfill the expectations set for them by the police department and the community.

Bratton believed that the significant resource increases allocated to the NYPD under the 'Safer Streets/Safe Cities' legislation were in danger of being squandered. To counter this there would be a shift from 'prozac' policing to proactive policing of the community. Bratton made the dramatic declaration that the NYPD would retake the city from the criminals block by block, street by street and house by house (see Lardner and Repetto, 2000, p. 321). The re-civilization of Gotham City was the overall aim. To do so would require the re-structuring of the NYPD's organizational infrastructure and the re-definition of the core police mandate. Bratton once more turned to a mixture of private sector management principles, Wilson and Kelling's 'broken windows' thesis and problem-oriented policing tactics to produce what he has defined as a policing blueprint for the twenty-first century metropolis, consisting of: organizational restructuring; high definition policing philosophy and problem-oriented policing tactics (see Bratton 1995; 1996; 1998).

Organizational restructuring

For Bratton and Giuliani, municipal authorities could not afford to economise on police officers. They must be prepared to budget for the employment of additional professional police officers and make the most of other uniformed policing and regulatory agencies and private security personnel. Verifiable crime control advantages can also be gained from the consolidation of available policing and regulatory resources. In addition, urban police departments need to be strategically re-engineered towards a results-oriented, pro-active crime fighting mentality. As many officers as possible need to be incorporated into the re-structuring process, providing middle managers and front line supervisors with the opportunity to get inside the department's way of thinking and to identify what needs to be done to improve departmental functioning. Organizational decentralization is of vital importance because it reinforces the authority and power of front line managers for all forms of patrol and detective work in their locality. The 'all crime is local' model points to precincts becoming self-contained mini-police departments. The degree of control managers exercise over personnel, resources, priorities and tactics should also expanded. They were empowered to decide 'how many plainclothes officers to assign, how many to put in COMPOL, on bicycle patrols, and in robbery squads. They were empowered to assign officers as they saw fit – in uniform or in plain clothes – to focus on the priorities of that neighbourhood … Whatever was generating the fear in this precinct, they were empowered to address it by prioritizing their responses' (Bratton 1996, p. 99).

Police departments needed to develop evidence-based data systems. The quality of the spatial and chronological crime data that the department works with needed to be enhanced. This necessitated overhauling the recording and reporting practices to produce accurate real time intelligence on crime patterns and trends and introducing relentless follow-up and assessment of the impact of police tactics. Once a crime pattern had been identified, an array of personnel and other necessary resources could be promptly deployed to deal with it. Although some tactical plans might involve only patrol personnel, experience proved that the most effective plans required personnel from several units. A viable and comprehensive response to a crime or quality of life problem generally demanded that patrol personnel, detectives and support personnel use their expertise and resources in a co-ordinated effort. In order to avoid merely displacing crime and quality of life problems, and in order to bring about permanent change, tactics had to be flexible and adaptable to shifting crime rates.

New forms of private sector productivity review were required. In the case of the NYPD this was realized through COMPSTAT, the 'Swiss Army knife of police management' (Maple, 1999; Walsh, 2001). This was where problem solving methods were used to generate hard data to pinpoint 'real time' crime patterns of 'who, what, when, where, why and how' and identify city wide trends and emergent 'hot spots'. Maple, the architect of the system, premised

COMPSTAT on four questions: was the precinct or division's crime information timely and accurate?; was deployment rapid, synchronized and focused? were the tactics effective?; were supervising officers relentless about follow-up and assessment?

These questions were intended to 'reset the standards by which operations were assessed at every level of the organization, from the executive camp, to the borough commanders, to the precinct commanders, to the cops we sent out on the streets' (Maple, 1999, p.23). At 'blood on the carpet' COMPSTAT performance review meetings held at NYPD headquarters, precinct commanders and those in charge of specialist units and teams were cross-questioned about what was being done to tackle crime 'hot spots', emerging crime trends and significant cases in their areas. These meetings were attended by senior NYPD officers as well as representatives from other municipal departments criminal justice agencies and the news media. As the presentations became more sophisticated, computerized, colour-coded maps and graphs of 'real time' crime and enforcement data were projected onto screens to offer a much more detailed, multi-levelled analysis of how police tactics were impacting on crime and disorder across different neighbourhoods. COMPSTAT was expanded to cross-reference data on 'quality-of-life' offences as well as data on neighbourhood demographics and dynamics gleaned from other municipal agencies and departments. It was also used to generate officer profile reports and upgrade the quality of information concerning the human resources at the disposal of the department. As a result of the intensity of early COMPSTAT meetings, a significant number of precinct commanders opted for early retirement or were replaced. Full meetings were subsequently supplemented by precinct and borough debriefings. According to Maple (1999) COMPSTAT was used to drive a variety of organizational requirements: install an aggressive results oriented accountability culture; identify and reward high performing senior officers; encourage a problem solving, evidence-based mentality; track the impact of different forms of police activity and deployment levels; break down departmental insularity and a fiefdom mentality; motivate senior officers to think outside of the existing bureaucratic box; match resources and personnel against priorities and provide evidence that the NYPD was a crime fighting machine (see also Massing, 1998; Henry, 2002; Kim and Mauborgne, 2003; McDonald, 2004).

High-Definition policing philosophy

In line with Wilson and Kelling's 'broken windows' thesis, the operational philosophy of metropolitan police departments must re-assert the 'sovereign' character of policing and affirm the role of the police as *the* custodians of the public realm. Re-establishing a doctrine of 'NYPD Blue' primacy and the 'will to police' and a mandate to re-civilize the streets requires policing to be re-dramatized. As was noted above, according to Bratton et al., police officers had been allowed to view many of the disorderly activities they encountered as not a police problem. If persistent or particularly annoying or if citizens complained, an officer might have asked troublemakers to move on, ask them to desist, or impose a fine. Given the bureaucratic consequences of arresting individuals for public disorder violations, it was considered to be a pointless exercise and such arrests only took place as a last resort. Bratton's retro-policing blueprint determined that rather than waiting for 911 calls, officers should 'go out and be cops: to arrest criminals, not to drive past them; and to investigate cases, not just write reports on them' (Bratton, 1998, p. 323).

Municipal police forces must of necessity manipulate appearances as well as reality. The heavily mediaized urban environment and the dramatic newsworthiness attached to crime and policing means that Guilliani and Bratton paid close attention to how news about the NYPD was produced, communicated and consumed (Silverman, 1999; Karmen, 2001; Manning, 2001). This required careful management of journalists and reporters and indeed all types of media personnel in order to market what would become known as the 'New York Crime Miracle' and rebut its critics. Proactive impression management to re-symbolize the NYPD's 'zero tolerance' policing style co-existed with the intensification of relationship building with key decision makers and stakeholders. During Bratton's two year reign in New York he publicly challenged the prevailing view among criminologists and police scholars that police actions could have nothing other than a marginal effect on the intractable crime problems that plagued urban neighbourhoods. It might not be possible to eradicate crime and disorder problems but Bratton argued that they could be managed more effectively, their social damage and visibility lessened and the message disseminated that crime, disorder and anti-social behaviour would not be tolerated.

Problem-oriented policing tactics

Re-establishing public confidence in the capacities of the police necessitates implementing what can only be described as high definition 'sovereign policing' tactics. The NYPD was reoriented towards the crime categories that would make an obvious statistical difference: getting guns off the streets; curbing youth gang violence; removing drug dealers from neighbourhoods; tracking down wanted criminals; reducing vehicle-related crime and breaking the cycle of domestic violence. Underpinning 'pressure policing' was paying close attention to the visible physical and human 'cues' of disorder in the public spaces of the city. 'Police Strategy No. 5' required officers to respond proactively to minor crime, unruly behaviour and 'quality of life offences'. Officers were told that it was their responsibility re-occupy streets and neighbourhoods to fix the broken windows 'and prevent anyone from breaking them again' (Bratton, 1998, p. 229). The police must promote corporate multi-agency problem-solving strategies based on data collected from all the municipal departments and be imaginative in its use of civil injunctions and municipal ordinances to

Figure 5.1   NYPD patrol cars, Times Square, New York

solve problems. For example, zoning restrictions and property regulations, in conjunction with proactive policing, were used to drive porn shops, pimps, prostitutes, drug dealers, beggars, street drinkers etc. out of central neighbourhoods. In addition, officers should be deployed in high visibility, high-media impact 'zero tolerance' targeting of begging, jay walking, truancy, illegal street vending, street hustling, excessive noise, double parking, graffitti writing, prostitution, sleeping on public benches, trespassing, fare dodging, public drunkeness and public urination, obstructive behaviour, etc. These activities make city thoroughfares look and feel even more unsafe and risky than they actually are.

The quality of policing matters as much as quantity. NYPD officers were mandated, for example, to use 'quality of life' policing tactics to 'crawl under the skin' of drug dealers. Identification checks were to be made, stop and searches carried out not just for their own sake but to facilitate further police attention. Working closely with the courts, the NYPD was able to impose penalties for relatively minor offences. In addition, those detained were finger printed, strip searched, checked for outstanding warrants and interrogated for information about other crimes. Street level policing was re-incentivized when officers realized that what was previously viewed as low level work was worthwhile because it was generating arrests and demoralising criminals. The 'broken windows' philosophy was the sharp elbowed tactic that enabled police managers to 'fold' the rank and file into a much more sophisticated set of policing strategies associated with intelligence-led and problem-oriented policing.

A remarkable decline in violent, property and street crime categories allowed Gotham to shake off its reputation as one of the world's most dangerous cities (Lardner and Reppetto, 2000; Kelling and Sousa, 2001; Travis and Waul, 2002). Equally significantly, there was a marked increase among New Yorkers of positive feelings about the overall quality of life of the city and about city governance (see *Time* 15 January 1996). The public was particularly impressed with the transformation of Times Square from what has been described as a 'sinkhole' of sleazy arcades and sex shows into a rejuvenated commercial entertainment complex. In addition to the neon advertising signs, restaurants, hotels, chain stores and Broadway theatres, Times Square has also become a major financial and media centre with Disney, Viacom's MTV Studios, the Condé Nast skyscraper and a giant video screen.

And as the decline in the crime rates continued into the early years of the new century, NYC's tourist office was able to boast that it was the safest US metropolis. Many, including Giuliani and and Bratton publically credited 'broken windows' policing for the New York 'crime miracle', Bratton insisted that, 'We have shown in New York City that police can change behaviour, can control behaviour and, most importantly, can prevent crime by their actions – *independently of other actors*' [italics added] (Bratton, 1998, p. 41).

Without doubt the high-profile spectacle associated with the 'NYPD-slashes-crime' experiment created extensive global media interest. What was newsworthy was the NYPD's reassertion that high definition policing could not only reduce crime and fear of crime but revitalize the police organizationally, stimulate public legitimacy and defy commentators who argued that there was no future for the publicly funded policing:

> What we learned above all from the New York experience is that the police can control and manage virtually every type of crime in virtually every neighbourhood. No place is un-policeable; no crime is immune to better enforcement efforts. Though underachieving in the past, American police departments can take the lead in restoring safety and order to communities all over the country. After a generation of police executives who were convinced that the cops couldn't cut crime, a new group of leaders is following the New York example and sending the message that police can make a difference. These leaders are junking the old reactive model, in which police responded to crimes and filed reports, in favour of a new strategic policing that gets criminals on the run and keeps them running. American police departments are beginning to live up to the boast posted by an anonymous officer in the NYPD Command Centre in 1995: 'We're not report takers', it reads, 'We're the police.' (Bratton, 1998, p. 9)

By the late 1990s the NYPD had mythologized itself as the high recognition 'power brand' in urban policing globally. As a consequence, foreign politicians and police departments made their way to NYPD Plaza One headquarters to find out whether New York style policing would work when transferred to other cities. In addition, key personnel involved in the New York 'crime miracle' were recruited to command other US police departments and to advise police forces world-wide on how COMPSTAT driven crime strategies could fix 'broken windows' and keep them fixed. The evangelic 'truth regime' constructed by the entrepreneurial NYPD would be crucial in debates about how to police anti-social behaviour in the UK (Upton Sahm, 2005).

The dimming 'blue lamp': the London policing model

Towards the end of 1992 the UK news media coverage of the seemingly inexorable rise in crime began to focus on a hardcore of persistent offenders who were deemed to be out of control and defied all attempts to control them. This was the 'crime panic' context within which the abduction and murder of two-year-old James Bulger by two ten-year-old boys occurred in Liverpool on 12 February 1993. The murder triggered an anguished public debate about the moral and spiritual malaise that had produced such a monstrous crime. Commentators across the political spectrum warned of the dreadful implications of an escalating number of anti-social 'underclass' neighbourhoods where law and order and virtually all notions of civility had broken down and crime, violence and disorder had become endemic.

Throughout the first half of the 1990s the news media presented numerous stories on 'de-civilized Britain', a country where the law-abiding were living under a self-imposed curfew and crime had spread virus like from the inner city, and the 'sink estates' to suburbia and the village. There was also an increasing number of incidents reported where 'active citizens', frustrated with the inability or willingness of the authorities to deal with local criminals had taken the law into their own hands, set up their own forms of DIY protection or hired private security companies. As panic raged about the UK's deepening law-and-order crisis, Tony Blair, Labour's newly appointed spokesman on home affairs, moved centre stage with a series of carefully crafted statements warning that the crime crisis was so serious in the UK that it had become a test, 'not just of law and order, but of our ability to function as a coherent democracy' (Blair, 1993, p. 25). For Blair the dangerous social tensions and levels of violent alienation on many council estates posed a strategic threat to the very possibility of state governance. This was the context within which Blair forged and popularized the 'tough on crime and tough on the causes of crime' soundbite both to reconnect Labour with its traditional heartland constituencies and to convince the broader electorate of 'middle England' that the party could be trusted on law and order.

The enthusiastic news media coverage of 'tough on crime, tough on the causes of crime' speeches, alongside extensive criticism of the Conservative government for its abdication of responsibility and failure to address public anxieties, enabled Blair to underline his left-realist inspired approach to crime. When he became leader of the Labour Party in 1994, it fell to Jack Straw to consolidate the party's 'tough on crime' stance and deepen the determination to re-moralize and re-responsibilize of the social. In July 1995 Straw made an undisclosed fact finding visit to the NYPD. What Straw learned during his briefing by Mayor Giulliani, the Police Commissioner William J. Bratton, and his deputy Jack Maples about the new policing model being rolled out by the NYPD would 'send shock waves through British politics' for years to come' (*Sunday Times*, 10 September 1995). The 'zero tolerance', 'broken windows' and 'quality of life' soundbites associated with the New York policing model began to percolate deep into British popular cultural and political consciousness.

Straw unveiled a batch of headline-grabbing plans promising that New Labour would authorize the police to reclaim Britain's increasingly brutalized urban spaces from winos, addicts, 'squeegee merchants', graffiti taggers; louts; and disorderly youths. This 'disorganized criminality' when co-joined with the threat posed by street muggers represented the 'most potent symbols of social decay', undermining the possibility of a 'peaceful street life', people's sense of security and their ability to participate in the everyday life on the community (*Independent*, 5 September 1995; *Guardian*, 7 September 1995). The speech had the desired effect with the news media reflecting on how the NYPD had provided New Labour with a 'zero tolerance' governmental script on policing and crime control. These highly controversial 'defining deviance up' speeches also provided evidence of the breadth of New Labour's unfolding anti-crime agenda and attestation of its readiness, if elected, to use the legislative powers of the national and local state to intervene in 'disorderly' communities and 'dysfunctional' families. In October 1996 Straw declared that 'securing people's physical security, freeing them from the feat of crime and disorder is the greatest liberty government can guarantee':

> It is not just specific crimes which affect our quality of life. The rising tide of disorder is blighting our streets, neighbourhoods, parks, town and city centres. Incivility and harassment, public drunkenness, graffiti and vandalism all affect our ability to use open spaces and enjoy a quiet life in our homes. *Moreover, crime and disorder are linked* [italics added]. Disorder can lead to a vicious circle of community decline in which those who are able to move away do so, whilst those who remain learn to avoid certain streets and parks. This leads to a breakdown in community ties and a reduction in natural social controls tipping an area into decline, economic dislocation and crime. Crime and disorder strike not only individuals – they can affect whole communities and the commercial success of town and city centres. (Straw and Michael, 1996, p. 4)

Speeches were made immediately after the 1997 election to different audiences confirming that the New Labour government remained serious about introducing 'zero tolerance' policing (see for example, Straw, 1997).

The legislative approval of the Crime and Disorder Act 1998 was a defining moment in New Labour's 'politics of behaviour'. Home Office officials assured journalists that although the term 'zero tolerance' had not been actually mentioned in the new legislation, its underlying principles had been folded into: anti-social behaviour, parenting, child safety, curfew and truanting orders. To facilitate this multi-pronged attack on anti-social behaviour, the legislation also required newly established statutory Crime and Disorder Reduction Partnerships, led by the police and local authorities to: carry out an audit of local crime and disorder problems, consult with local communities, publish a crime and disorder reduction strategy based on the needs and priorities of local communities, identify targets and performance indicators for each part of the strategy, with specified time scales, publish the audit, strategy and the targets and report annually on progress against the targets. Critically, tackling anti-social behaviour was to be mainstreamed within the co-joined decision-making processes and practices of the police and local authorities.

Despite the flurry of post-1997 crime reduction developments and the statutory requirement to conduct a crime and disorder audit and community consultation exercise, there was evidence of deep institutional resistance to prioritizing action against anti-social behaviour in major cities, most notably London.

First, local councils did not really take the audits seriously and for the most part, continued with what they had been doing by way of community safety and crime prevention since the mid-1990s. There was also a strong desire in Labour controlled councils to balance policing and situational crime prevention with long-term work on unemployment, poverty and deprivation in order to tackle the underlying causes of crime. There were no quick fixes to the deep seated problems resultant from 18 years of neo-liberal government. Without a massive investment of resources, many low level social problems were intractable. Local councillors who were drawn from social and educational services backgrounds were also concerned that targeting the anti-social would encourage the police to harass, intimidate and arrest people whose only crime was being poor, helpless and or vulnerable.

Second, a dominant Home Office managerialist discourse insisted that irrespective of political rhetoric, the ability of the police to control crime was limited. High visibility 'bobbies on the beat' strategies were an extremely expensive and inefficient use of scarce police resources, were often in competition for staffing of other high priority specialist activities and did not register well on productivity indices of making arrests and clearing up crime. The Home Office explicitly cautioned against the adoption of 'broken windows' and 'zero tolerance' policing strategies (Jordan, 1998; see also Weatheritt, 2000: Young, 2000). The police were encouraged instead to target resources on known crime 'hot spots', prolific offenders, repeat victims, persistent callers and conduct specialist raids to disrupt serious, crime markets and put more offenders before the courts rather than providing a visible police presence. In the long term the 'less police/better policing' Home Office perspective argued for a full-blown intelligence led, 'problem-oriented policing' paradigm and paying more attention to developing the effective use of scarce resources. The Home Office would also introduce a package of performance evaluation measures to allow for inter-force comparison on serious crime categories, particularly residential burglary, drugs and violent crime. Hence, policing was to be 'narrow banded' to effective crime management. Ian Blair, the then chief constable of Surrey, went so far as to suggest that the police were no longer committed to a preferred model of beat policing:

> We stand at a turning point in the history of policing in Britain. The past 50 years have seen an accelerated loss of our share of the security market – the loss of guarding of cash in transit, the monopoly of control of sports events, prisoner escorts, and above all, the subtle redefinition of what was once public space – the High Streets – into private spaces in the form of shopping centres, patrolled by private security. This tide will continue. Within 10 years it is possible that a substantial proportion of the police function may be absorbed by other local authorities and an unregulated private security sector. Alternatively, the police service can put itself forward as the central point both of cooperation to strengthen communities, and of patrol services carried out by a mixture of police, volunteer, local authority and private sources. It is not abandoning a monopoly of patrol. It is admitting that we haven't had one for years. The bobby on patrol, alone, has been seen as, somehow the point of the service. Yet you and I know the very small number of police officers who are actually patrolling. Chief officers and police authorities are simply choosing not to spend particularly heavily on patrolling officers ... Community security should not, however, merely be left to a matter of consumer choice. I would want local constables to co-ordinate all that activity. We already train and accredit door supervision – 'bouncers' – who carry out a much more confrontational task. Why shouldn't we do the same with private security and local authority patrols? (Blair, 1998, p. 20; see also Blair, 1999)

This 'mixed economy' model of 'franchise policing' would of course consign the post-war Dixonian notion of the omni-competent 'bobby on the beat' to the history books.

Third, since it was difficult to define 'anti-social behaviour' with legal precision, the police were also extremely loathe to expand their mandate to get involved in disputes and sub-criminal matters that were woven into the fabric of certain neighbourhoods. The liberal orthodoxy within the police argued that the publicity hungry NYPD's triumphalistic assault on crime dealt with the symptoms of social breakdown in multi-cultural societies without addressing the underlying causes (see Pollard, 1998; HMIC, 1999a). Also the volatile communal dynamics on certain housing estates militated against a routine uniformed police presence and only acted to amplify the fear of crime and disorder. This was a particular concern given that the majority of street police work being carried out by probationary officers who were not really experienced enough to manage complex sub-criminal policing situations. A very real concern was that officers could become involved in a partisan manner in neighbourhood, street and/or family disputes where there was an element of blame on both sides or where they were in danger of being used to settle scores. Supervising officers wanted young constables to be able to take a 'standback' position and to avoid being socialized into an 'easy results' culture of 'criming' as many trivial incidents as possible.

Fourth, there were also concerns about the unintended effects, displacement and otherwise, of aggressive crackdowns. The police were in many respects content to 'localize' and therefore manage particular crime problems, particularly those relating to the established drugs market and unofficial 'toleration zones' for prostitution, in particular parts of the city.

Fifth, there was the problem of motivating officers when an ineffective criminal justice system was being guided by the Home Office to prioritize the control of prison numbers rather than punishing offenders. Finally, despite the rhetoric, police officers were not convinced that the 'partnership' approach advocated by the Crime and Disorder Act added any real value to routine police practices. The police perspective was that there was every possibility that council departments would pass their 'rubbish collecting' responsibilities over to the police. The police, councils and the government all took comfort in the indications that overall crime was falling and would continue to fall. This would allow for a much more rational approach to crime and policing and criminal justice policy-making.

However, there were mounting pressures for the police and local councils to do something tangible about the mini-crime waves engulfing different localities and this was producing an incredibly localized anger about crime. The increasingly common complaint across working-class and middle-class residents was that localities were not being adequately policed or looked after. The police stood accused of having withdrawn from neighbourhoods, closing police stations or cutting back on opening times, unofficially given up trying to tackle certain forms of crime, tolerating disorder, raising the threshold of what they would respond to via prioritization or defining incidents as not a police matter. The inability of patrol officers, when they did respond to a call, to communicate properly with residents was another common complaint. Crime victims were less than satisfied to hear police officers telling them that there was little or nothing that could be done to apprehend perpetrators.

In the social housing sector, concerns about de-policing/non-policing were heightened because of residents' fears that their estates were being abandoned by councils that wanted to get rid of them or were willing to let them deteriorate into 'sink estates'. Respectable families found themselves under siege because empty properties were being taken over by drug dealers, junkies, prostitutes, the mentally ill and emotionally disturbed and illegal immigrants. Gang activity was flourishing and levels of physical violence had intensified and whole estates were on the verge of socio-economic disintegration. The deteriorating physical appearance of housing estates was compounded by the unwillingness of the council to tackle vandalism, graffiti, noise nuisance, dog mess, broken street lamps, unsecured entrances, drug paraphernalia, harassment and disorder. Underground carparks, alleyways, side streets and parks had become public urinals for the homeless. The changing mix in nearby hostels and refuges was also concentrating a much more volatile population in already de-stablising and disorganizing localities.

Middle-class neighbourhoods that had traditionally been able to spatially guarantee a high degree of order, civility and respectability had become crime scenes with a perceived increase in burglaries and stranger violence as well as the vandalizing of cars, gardens, common spaces and shopping parades. As a consequence, fear of crime was keeping people off the streets, especially after dark and out of public spaces such as parks. In this context, the police faced the most withering criticism on the virtual disappearance of the 'bobby on the beat' and the inability or unwillingness to tackle anti-social behaviour and 'quality of life' issues.

What united residents and indeed local businesses was the sense that they were being put in the front line of escalating crime, lawlessness and disorder as a result of police, council and government inaction. The general dissatisfaction with the police and local councils was heightened as a result of the accumulation of news-media reports of street crimes and violence against persons, attacks on joggers in parks and people using public transport, rapes, gang shootings, muggings of tourists, high profile crimes, and a 'drink-violence-disorder' culture associated with the ever expanding 'night time economy'. This created an overwhelming sense that Britain's cities were not just crime racked but tipping over into a deeper level of social disorder.

The police crisis

Frustrated by high levels of crime, the increasing disorderliness of urban neighbourhoods, the perceptible unravelling of both informal and formal social controls and the seeming indifference of the police and local councils, we see the acceleration of private responses. First, and most obviously, there has been the expansion of private surveillance cameras and security staff outside bars, clubs, restaurants and shops in the high street. Second, businesses in many towns and cities have clubbed together to sponsor a timed police presence. Private security personnel have also begun to patrol sections of main shopping thoroughfares to provide a reassuring presence, deter crime and enhance the overall shopping experience. And of course there has been the construction of a new generation of inter-connected shopping 'concourses' and 'mini-malls' which have 'designed in' hi-tech security and surveillance systems. Third, private security patrols now routinely patrol in wealthier neighbourhoods. Fourth, we have seen the spread of mini or 'outpost' gated private residential developments. Fear of Rolex robbers and car jackers who target BMWs, Mercedes Benz and Porsche and a lack of a visible police response has persuaded the privileged to build themselves secure, segregated 'guilded ghettoes'. Visible defence measures such as decorative walls and railings are for the most part symbolic. Exclusive postcode location, landscaped gardens, CCTV cameras, smart cards, underground parking and security guards do the real security work. Attempts by local authorities to curb these developments has seen the development of built-in 'stealth security' such as imaginative landscaping and 'natural defense' spaces.

What is most significant is that the market for 'gated communities' has begun to reach beyond élite protected estates for celebrities and new wealth. More modest developments, many built by mid-market companies, cluster around old converted churches and schools in less desirable postcodes. There may or may not be CCTV camera systems or security guards but there are gates and walls and secure parking facilities. Because of their location, these developments are in many ways having a far more significant impact on the social mix of the surrounding area. Neighbourhoods and communities are being slowly but surely remade as a result of the ongoing process of gentrification. The other side of urban renewal is ghettoization, represented by notorious sink estates where to all intents and purposes the writ of the local authorities has ceased to have meaning. These are effectively 'no-go areas' with a pervasive aura of decay where many public services have either been withdrawn or are pared down to the minimum. Left to their own devices they have turned in on themselves. Residents have transformed their homes into DIY fortresses with reinforced doors, grills and guard dogs. In many respects power, authority and respect within these clearly demarcated estates passes back and forth between the police and local authorities and the young and the strong. It is they who have the physical capacity and visible presence to enforce some form of order and act as a conduit between the legitimate and criminal local economies.

However, post-2000, the pressures around law, order and policing began to intensify. First, unexpected race riots in spring and summer 2001 in Bradford, Oldham and Burnley provided irrefutable evidence of the failure of New Labour's social policies to impact positively on fractured and volatile post-social Britain. This produced a flurry of initiatives that foregrounded the need to develop community cohesion (Cantell, 2001). Second, post 9/11 led the police to forewarn the public that the priority was to upgrading security policing as part of the preparations for an inevitable major terrorist incident in Britain. Third, the government and the Police Federation were involved in an increasingly acrimonious public row about what they viewed as the government's market-based reform agenda for workforce modernization. Finally, in the first months of 2002, the tabloid and mid-market newspapers launched a campaign to force the government to act against what was defined as a US-style epidemic of violent street crime and lawlessness. Intense news-media coverage took the form of melodramatic front pages, outraged editorials and double page specials on gun crime, stabbings, muggings, burglaries and 'new' crimes such as mobile phone thefts and carjackings. In addition, major newspapers produced 'crime specials' such as the *Daily Mirror's* 'Crime UK/Crime

2002'; the *Sun's* 'Crusade against Crime' and 'Anarchy in the UK', the *Daily Mail's* 'Wild West UK'; and the *Daily Express's* 'Is Britain Safe in 2002?'. As the crisis unfolded, incorporating a wide range of anxieties and Police Federation preparations for a strike, opinion polls indicated that crime had emerged as the single most damaging electoral issue for the government. This was reinforced by the Home Secretary's acknowledgement that violent street crime was spiraling out of control and that Britain's streets were unsafe. In an unprecedented move the Prime Minister declared that soaring street crime constituted a national emergency. He convened the first 'National Crime Summit' at Downing Street on 20 March 2002 to launch an anti-street crime initiative. The Home Secretary informed the newsmedia that:

> We are facing head-on the thuggery and violence on our streets. We literally must reclaim our streets for the decent law-abiding citizens who want no more than to be able to walk safely, to live peacefully and to go about their business freely, untroubled by the fear of attack. We want more police visible on the streets, immediate action to speed the perpetrators through the system, action to protect the victims and witnesses, and to ensure that those who are remanded or convicted don't walk freely on our streets. (David Blunkett, *Times*, 18 March 2002)

The startling pledge was made by the Prime Minister that the police would bring street criminality under control by the end of September 2002. There was also acknowledgment that the Home Office had re-oriented the police from the symbolic and emblematic qualities of front-line policing, most notably order maintenance, the general service function and the exercise of sovereign power toward a much narrower instrumental emphasis on rapid responses times and measurable targets to prevent and detect volume crime.

The police and local councils have been forced into a noticeable step change as a result of the prioritization of the 'politics of behaviour' and the proliferation of private security initiatives. There have been numerous declarations that the number one strategic priority is to demonstrate that minimum standards of public conduct and respect an be re-imposed. There was a notable public toughening of language, most of it expressly based on acceptance of the core 'grime to crime' tipping point and ripple effect principles of Wilson and Kelling's thesis. This is not surprising when it is remembered that the British newsmedia began to run 'NYPD shows the way' type headlines, drawing a direct comparison between New York's crime miracle and London's crime crisis. In February, 2002 Rudy Giuliani arrived in London to brief politicians on how the NYPD had used the 'broken windows' thesis to slash New York's crime rates. The *Sun* newspaper, as part of its 'Crusade Against Crime', devoted a double page special to by William J. Bratton's 'How you can win back the streets of Britain by the man who tamed New York' (*Sun*, 25 March 2002, pp. 14–15). This provided readers with a detailed account of policing philosophy and tactics that had 'revolutionized crime fighting in America and amazed politicians who had written off New York as uncontrollable':

> I'm aware of the situation in Britain. A lot of what occurred here in New York is transferable and can be tailor made for your situation. You need a combined attack on serious crime and quantity of crime. Quality of life seems to be something where increasingly your resources have become more restricted. A number of your chief constables have pulled away from focusing much attention on some of those issues. You have got to focus energy on serious crime and also on the so called signs of crime, such as broken windows, which is what generates most of the fear among citizens. The average citizen is not going to be the victim of crime. But the majority are going to victimized everyday by seeing people smoking marijuana without fear of interference by the police, selling drugs without interference, carrying out graffiti, aggressive begging and hooliganism. All these things create a climate which implies you can get away with disorderly behavior without fear of being restrained. What citizens fear is a deterioration of their neighbourhood. (Bratton, *Sun*, 25 March 2002, p. 14)

Building upon Bratton's thesis, New Labour's re-civilizational discourse began to emphasize that anti-social behaviour: *created* the environmental conditions in which more serious criminality and disorder can flourish; *undermined* community cohesion by increasing fear and anxiety and social withdrawal; *fostered* an ethos of intimidation and threat that was leading to a reluctance to intervene or co-operate with the authorities; wasting scarce public resources; *impeded* neighbourhood renewal strategic and commercial regeneration plans; and *destroyed* basic human rights ands civil liberties (see Home Office, 2003b).

Communities were encouraged to be intolerant of both crime and anti-social and disruptive behaviour that was ruining the lives of respectable, law abiding people. Council leaders and police officers promised that they will move vulnerable neighbourhoods from being a 'high crime' to not just low but 'no crime' localities. This would require the police and local authorities to demonstrate to residents, businesses and visitors that they exercised sovereign control over the disorderly streets, deserted parks and fearful neighbourhoods and housing estates and could 'security proof' communities. This was to be realized through a shift to 'safer neighbourhood policing'.

Re-lighting the 'blue lamp'?

As a result of the political fall out from the local law and order crisis, the 'bobby on the beat', or 'retro-policing', has been revalued in a variety of ways. The most obvious is in terms of government promises to deliver on what have been defined as 'NYPD levels of resourcing'. Ideologically the police have also been conceptualised by government as a 'vital civic institution' as embodied in the 'office of constable'. The police are being offered a key leadership role in the local community with highly visible local commanders being mandated to work with local authorities, Crime and Disorder Reduction Partnerships and local organizations. We have also seen the move towards what has been tagged as a 'reassurance' or neighbourhood policing philosophy. It was recognized that public reassurance, like anti-social behaviour, was a complex and multi-facetted concept that extended well beyond the capacities of the police. Nevertheless, the argument was advanced that 'reassurance', defined as the levels of *security* (personal and property) and *order* (behavioural and physical) that exist in a locality, could be operationalized through a visible, accessible, familiar, responsive, intelligence-led consistent police presence (ACPO, 2001; HMIC, 2001a; see also Innes, 2004 a,b; Millie and Hetherington 2005; Crawford, 2006). The hope is that reducing both the physical and psychological distance between uniformed officers and the community will result in increased levels of personal safety and neighbourhood security. The long-term hope is that a virtuous circle will develop in which communities will develop more confidence that the local police and will come forward with more information about crimes, leading to more arrests, which will in turn, generate a greater readiness on the part of people to work even closer with police officers. This shift in emphasis has been justified by reference to both the NYPD's 'broken windows' tactics and more recently to the Chicago police department's model of deep community engagement. In this model the police are expected to move from service delivery to leadership of and support for the community (Skogan, 2006).

There have also been moves to re-anchor the police in the community via providing a high visibility unformed police presence in key places at key times to maximize public reassurance. In an attempt to meet the public's insistent demand for a uniformed presence, there has been a commitment to significantly increase the proportion of officers working on frontline policing and to put as many police officers and civilian staff as possible back in uniform. 'Neighbourhood Policing Teams' are being deployed on a permanent basis to work within specified communities to identify 'background noise' such as low level nuisance, the 'signal' crimes, disorders and environmental issues that have a disproportionate impact on the public's sense of safety and the 'comfort factors' that might reassure people (see Innes 2004 a:b; O'Connor, 2002, 2003).

Localization necessitates giving Neighbourhood Policing Teams the autonomy to arrange their own working patterns and develop proactive problem-solving policing styles to correspond to local needs and problems. Underpinning this shift to retro-policing is the recognition that relationship building, beyond conventional notions of community consultation and responding to 999 calls, is crucial to improving the quality of intelligence available to the police and public co-operation during criminal investigations. The promise has been made that organizational structures will be reformed to ensure that Neighbourhood Policing Teams are not subjected to the tyranny of answering the police radio or redeployed from their core duties to special operations.

However, this latest resurrection of the Dixonian 'bobby on the beat' has several novel twists (see Blair, 2002a). First, a significant percentage of street patrol responsibilities have been passed to Police Community Support Officers (PCSOs). This auxiliary tier of 'cut-price' officers, who were championed by Sir Ian Blair as a response to his fears of a proliferating 'mixed economy' of policing, are not mandated with full constabulary powers. They are being deployed on the streets to: provide a visible presence; help prevent crime; maintain public order; assist the public to receive reports of crime; get to know the locality and act as 'the eyes and ears' of the police. The PCSOs can issue fixed penalty notices for a variety of anti-social behaviours and can detain someone who does not comply with a request to provide his/her name and address until police constables arrive. Neighbourhood policing teams can also include a mix of special constables, and 'badged up' local council street wardens, park wardens, community safety officers, private security guards and private security patrols. Second, neighbourhood policing is part of a broader toughening up of the government's 'community safety' efforts. Most obviously local authorities and their partner agencies are financing the integration of key situational crime prevention aspects into their properties, securitizing access points, adding concierge services, fencing and gating off estates and closing down entrances and organizing warden patrols. In addition, there have been moves to tighten up the sanctions associated with tenancy agreements to reinforce obligations and responsibilities.

Third, the police and councils have been given new powers to deal with the threat of anti-social behaviour. It has been the introduction of Anti-Social Behaviours Orders that has symbolically marked the shift in the policing of low-level, sub-criminal behaviour (see Millie et al., 2005). As was noted above, the Anti-Social Behaviour Order (ASBO) was introduced under the Crime and Disorder Act 1998 and strengthened under the Police Reform Act 2002 and the Anti-Social Behaviour Act 2003. The ASBO is a civil order that can be applied for by the police or a local council, or acting in partnership, where it can be demonstrated that a person aged ten or over has been acting 'in a manner that caused or was likely to cause harassment, alarm or distress to one or more persons not of the same household as him/herself and where an ASBO is necessary to protect relevant people form further anti-social acts by him/her'.

This definition is meant to include behaviour where members of the public are put in fear of crime. ASBOs should be restricted to chronic, intentional problematical behaviour and not used to settle petty neighbourly disputes, minor disorderly acts or penalize those who are 'different'. Where the anti-social behaviour is the result of drug and/or alcohol misuse or homelessness, the ASBO should be deployed if it is not possible to get the individual to regulate their behaviour. The police must demonstrate that there is a pattern of anti-social behaviour that has happened over a period of time that cannot be dealt with easily or adequately through the conventional criminal justice system (Home Office 2003b). Applications for an ASBO are made in a magistrates

Figure 5.2   Safer neighbourhood policing, London

court, acting in its civil capacity. The complaint must be made within six months of the time of the anti-social behaviour. A summons together with the application should be either given to the defendant in person or sent by post to the last known address. Where it can be shown that there is an urgent need to protect the community an application for an interim order can be made with the application for the main order. The police take the lead in putting the package of evidence together, including police reports, first hand witness statements, hearsay and professional witness evidence and, if it is available, back up information from CCTV footage.

The ASBO, which can last for a minimum of two years, is preventative in effect, containing restrictions prohibiting the offender from specific anti-social actions and from entering specified geographical areas. 'Exclusion zones' can be used to ban individuals from: streets, housing estates, residential properties and neighbourhoods; being out at night; associating with named individuals; carrying a weapon; swearing or using racist language. A map showing any 'exclusion zone' and information regarding other prohibitions is circulated among the police, particularly those working in relevant areas. Data is also automatically fed into police intelligence systems. Originally, the prohibitions could only be applied to the geographical area of the authority applying for it and this raised concerns about displacement. The Police Reform Act 2002 remedied this problem so that the restrictions could extend to anywhere in England and Wales if a convincing case could be case could be put together. Breaching an ASBO is an arrestable offence which can result in a custodial sentence of five years imprisonment for an adult offender. ASBOs are being used to target: anti-social street behaviour (rowdy or threatening group behaviour; drinking alcohol; drug abuse and dealing; joyriding; begging; prostitution; kerb-crawling; public nuisance; depositing litter); problem neighbours (harassment and intimidation of residents: racial and homphobic abuse; noise nuisance; waste dumping; animal related problems; vehicle related problems); and broader environmental problems (vandalism; grafitti and environmental damage; fly-tipping; fly-posting; abandoned vehicles; illegal lockups, misuse of fireworks).

The police and council are using the news media and internet as well as leaflets and posters to both 'blame, name and shame' offenders and inform residents of the prohibitions imposed by the order so that they will be able to identify and report breaches (Home Office, 2005). The police and local authorities can also use curfew and dispersal orders to clear streets and neighbourhoods of those who are deemed to be behaving in an anti-social manner.

Fourth, we see the deployment of high-definition 'sovereign policing' actions to spectacularize neighbourhood policing. More officers and wardens are on regular foot patrol wearing bright yellow vests in key locations across the city, backed up with considerably more clearly marked police vehicles. There are also high profile, media-staged 'zero tolerance' or 'pulse' policing crackdowns involving both local and specialist police units which are undertaken to demonstrate that the local police are capable of reclaiming streets and neigh-bourhoods. As a result of prior undercover surveillance operations and use of CCTV, we see New York style initiatives against: street crime; illegal trading; street drinking; begging; prostitution and drug dealing. We also see the pulling together of the different policing and wardens in dramatic 'hotspot' corporate policing actions. This normally consists of removing abandoned cars to stop them being used for sex and drugs; stripping phone boxes of sex cards; visiting off-licenses to encourage them to stop selling alcohol to street drinkers; raiding drug locations and illegal sex, drinking and gambling clubs; removing rubbish and graffiti; and securing derilict buildings. Policing teams also move into 'over-spill' areas to mop up on displacement effects. And in presentational terms the news media is routinely invited along to record and communicate the scale of these policing operations. Police video cameras also record what is happening. What is significant is that in major crackdowns it is the upgraded paramilitary weaponry and clothing of the specialist police units that now marks out real police officers from uniformed PCSOs and the plethora of wardens.

Conclusion

The purpose of this chapter has been to delineate the overlapping attempts to de-intensify and control the unpredictable social interactions that are charac-teristic of the contemporary city. Although commentators agree that the shift to new modes of regulation and policing is generating a hyper-spatial reorder-ing of whole or certain parts of the cityscape and everyday interactions they cannot predict with any confidence how things will unfold.

John Pratt (2000) has made a valuable contribution to the general crimino-logical discussion about the new social control dynamics that are currently manifesting themselves across 'high crime' societies. He picks up on a little commented upon section of Stan Cohen's original 'visions of social control' the-sis that notes that sitting alongside the fear of the powerful state machine is: 'the fear that the machine is breaking down by itself, and that 'outside' in the chaos of urban life, in the desolate city streets abandoned to the predators, lies the ultimate horror – chaos, disorder, entropy' (Cohen, 1985, p. 210). And as we have discussed in this chapter, there is a widespread concern that the famil-iar structures of certainty and security which provided the glue to hold 'social' together are fragmenting and crumbling. Accompanying all the emphasis on individualization is also a pervading sense of anxiety, fear and insecurity. This is compounded by the fact that state authorities are more willing to acknowl-edge that in a globalizing context there are limits to what they can do and that citizens are responsible for looking after themselves. For Pratt we:

> become fearful when it appears to us that the machinery of state control is
> breaking down, or that the state no longer seems to have much interest in

coming to our assistance when needed, or that neither the state nor its organisations seem to have the solution to our fears of disorder and personal
threat. It cannot even recognise the dangers to us, however obvious they
appear to the general public (2000, p. 175)

However, significant sections of the public still want 'proof' that the state is
not 'withering away' or 'hollowing' itself out or 'governing at a distance' but
is capable of representing their interests and acting decisively on their behalf.
The desire is for the social to be transparently governed, policed and cared for.
This may explain why 'forms of social control that have an ostentious presence and are calculated to bring out the emotive sentiments of a watching public are gaining ascendancy, precisely because of the growing demands on the
central state to show that it still working' (Pratt, 2000, p. 176). At a time of
insecurity we desire and indeed demand symbolic acts of security and evidence
of the ability and willingness to exercise sovereignty over the streets, parks
and the estates. Hence the public's willingness to support high levels of
imprisonment and the introduction of expressive, ostentatious sanctions that
are designed to blame, shame and humiliate.

High-definition 'sovereign policing' tactics such as those blueprinted and
branded by the NYPD have captured the public imagination because they
have an invaluable role to play in symbolizing norms of public behaviour that
are vital to virtually every facet of a civilized urban life. There is still the desire
to inhabit public 'spaces of trust' that naturally and 'softly' police and regulate themselves. For writers such as Jane Jacobs (1961) the bedrock principle
of a humane and democratic urbanity is one of providing both for safety for
and safety from strangers on the street. Safety nourishing streets and parks
manage to strengthen the network of social reassurance across people of all
incomes and races through balancing people's right to privacy and their
co-existent desire for degrees of contact, excitement or assistance. Public
spaces if they are to foster trust relations must have the capacity to bring
strangers together and manage and transform their presence into 'a safety
asset'. However, Jacobs is also only too aware that historically cities and areas
within cities have differed considerably in their capacity to facilitate and manage safe interactions among strangers. Indeed she stresses that the breakdown
of trust between strangers and the heightening of a sense of fear, insecurity
and anxiety undermines core aspects of city and/or neighbourhood life.

To function, contemporary urban space necessitates the de-intensification and
management of incendiary extremes of wealth and privilege and poverty and
marginalization. Lawlessness and de-civilization could be the end result of dramatic increases in violent crime, menace, disorder, chronic insecurity and
extreme conflicts and struggles associated with the neo-liberal intensification of
material inequalities and/or racial and ethnic conflict and cultural divisions. The
contemporary city is a frenzied criminogenic entity, being a natural 'safe haven'
for organized criminals who are integrated into global crime networks. We see

the proliferation of criminal opportunities with the demand and supply of goods and services (human trafficking; money laundering; drugs; weapons; pornography; prostitution; fraud; extortion; counterfeiting; forgery; body parts; personal security services). This reconstructs the lower levels of the criminal 'marketplace' with the emergence of explosive forms of dis-organised, irrational crime. 'Third worlding' produces forms of criminality linked to pre-modern family, kinship, community, and ethnic culture, e.g., witchcraft; exorcism; honour killings, etc. Allied to this, fears for public safety and personal security and distrust of strangers is intensified in neighbourhoods with poor lighting, boarded up shop fronts, squalid streets, offensive graffiti, vandalised public utilities, inadequate public transport and the presence of the homeless, the mentally ill, drug dealers, prostitutes and gangs and the emergence of 'no go areas'.

It could be argued that NYPD style high definition 'sovereign policing' can re-establish the freedom of movement in public places that is essential to all social groups who inhabit the city. Although no policing strategy can be expected to eradicate the root causes of crime, such policing methods can be supported as progressive if they galvanize the police to act 'where many would, for a quiet less risky life, prefer to allow illegal economies and bullies to operate with unhindered dominion in poor neighbourhoods' (Stenson, 1999 p. 284; see also Taylor, 1999). Policing actions that displace 'yob culture' can create the much needed breathing space for the implementation of longer-term local state build-ing programmes, neighbourhood renewal, community safety schemes, and 'place-making' programmes. In the long run of course there is the intriguing pos-sibility that this much more clearly defined localized policing tier will be politi-cally anchored within the micropolis rather than national state. This is something we will discuss in more detail in Chapter 7.

Critics of high definition 'sovereign policing' insist that what we are really witnessing is the latest staging post in the mobilization of core coercive gov-ernmental capacities to facilitate and protect the interests of multinational cor-porations and the bourgeois habitus of cosmopolitan elites. The relentless neo-liberalization of the contemporary city is not only a response to, but con-tributing to and deepening racial/ethnic/cultural/economic segregation and polarisation. The way in which municipal authorities and private corporations now co-produce and co-govern significant expanses of urban space suggests a police-led form of urban governance that prioritizes punitive control over welfarist policies to alleviate the deeply divided, unequal city. Attempts to manage 'public' space through mallification, gated communities, techno-surveillance and high-definition 'sovereign policing' whilst enhancing public confidence for some, generates chronic levels of individual anxiety, lower lev-els of communal trust and indifferent or defensive social encounters. There is an obvious redistribution of risks involved in the entrenchment of 'innocent populations' in over-protected consumerist 'citadels', insulated residential 'enclaves' and heavily policed thoroughfares and the containment of 'suspect populations' in outcast, under-protected, disordered peripheral 'ghettos'.

Central to all this is the emergence of a politics of behaviour that attempts to heighten public insecurity through the demonization and criminalization of the 'anti-social'. Authoritarian populist modes of governance encourages the authorities to publicize their actions to provide reassurance to residents; enable communities to identify breaches and violations; and send out the message that anti-social behaviour will not be tolerated. The result of a 'show not tell' mentality is that sections of the newsmedia expose ever more outrageous examples of anti-social behaviour. Popular television is saturated with docudramas that use CCTV and police footage to give us an insight into 'neighbours from hell' and 'yob culture'. Local news media work closely with police forces and council departments to profile 'prolific' or persistent offenders'. The stated intention, as was noted previously, is to 'blame, name and shame' criminals; discourage others and to reassure the public that the authorities are in control. It also permits the use of a public language that not just stigmatises but dehumanisies and makes certain people 'untouchable'. The populist news media also silences or marginalizes or ridicules alternative social policy options. It requires of the police and local councils that they put a spin on policies to prove that they are tough and stage dramatic incidents to publicize and market their 'get tough' credentials.

The stark inequities of the 'contemporary city' will require the deployment of a much wider and spectaclar-'shock and awe' range of means of disciplinary regulations and controls. Ever more sophisticated surveillance and monitoring devices, target-hardening techniques, private security guards, and 'stone age' order maintenance policing practices will be a central part of what Parenti (2001) defines as the corporate 'security matrix' upon which the profit potential of the fractured and fragmented postmodern metropolis depends. They require the police to operate in a high definition manner across the 'public' parts of the cityscape not only to promote particular forms of public reassurance and the illusion of order but to track the movements of the visibly 'deviant', 'troublesome', 'out of place', 'surplus population', residual social groups. The power relations that constitute and drive high definition, maximum impact policing inaugurates the shift to a proactive, paramilitarized, media-amplified policing regime that is mandated to (a) re-establish control over economically significant and culturally symbolic city centre sites and gentrified/gentrifying neighbourhoods and (b) sweep 'problem populations' and the social problems they represent to carefully screened 'vanishing point' parts of the city or its hinterland with the least political and economic power (Nelson, 2000; Bass, 2001; McArdle and Erzer, 2001; Karmen 2004). High levels of crime and minimal policing will be normalized and DIY protection routinized in ways which exacerbate rather than resolve poor neighbourhood problems. Irrespective of the 'neighbourhood policing, 'quality of life' rhetoric, high definition 'sovereign policing' styles have meshed seamlessly with privatization strategies to secure the postmodern city against those who actively challenge, resist, disturb or offend the relentless neo-liberalization of urban spaces.

One final point needs to be noted. Police forces have learnt a number of important lessons from NYPD developments. First, and most significantly, it would seem that the contemporary metropolis cannot do without the spectacle 'sovereign policing'. There has been increased recognition that the police can have a significant impact on crime levels and the fear of crime through controlling the 'anti-social' and reassuring the law abiding. Second, the NYPD formulated a retro-policing blueprint that has allowed for an organizational re-conceptualization of how to control crime and disorder. Despite the warnings of their critics, it is possible, for example, to deploy aggressive street policing tactics without provoking a full scale riot. And equally importantly the possibility of a riot breaking out can be factored in to planned operations and paramilitary police units put on standby. Finally, the mobilization of a politics of behaviour that targets the 'anti-social' can provide the police with a powerful if volatile source of sovereignty. The Metropolitan Police have also learned that operational revitalization and cultural validation can be achieved through symbolically allying themselves with not just the expertise but equally significantly the media amplified 'brand authority' of leading US police forces. In order to officially launch the Neighbourhood Policing Team initiative in London, for example, in March 2006 the Metropolitan Police felt it necessary to ensure that it was personally validated both by William J. Bratton and the Chicago Police Department. This does of course in the long term make British urban policing philosophy and practice and wider governmental thinking about how to regulate the postmodern metropolis increasingly dependent on, and perhaps subservient to, tabloid media validation and US technical know-how.

Police Culture

As was established in Chapters 2 and 3, police scholarship, in a variety of different jurisdictions, established that certain orders of thought and feeling and behavioural tendencies develop as rank and file officers gradually internalize and adapt to the requirements of routine police work. The norms and values associated with the workplace culture exercise a significant influence in everyday decisions in policework. However, the self-protective, self-reinforcing, culture is not just the result of the inter-personal dynamics of the work group or the collective experiences of rank and file officers. Rather, as we have seen this culture is constituted within situated work practices that produce and sustain the core discourses and symbolic categorizations of the imagined police community. What was also established in the Anglo-American sociology of policing, from Westley and Banton onwards, was that racialized 'identity work' was deeply embedded in organizational processes and practices and also in the cultural notion of who was entitled to be a 'real' police officer.

The aim of this chapter is to offer a critical analysis of how and why the construction and reproduction of racialized relations within policing continues to challenge the core conceptualization of the police. This is of course within an overall context of the seismic transformations to the macro-policing landscape referred to in the previous chapters. The chapter begins with a brief reconsideration of the attempted 'Scarmanization' of the police to prepare it for the challenges of policing a multi-cultural polity. The second part assesses the nature and effects of the cultural meltdown and identity crisis unleashed within the police by the 'institutional racism' finding of the Macpherson inquiry. I then analyse the contents of the BBC 2003 *The Secret Policeman* documentary which sent shockwaves through the police and reignited the debate about the extent, nature and causes of rank-and-file police racism. Finally I discuss the new round of post-Macpherson reforms to reform police culture and 'de-contaminate' it of what was defined as 'stealth racism'. The critical question is whether we are witnessing the painful birthing of the multiple police identities that can symbolise the complexity of a fractured police culture?

Policing the multicultural society

In the UK, the philosophy and techniques of policing multi-racial neighbourhoods came under official scrutiny in the aftermath of the 1981 inner city riots. These riots highlighted the conflictual relationships between police and new immigrant communities that dated back to the late 1940s and the docking of the *SS Empire Windrush* at Tilbury Docks. Lord Scarman's inquiry listened to evidence that ethnic minority communities were over policed as exemplified by allegations relating to the discriminatory use of police powers, harassment; excessive use of force; aggressive policing tactics; and unfairness in the application of stop and search tactics. As well as incidents of individual harassment, minority communities also complained about racial profiling of certain crime categories, saturation policing by specialist police squads, incursions on cultural and political events, and immigration raids. In addition, there were complaints that the police were providing inadequate levels of protection to ethnic minority communities, as exemplified by the general quality of service in these neighbourhoods and the response to racist violence and harassment (see Hall et al., 1978; Cashmore and McLaughlin, 1991; Keith, 1993; Bowling and Phillips, 2002, 2003). And for those communities, the evidence was suggestive of institutional or systemic racism rather than the racist attitudes and actions of individual officers. There were also complaints that police racism was not adequately controlled by the existing structure of police accountability. From the police, Lord Scarman heard evidence that officers were trained to 'serve without favour or distinction'. A robust police response had been necessary because Britain's multi-racial inner cities were experiencing extremely high levels of violent street crime in which there was irrefutable evidence of the over-involvement of young black men.

Lord Scarman's overriding goal was to achieve a settlement which would square a series of circles by re-imagining police–community relations and re-ordering the relationship between ethnic minority communities and British state and society. He rejected allegations that the police was 'institutionally racist' and also released the Metropolitan Police from the accusation that it was a racist organization (Scarman, 1981, para 4.62). For Scarman the police could not be held solely responsible for the tensions and conflicts that were manifesting themselves in multi-racial Britain. However, the police was going to have to give serious consideration about how organizationally it responded to larger social transformations. It was his opinion that part of the problem was 'ill-considered, immature and racially prejudiced behaviour' which manifested itself 'occasionally in the behaviour of a few officers on the streets' (para. 4.63). He recognized that the UK police, like their US counterparts, needed to be much more attuned to the demographic shifts reshaping Britain's inner city neighbourhoods. As a matter of urgency the police had to address the implications of predominantly white forces patrolling increasingly ethnically and culturally diverse neighbourhoods. In addition, as a general principle of 'policing by consent', officers would be required to strengthen their community links and demonstrate their ability to enforce the law and prevent crime in an effective, impartial and equitable manner in such neighbourhoods.

While recognizing that training alone would not guarantee improved police–community relations, Scarman insisted that education in community and race relations was necessary for the development of a racially and culturally sensitive police force that could cultivate community trust and confidence. Efforts would have to be oriented towards producing an ethnically representative workforce. This would, in turn, require action to ensure that the selection methods and the internal occupational culture were free of racial prejudice and discrimination. He also recommended that recruits be screened for signs of overt racial prejudice and that racist officers be dismissed from the force. Combining equal opportunities with an operational philosophy of non-discriminatory 'community policing', rule-tightening and enhanced community involvement would, for Scarman, transform the white masculine working-class police culture and get rid of 'rotten racist apples'.

Beyond Scarman

Throughout the 1980s and early 1990s, the police was immersed in reform initiatives that were intended to neutralize the impact of race on policework (for an overview see Holdaway, 1996; HMIC, 1996; HMIC, 2000; Bowling and Phillips 2002: 2003). First, forces in areas where there was a substantial ethnic minority population launched outreach initiatives and recruitment drives to produce a work force whose demographics matched those of the community. Second, US sourced racism awareness training courses were introduced to ensure that officers treated all members of the public in an equitable, fair, 'colour blind' manner (see Oakley, 1989, 1993; Tendler, 1991; HMIC: 2000). Finally, there was a broader reform programme to develop professional standards of conduct and the formulation of a 'force to service' paradigm. In 1985, Metropolitan Police officers received *The Principles of Policing and Guidance for Professional Behaviour,* a wide-ranging code of ethics which reminded officers that it was their professional duty to provide a courteous service to all sections of the community. In April 1989 *The Plus Programme – Making it Happen* was unveiled committing the organization to what was described as a 'revolution' in customs, practices and values. The overall aim was to ensure that the force could provide a quality of service to Londoners, which met their different needs, priorities and expectations. At a *Fairness, Community, Justice* conference in February 1993, which examined the relationship between the Metropolitan Police's internal equal opportunities policies and quality of service issues, Sir Paul Condon, the newly appointed Commissioner of the Metropolitan Police, stated:

> We must be equally intolerant of our own colleagues who fail to reach the required standards. We demand exemplary conduct from those we employ. We hold a position of trust in society and it has the right to expect the very best conduct from us ... We have a moral duty to the communities we serve, not only in the way we police them, but also in the way we conduct our own affairs. How will the public expect us to treat them if we cannot even treat each other fairly? (*Independent*, 2 February 1993)

The default police position was to continue to highlight its successes in relationship building with ethnic minority communities and to reiterate that it treated everyone fairly regardless of racial or ethic origin.

However, countering these initiatives were indications that racialization remained central to police culture. A new generation of officers was socialized into an anti-Scarman police culture that insisted there was a relationship between race and criminality and advocated a tough policing response to what was perceived as the increasing lawlessness of black neighbourhoods. This of course fed into and was fuelled by periodic police backed media campaigns for the racial facts of 'mugging' to be acknowledged and debated. Despite officers being trained in specialist community and race relations courses, there were suggestions of a tacitly condoned casualized racism. Equally significantly, there were also indications that ethnic minority officers as the classic 'outsiders-now-enemy-within' were encountering significant levels of cultural resistance in the form of racial prejudice, disadvantage and discrimination within certain police forces (Smith and Gray, 1985). In the early 1990s, the inability to integrate ethnic minority and female officers into the ranks generated a series of high profile cases of institutionalized racism and sexism (see McLaughlin, 2001). At the same moment as the police were having to defend themselves against a record number of complaints of malpractice and corruption, the fabled 'blue shield' was breached from within. What was revealed was a claustrophobic workplace culture which presumed conformity to a hegemonic white, male, heterosexual culture and condoned vituperative sexist and racist attitudes and behaviour. Unacceptable attitudes and behaviour were going unchallenged and ethnic minority officers, women and gay officers were tokenized, isolated and extremely vulnerable (see Holdaway, 1996). These cases produced two significant outcomes in the mid-1990s. First, ethnic minority officers established a Black Police Association (BPA) in 1994 claiming that the Police Federation was unwilling and unable to promote racial equality in the workplace. The BPA replicated their US counterparts in focusing on complaints arising out of the conflictual racial dynamics within police forces and poor relationships between the police and black communities. Holdaway

(1996) pointed to the radical implications of this development arguing that the formation of the BPA would amplify the racialized identity of its members.

The establishment of the BPA disrupted traditional rank and file-management relations within police forces and provided the news media with a distinctive voice on policing issues. It also set the equally important precedent for other marginalized officers to set up their own representative bodies. Second, two years later, ACPO (Association of Chief Police Officers) sought the help of the Commission for Racial Equality (CRE) to produce an 'action plan' on race and equality issues. This plan was premised on the baseline benefits of main-streaming equal opportunities at all points of the employment cycle: enhanced corporate 'brand reputation'; improved operational effectiveness; deepened public trust and the easing of conflict between police officers and the public. It also spelt out the long-term consequences for the police of having to fight further discrimination cases: more financially costly industrial tribunals; extremely negative publicity; damaging community relations; staff de-moral-ization and poor performance; absenteeism and high wastage rates. So long as the police remained overwhelmingly white and male, it would be vulnerable to charges of racism and sexism. The result would be that it would be extremely difficult to recruit or retain high calibre ethnic minority staff and women (Commission for Racial Equality, 1996; HMIC, 1996; 1997).

Macpherson: institutional racism and cultural crisis

At 10.40 p.m. on the night of 22 April 1993, two young black men, Stephen Lawrence and Duwayne Brooks, were waiting at a bus stop in Eltham, South London. After the words 'What? What? Nigger!' were shouted, they were sud-denly confronted by a group of white youths. Duwayne Brooks shouted 'run, run' but Stephen Lawrence was surrounded and stabbed by one of the youths who then ran away. He managed to run for about 200 yards up the road before collapsing and bleeding to death. His friend ran to a public telephone, dialled 999 and requested an ambulance. He also asked passerbys for help. When police officers arrived at the scene an hysterical Duwayne Brooks managed to tell them that he and his friend had been attacked by a group of five or six white youths who had used the term 'nigger' and that the attackers had run down an adjoining road (Brooks, 2003).

Despite an extensive police investigation nobody was convicted of the fatal stabbing. Two of the five white suspects, Neil Acourt and Luke Knight, were charged with murder but the CPS (Crown Persecution Service) ruled that the evidence against them was not strong enough and refused to proceed with the case. During a re-investigation, the suspects were secretly recorded on video playing with knives and expressing a shocking level of racial hatred of black people. However, on the video recording they also denied having anything to do with the Stephen Lawrence murder.

Neil Acourt, Gary Dobson and Luke Knight were acquitted when a private prosecution brought by the Lawrence family in 1996 collapsed. Charges against two other suspects, Jamie Acourt and David Norris, were dropped before the case came to court. On 17 February 1997, after the reconvened inquest into Stephen Lawrence's death returned a verdict of unlawful killing, the *Daily Mail* published its infamous front page cover with the photographs of the five suspects under the headline 'Murderers – If we are wrong let them sue us'. Following persistent campaigning by the Lawrence family and the intervention of Nelson Mandela, the Home Secretary established a judicial inquiry in July 1997 under the chairmanship of Sir William Macpherson. The remit of the inquiry was to re-examine the failed investigation of the murder of Stephen Lawrence and subsequent events. Its primary purpose was to 'identify the lessons to be learned for the investigation and prosecution of racially motivated crimes' (para 3.1). The inquiry was also authorized to look at wider issues relating to the lack of trust and confidence in police amongst ethnic minority communities.

Almost every part of the Metropolitan Police and every level of personnel was found wanting in some respect. The extent of the organizational disintegration – particularly the catalogue of failures, mistakes, misjudgements and lack of direction and control – is something that the inquiry team was unable to comprehend. In many important respects from beginning to end the Macpherson inquiry was also a battle for public opinion and political support that was fought out across the media and it is a classic case study of how a local tragedy can be transformed into a media crisis for the police (see Chapter 4). The Metropolitan Police found themselves in the unprecedented position of allegations of incompetence, racism and corruption being repeatedly flashed across not just on the front pages of newspapers, editorials, commentary pieces, news broadcasts and documentaries but also detailed in a prime-time ITV docu-drama *The Murder of Stephen Lawrence* (18 February 1999). On 21 February 1999 the crisis of representation deepened further when the BBC2 broadcast *The Colour of Justice*, the dramatized reconstruction of key moments in the Stephen Lawrence Inquiry that had already played to packed houses in various London theatres. The inquiry was a public relations catastrophe with even the Metropolitan Police's political friends and stakeholders beginning to distance themselves from the force (see Cathcart, 1999; Hall, 1999; McLaughlin and Murji, 1999)

The publication of the Macpherson report on 24 February 1999 generated global news media coverage and passionate public commentary. The report was the hardest hitting official statement on race and policing ever published in the UK. Race relations were catapulted into the forefront of the nation's consciousness. Almost 20 years after Scarman's report, Macpherson concluded that the culminative effect of decades of the over-policing and under-protection had undermined ethnic minority trust and confidence in the police.

The report was a devastating indictment of the Metropolitan Police force. Individual officers of all ranks were 'named and shamed' for their mishandling of a murder investigation that was marred by 'a combination of professional incompetence, institutional racism and a failure of leadership by senior officers' (Macpherson, 1999: para 46.1). In the course of the inquiry it became clear that the much lauded post-Scarman 'colour blind' policing initiatives had had little discernible affirmative impact on the police. This was evidenced most obviously in the inability of officers of all ranks who gave evidence to understand how racism might be embedded in and constitutive of policework. The intensity of newsmedia criticism of the Metropolitan Police's handling of the Stephen Lawrence murder, as documented in the report, was unparalleled.

The report concluded that key parts of the unsuccessful police investigation of the Stephen Lawrence murder could be accounted for only by the presence of insidious and persistent 'institutional racism', which was defined as:

> the collective failure of an organisation to provide an appropriate and professional service to people because of their colour, culture or ethnic origin. It can be seen or detected in processes, attitudes and behaviour which amount to discrimination through unwitting prejudice, ignorance, thoughtlessness, and racist stereotyping which disadvantage ethnic minority people. It persists because of the failure of the organisation openly and adequately to recognise and address its existence and causes by policy, example and leadership. Without recognition and action to eliminate such racism it can prevail as part of the ethos or culture of the organisation. It is a corrosive disease ... Unwitting racist language and behaviour can arise because of lack of understanding, ignorance or mistaken beliefs ... from well intentioned but patronising words or actions ... from unfamiliarity with the behaviour or cultural traditions of people ... from racist stereotyping of black people as potential criminals or troublemakers. Often this arises out of uncritical self-understanding born out of an inflexible police ethos of the 'traditional' way of doing things. Furthermore such attitudes can thrive in a tightly knit community, so that there can be a collective failure to detect and to outlaw this breed of racism. (Macpherson, 1999, para 6.34)

Macpherson's proposals to 'outlaw this breed of racism' had repercussions for every aspect of policing. The report insisted on: new procedures for the reporting, recording and investigation of racist crime; rule-tightening of discretionary stop and search powers; targets for recruitment, progression and retention of ethnic minority officers; making racism a disciplinary offence punishable by dismissal from the police force. Proposals were presented for revising race awareness training to make certain that all police personnel were educated to not just understand but positively value cultural diversity; recognize the connection between the cultivation of good community relations and effective policing and to hammer home that 'a racist officer is an incompetent officer' (Macpherson, 1999, p. 332). It was also recommended that the Race Relations Act should be amended to apply to the police and that an independent police complaints system be established.

Following publication of the report, Jack Straw, then Home Secretary, set out an action plan for implementation of the core recommendations referred to above (Home Office, 1999). A Lawrence Steering Group (LSG) was established in the Home Office consisting of independent representatives from ethnic minority communities, the police and other statutory agencies. In addition to ensuring that the Macpherson recommendations were being actioned, the LSG was expected to monitor the impact of the report on the public's experiences and perceptions of the police; the way policing was being delivered; and the relationship between the police and ethnic minority communities. It also had a role in advising on the implementation of the Race Relations (Amendment) Act 2000, which came into force in April 2001. This gave public institutions a statutory duty to promote race equality by: eliminating unlawful discrimination; promoting equality of opportunity; and furthering good relations between different racial groups. Individual officers could not discriminate directly or indirectly, or victimize one another in discharging their public functions (Bhavnani et al., 2005). Chief police officers were made vicariously liable for all aspects of discrimination carried out by an officer in the exercise of his or her public duty unless it could be demonstrated that all reasonable steps were taken to prevent the discrimination. The Commission for Racial Equality was given responsibility for ensuring compliance with the act.

Beyond Macpherson

The Metropolitan Police's 'Policing Diversity: Protect and Respect' strategy was intended to signify the movement from a (pre-Macpherson) 'colour blind' to a (post-Macpherson) 'anti-racist' policing philosophy (see Condon, 1998; Metropolitan Police, 1998; 1999 a,b; 2000; HMIC, 1999b; 2000; 2001b; Blair, 2002b). Constructing what was defined as the world's first anti-racist police force would require three inter-related practical adjustments regarding (a) recruitment, retention and career development, (b) cultural diversity training, and (c) the race-proofing of operational practices.

There would be renewed efforts to ensure that the police force, at all levels, visibly reflected the diversity of backgrounds, cultures and characteristics of the communities it worked in. This would require eliminating discrimination by identifying the barriers in the recruitment and selection process which adversely impacted on ethnic minority candidates. In August 2000 the Home Office hired the Saatchi advertising agency to run the country's first national police recruitment campaign costing £7 million to 'rebrand' the force and to boost the number of visible ethnic minority and women officers. This was followed up in August 2001 by the launch of the high profile 'Could You?' advertising campaign. The Metropolitan Police also considered recruiting from

Figure 6.1   Positive Action Poster: Police Federation

Figure 6.2   Positive Action Poster: Gay Police Association

the Caribbean and Indian sub-continent to meet the government's targets for increasing the number of ethnic minority officers. Under a 'Refer a Friend' scheme, cash incentives were offered for the recruitment of ethnic minority staff. An 'ethnic minority only' intake of recruits was also contemplated in order to create a critical mass as was positive discrimination to compensate for under-representation at senior command levels of the organization. Sir Ian Blair's Police Community Support Officer scheme was also folded into the post Macpherson recruitment agenda. This initiative, as was noted in the previous chapter, was originally developed to meet public demand for more 'bobbies on the beat' and to respond to the pluralization of policing. However, it was realized that if it was advertised properly it could attract ethnic minority recruits that might not normally consider a police career.

It was stressed that recruiting more ethnic minority officers and facilitating their career development would fail unless it took place in a working environment that appreciated and positively valued cultural diversity and inclusivity. Police racism and intolerance would be addressed through unprecedented Home Office investment in a new generation of community and race relations programmes run by Ionann Management Consultants (2000; see also Garland et al., 2003; HMIC 2003). The Metropolitan Police rolled out a cutting edge 'united in diversity' programme to create a working environment that was both neutral and multicultural and ensure that police officers were attuned to the differences between London's multitude of ethnic and religious communities. The force also encouraged the establishment of staff associations of different racial, ethnic, national, religious and social backgrounds.

There was acceptance that the relationship between the police and ethnic minorities was shaped to a considerable degree by the historic complaint of over policing as crime suspects and under protection as crime victims. In line with Macpherson, action was taken to 'race-proof' operational strategies, policies and practices. Officers would be required to demonstrate fairness and impartiality in the use of their powers during 'critical encounters' on the streets. For example, 'stop and search' was reviewed to identify how it could be used lawfully, fairly and professionally on the basis of intelligence and verifiable crime patterns (see Fitzgerald, 1999, 2000). Operational responsibility for responding to racist incidents was handed over to a specialist Racial and Violent Crime Task Force led by Deputy Assistant Commissioner John Grieve, the former head of the anti-terrorist squad. This high-profile Task Force took lead responsibility for investigating the Stephen Lawrence, Ricky Reel, Michael Menson and McGowan murders.

The establishment of the Task Force, an Independent Advisory Group and borough-based Community Safety Units (CSUs) represented the latest attempt to close the gap between the Metropolition Police and those groups and communities who complained that they were underprotected and particularly vulnerable. Initially the Metropolitan Police concentrated on 'race hate crime' with John

Grieve declaring war against the racists. The no-warning nail bomb attack on the Admiral Duncan pub in Soho during April 1999 by David Copeland, a self-declared neo-nazi, resulted in calls for tough new penalties for anti-gay 'hate crime'. As a result a new squad dedicated to fighting homophobia was established. The discovery that the majority of incidents being referred to the new CSU's were incidents of domestic violence widened the definition of 'hate crime' used by the metropolitan Police. On 8 June 1999 the first co-ordinated 'hate crime' arrests took place in early morning raids in South London.

To raise public awareness about the realities of 'hate crime' in London, a high-profile multi-media campaign also ran initially through autumn 1999 and early 2000. Further publicity for anti-'hate crime' initiatives in London was garnered on the first anniversary of the publication of the Stephen Lawrence Inquiry report. Finally in October 2001, a £250,000 advertising campaign was launched by the Metropolitan Police to discourage young people from committing race hate crimes. Advertorials were placed in youth magazines to support television advertisements featuring some of the country's best-known pop stars. Nationally, the release of a detailed ACPO guide to 'Identifying and Combating Hate Crime' in September 2000 represented another significant step in the mainstreaming of the initiative. The guide stressed that 'hate crime' would be a priority for not just the Metropolitan Police but all police forces because it was 'exceptionally pernicious and damaging to individuals and communities'.

Culture wars

In the final countdown to publication of the Macpherson report it became clear that the Metropolitan Police recognized the need to get to grips with what was in many respects the equivalent to the fall of the Berlin Wall. Consequently, it intensified its efforts to promote its diversity reform agenda across the news media. As was noted above, the force made a concerted attempt, for example, to resuscitate the myth of Scotland Yard by highlighting the Racial and Violent Crime Task Force's 'war on racist criminals'. A charm offensive was also launched which involved targeting of government ministers, civil servants, media figures, the clergy and community leaders. The force let television cameras into Scotland Yard to record the efforts of Sir Paul Condon and his senior officers and public relations department to build a post-Macpherson police force (Channel 4, 1999; see also BBC, 2001a). However, the reactions to the Macpherson report from within the Metropolitan Police revealed a volatile, litigious workplace racked with confusion and anger, criss-crossed with competing power networks and replete with highly racialized schisms and micro-conflicts. These conflicting victimization discourses were played out in the full glare of the newsmedia.

First, a radicalized BPA was extremely vocal in its criticism of what it viewed as the glaring gap between, on the one hand, the 'hand-on-heart' speeches of chief officers and the glossy official publications that extolled the rhetoric of 'institutionalizing diversity' and on the other, the reality for visible ethnic minority officers confronting a groundswell of hostility to Macpherson's reform agenda. According to the BPA:

1   The cultural diversity training programmes were accommodating rather than challenging police racism.
2   A significant percentage of ethnic minority applicants were being rejected for racist reasons at the selection stage in the recruitment process.
3   A racist culture was being allowed to develop unchecked within the training schools with ethnic minority recruits facing insults, discrimination and intimidation by white colleagues and training staff.
4   Ethnic minority officers were being frozen out of specialist policing units and departments.
5   Ethnic minority officers were being set up by colleagues to fail in prominent or prestigious roles.
6   Malicious complaints were being used to trigger serious disciplinary proceedings against ethnic minority officers who had played a public role in the Macpherson inquiry.
7   Ethnic minority officers had lack of support from the Police Federation.

The overall intention of this orchestrated attack was to decapitate the BPA leadership, destroy its reputation and sabotage core recommendations of the Macpherson report (Holder et al., 2000; see Ousley 2000; Cashmore 2001, 2002; Muir, 2001; BBC, 2001b:c; Fitzgerald et al., 2002; Holdaway and O'Neill, 2004).

Second, the sensitivities of white Metropolitan Police officers were at an all time high, provoking protests that the finding of 'institutional racism' was an affront to their professionalism. What might be defined as a dissident white perspective complained that:

1   The Stephen Lawrence murder investigation had failed not because of the police but because of the incompetence of the legal team representing the Lawrence family.
2   Operational policing had been handcuffed in multicultural neighbourhoods by the imposition of politically correct 'softly softly' policing tactics.
3   Criminal elements had been provided with the opportunity to make career damaging malicious or speculative complaints of racial harassment and discrimination.
4   They had been branded as racist bigots with regard to a murder investigation that had happened before many officers had joined the force.
5   'Politically correct', image-led chief officers were looking for scapegoats to demonstrate the force's commitment to rooting out racist officers.
6   'Reverse racism' was resulting in under-qualified ethnic minority candidates being fast tracked through the recruitment process.
7   Ethnic officers were using the 'race card' to gain preferential treatment in promotion and specialist placements and to block disciplinary action over poor performance and aberrant behaviour.

8　Senior officers and the Home Office were making cynical use of the 'diversity babble' of the Macpherson report to drive through new disciplinary rules and a much broader set of managerialist reforms.

The concerns of officers hostile to the 'political correctness gone mad' Macpherson report received prominent coverage and support in right-wing sections of the news media and among Conservative politicians and commentators (Green, 2000; Dennis et al., 2000). The broader anti-Macpherson backlash found full expression in the overwhelmingly negative reaction to the Parekh Report (2000) which had attempted to broaden the terms of the debate about the future of multi-ethnic, multi-cultural Britain. Such was the level of hostility to the report's anti-racist agenda that government ministers had to take the lead in denying that Britain was a racist society (McLaughlin and Neal, 2004). It should not be forgotten that direct connections were also made to the 'flags, badges and emblems' campaign being conducted by sections of the right-wing press to save the (RUC) Royal Ulster Constabulary from post-Patten abolition (see Ellison and Smyth, 2000).

Third, female and gay officers pressed to make sure that their respective interests and concerns were both included in the post-Macpherson cultural diversity agenda and recognized in their own right. This is not surprising given that there was continuing evidence of high levels of sexism and homophobia in the force. As far as they were concerned they would resist attempts to impose an internal 'hierarchy of oppression'. Fourth, there were signs that ACPO desired to move the force on from what was viewed as a de-motivating obsession with 'institutional racism'. Sir John Stevens, the Commissioner of the Metropolitan Police applied a tough-minded realism to the problem of repairing the divisions and 'rallying the troops'. He concentrated on rebuilding a sense of officer commitment by emphasizing the importance of teamwork and the corporate identity of the police family and highlighting the achievements rather than failures. The workforce was told to concentrate on the core business of: developing safer neighbourhoods; securing the capital against the post-9/11 terrorist threat; reforming the criminal justice system; developing effective policing strategies; implementing broader service delivery reforms; and campaigning for more resources and powers. He declared that 'Of course there will still be one or two racists in the force, and I'm determined to root them out. But we have moved on light years in the past two or three years. Even the most trenchant critics will give us that. *We are not institutionally racist'* (*Sunday Telegraph*, 20 January 2002). The Commissioner received official support in January 2003 when David Blunkett, the then Home Secretary, queried the usefulness of the term 'institutional racism' (*Guardian*, January 2003). On the tenth anniversary of Stephen Lawrence's murder, Cressida Dick, Commander of Scotland Yard's Diversity Directorate, complicated the debate further when she contradicted both the Commissioner and the Home Secretary, saying she could not imagine a time when the police would be able to proclaim that it was free of institutional racism (*Independent*, 22 April 2003).

The rumbling 'culture wars' centred on a series of truly extraordinary disciplinary investigations involving senior ethnic minority officers. The very public nature of the investigations into Superintendent Ali Dizaei, one of Britain's most senior ethnic minority police officers and the legal advisor to the BPA who was suspended from duty over a variety of allegations, provided a remarkable insight into the post-Macpherson conflict raging out of control within the Metropolitan Police. A post-Lawrence crisis point was reached when the BPA declared that the £7 million *Operation Helios* indicated that the Metropolitan Police had learnt nothing from the Macpherson inquiry. Senior officers stood accused of failing to stop an orchestrated 'racist witchhunt' against the leadership of the BPA. On the day that is was announced that Kent Constabulary had appointed Mike Fuller as Britain's first black police chief, the BPA confirmed that it was organizing a 'March of Solidarity' which would see ethnic minority officers protesting in full uniform outside Scotland Yard on 17 November (see Cohen, 2003). The Dizaei case was subject to investigation by both the Police Complaints Authority (PCA) and the Metropolitan Police Authority (MPA). The MPA inquiry chaired by Sir Bill Morris, the former general secretary of the Transport and General Workers Union, was tasked with investigating the Metropolitan Police policies, procedures and practices for handling complaints and allegations against individuals, grievances and workplace disputes, as well as Employment Tribunal claims. As we shall see later in this chapter, the Morris inquiry would publish a highly critical report in December 2004.

'An hour of painful truth': *'The Secret Policeman'*

In the midst of the increasingly bitter and damaging post-Macpherson culture wars, rumours began to circulate that a BBC undercover investigation team had obtained evidence of racist attitudes and politically incorrect behaviour among probationary police officers matching anything seen in the covert video footage of the five white men accused of murdering Stephen Lawrence.

The programme makers chose Greater Manchester Police (GMP) Britain's second largest police force, because in October 1998 David Wilmott, the then Chief Constable, had told the Macpherson inquiry that: 'society has institutionalised racism, Greater Manchester Police therefore has institutionalised racism. And it is our responsibility and duty to try and make sure that (a) that's eradicated and (b) that it doesn't interfere with discharge of our responsibilities to the community' (*BBC Newsnight*, 15 October 1998). This acceptance of 'institutional racism' came as a surprise to other chief constables and infuriated the Police Federation. Wilmot stood accused of contradicting the views of Sir Paul Condon and betraying his officers. GMP subsequently launched 'Operation Catalyst' to implement the Macpherson report (see Jenkins, 1999) as well as a new recruitment campaign that emphasized that GMP was 'the best police force in the world'.

The BBC documentary wanted to find out whether the first generation of post-Macpherson officers were racially prejudiced and equally importantly if they were whether they were prepared to ignore force policies and act upon their racial predispositions. The BBC justified using undercover investigation because of the distinct possibility that racism had been driven underground by post-Macpherson policy initiatives. In so doing, the BBC broke all the conventions that governed the relationship between the news media and the police with regard to filming in training schools.

It took BBC reporter Mark Daly approximately one year to infiltrate the force. In February 2003 Daly underwent 15 weeks training in Bruche Police Training Centre in Warrington along with officers from other police forces in North West England. In total there were 120 recruits, only one of whom was Asian. After successfully completing his training, Daly operated as a probationary constable in Greater Manchester. The investigation ended in August 2003 when the reporter was arrested outside his home by GMP internal affairs officers for: obtaining his police wages by deception; presenting false documents during the application process; and damaging a police uniform. The GMP officers confiscated cameras, recording equipment and note books from Daly's home.

There was considerable news-media coverage of the force's anger about what was defined as the irresponsible, underhand behaviour of the BBC. Michael Todd, GMP's Chief Constable, protested that 'if true, we deplore this tactic, which would appear to be an outrageous waste of public funds used to train, equip and pay this individual. It has also deprived a genuine recruit of the opportunity to join the service'. A GMP press officer added 'Greater Manchester Police is accountable at all times to the public. We serve and welcome legitimate scrutiny. But this behaviour, if true, is reprehensible and only serves to undermine the work of the police service. The journalist is also in breach of an oath of attestation that he made in becoming a police constable as he has failed to act with integrity. In condoning this act of unethical journalism, the media organisation may well have breached people's human rights' (BBC News website, 16 August 2003). In addition, the GMP announced that it was looking into every case handled by Mark Daly while he was a probationary police officer. This was a particularly sensitive moment for the country's second largest force as it had just received a highly critical HMIC report on sexism and racism within the workplace.

The Home Office and the GMP made a concerted effort to attempt to dissuade the BBC from broadcasting the documentary. The intimation was that post-Macpherson, the police could not survive another 'racist-to-the-core' scandal. However, a *Manchester Evening News* story (14 October 2003), 'BBC defies police on "racism" TV probe', disclosed that the BBC had secretly reworked its schedules to rush out the programme – with its 'damning' evidence of racist police recruits – at 9 p.m. on 21st October. Furthermore, the Corporation had not informed the GMP or Home Office about the scheduling of the programme and despite a high-level meeting, a police request for an advance screening had been refused. The initial focus of the weekend news media coverage was Home

Office and police anger with the BBC for the unethical methods it used both to get the footage and generate publicity for the programme. The *Daily Mail* (18 October) ran a story about the questionable methods used by the programme-makers and the following day had an 'exclusive' 'Blunkett fury at BBC Racist Police Stunt'.

> We have raised concerns with the BBC, not about their right to expose racism but their intent *to create not report* a story. And they have done so in a way that did not present the detail for action to be taken, but was a covert stunt to get attention. We want chapter and verse to deal with the issue, not media leaks to develop controversy. (*Mail on Sunday* 19 October 2003)

The Home Secretary inferred that the BBC had 'sexed up' the programme to justify its subterfuge. A Home Office spokesperson backed up Blunkett arguing that 'This reporter took the place of a much needed genuine policeman. The BBC have failed to produce hard evidence to back up their claims. If they do we will look into it' (*Mail on Sunday*, 19 October 2003). The *Mail on Sunday* provided a double-paged exclusive overview of the programme's 'shocking' contents. The other Sunday newspapers also focused on the extreme racist language used by some officers and remarkable footage of an officer posing as a member of the KKK and making threatening comments about an Asian recruit with headlines such as 'BBC reporter films Klan stunt' (*The Observer*); 'Police officer said Stephen Lawrence deserved to die' (*Independent on Sunday*) and 'Police 'Ku Klux Klan incident filmed' (*Sunday Telegraph*). This in turn generated commentary in reviews of the papers in other sections of the broadcast newsmedia. On the Monday the 'KKK cops' coverage continued to focus on the row between the Home Secretary, the police and the BBC.

At 9 p.m. on 21 October 2003 immediately before the broadcasting of the programme, a BBC announcer informed viewers that:

> Four police officers from North Wales and North West have been suspended following a long investigation by the BBC into racism in the police service. Reporter Mark Daly went undercover to see how the police are tackling racism in training and policing on the beat. His findings contain strong and racist language from the outset ...

In the opening credits Daly tells us:

> I have been 'PC2210' of Greater Manchester Police for the past seven months. But I am also a journalist for the BBC. I was doing both jobs in order to investigate racism in the police. But my double life ended this August when I was arrested. It's twenty four hours since my release from police custody. On Friday afternoon I was intercepted by two internal affairs officers. I can't express the shock I experienced when they arrested me for deception. We had no idea they were close to arresting me. In fact I was looking forward to the time that I would no longer wear the police uniform – the plan was to leave the

The programme cut to covertly shot clips of the racist views of the recruits Daly had made friends with in his class. Viewers are then reminded of the unhappy history of post-war police-race relations. Particular attention is paid to footage of the five white suspects accused of the murder of Stephen Lawrence, including the images of violent racism gleaned from covert surveillance cameras. Daly then recaps on the Macpherson report's definition of 'institutional racism' and Chief Constable David Wilmott's controversial statement.

Through micro-cameras hidden in his uniform, room and car, the nation was privy to covert footage of Daly having laser surgery to correct his poor eyesight, attending his final interview, being fitted out for his uniform and sworn into the police force, and his time at the training centre. This includes footage he records in classrooms, the bar, canteen, various external locations and his car. However, the primary focus is his bedroom where fellow recruits hang out after the bar is closed. Here the reporter gradually turns general conversations towards the issue of race and policing. In addition to watching covert footage of his fellow recruits, Daly also provides viewers with a video diary that fills us in on off-the-camera developments as well as his thoughts about what is unfolding around him.

Daly notes how in the Training Centre literature makes it clear that there is a zero tolerance policy with regard to racist, homophobic, sexist language and behaviour or harassment or intimidation of any form. In the first cultural diversity training class there is a discussion about racism in British society and in the police force. There is footage of recruits being warned about unacceptable behaviour, stereotyping and not to use the words 'Paki', 'nigger', 'wog' or 'coon' or they would be dismissed. A Police Federation representative reinforces the message that they should not use racist words. However, if they did they would still be represented by the Federation in any disciplinary proceedings. As was noted by Daly this was the first time that an alert recruit would see a discrepancy between official policy and practice.

The eight racist officers 'outed' by Daly in the course of his investigation were Andy Hall, Carl Jones, Tony Lewin, Adrian Harrison and Andy Turley of the GMP, Keith Cheshire and Rod Pulling of North Wales Police and Steve Salkeld based with Cheshire Police. In the course of a series of 'private' conversations between Daly and these officers they convey a visceral hatred of Asians and a willingness to discriminate on racial grounds once they picked up their warrant cards and were assigned to operational duties. PC Pulling is the most consistently extreme in his racist views, declaring his support for the KKK and Combat 18 and praising Adolf Hitler and the use of the gas chambers. He declares that 'I'm not fucking out of place, I'm not fucking one in a million I am the majority and I think like the majority of my town'. He also declares his willingness to vote for the BNP and rants and raves about the Stephen Lawrence case:

Daly:	Stephen Lawrence's killer – what are your thoughts on that?
PC Pulling:	Isn't it good how good memories don't fade. He fucking deserved it and his mum and dad are a fucking pair of spongers – and they've fucking seen a good opportunity and sponged it for every-thing they can get their hands on – including their MBE.
Daly:	What do you think about the boys that done it?
PC Pulling:	They fucking need fucking diplomatic immunity mate – they have, they've done for this country what others fucking should do. Macpherson report. I remember it as if it was yesterday. A fuck-ing kick in the bollocks for any white man that was.

At one point viewers see footage of Pulling posing in a makeshift KKK hood and visualizing how he would physically assault the only Asian officer on the force. This officer, from the North Wales force, had been fast-tracked through the selection process. This was interpreted as positive discrimination by most of the other officers in his cohort and was a source of festering resentment since they had been waiting for over a year to join up. As the programme unfolds, the Asian officer is marginalized by the group. Pulling, who has already defined Asians as 'Pakis', branded this officer the 'fucking curse of the class'. He goes so far as to attempt to get the officer thrown off the course by complaining to one of the trainers that he is using the 'race card'.

PC Pulling informs colleagues that he would like to kill him: 'I just fucking hate him … I'd pull my fucking hood on my head and fucking chase him down the road … I'd wrap a towel round my hand and he's gonna bump into some doors'. 'I haven't even fucking started with him yet. He'll regret the day he was ever fucking born a Paki'. Pulling's preference would be to eliminate the country of Asians. 'If I don't get that high like, my fucking bonus in life will be to get him out of the police service'. He confessed that he had beaten up an Asian man in a bar because he did not like him and confirms that if he could get away with it he would kill an Asian. Pulling declared that once he is assigned to operational duty he will use his powers to discriminate against Asians. Daly asked his fellow recruits what they would do if they saw an Asian driving a Jaguar. Pulling replied he would stop him 'cos he's a fucking Paki in a Jaguar – to put it bluntly like. A dog that's born in a barn is still a dog. A Paki, born in Britain is still a fucking Paki'. To general elation, one of the train ers informed the probationers that the Asian officer had withdrawn from the course for personal reasons and would not be returning.

When Daly catches up with PC Pulling socially after he has joined the North Wales force, the latter claims that many of his new colleagues share his views. He also provides details of how he has already picked on an Asian motorist for motoring violations.To make his point Pulling describes how he had used his discretion to let a white woman off for a similar motoring offence.

The views of PC Andy Hall were also extremely embarrassing for the force. This officer had spent 15 months with the Metropolitan Police before under-going 15 weeks re-training with Manchester Police. Hall is scathing about equal opportunities and post-Stephen Lawrence diversity training and illustrates the gap between training class and practical policing.

Daley: What was it like in the Met with all that stuff?

PC Andy Hall: Shit, because of that Stephen Lawrence stuff … 'Cos of that Stephen Lawrence thing they dedicated a week to it. My first opening week was called diversity week. You had members of the community coming in, black people, Afro-Caribbean really fucking – who hate the police saying like they think we all discriminate against them because they're black. The thing with London is the majority of street robbers are black. That's a fact that. And in Hackney in particular they just run riot, so they, they use that as reasonable grounds to go stop a black person and searching him … I would never say this in class, if you did not discriminate and you did not bring out your prejudices you would be a shit copper, do you know that? If you was on the street Mark and you wouldn't stop anyone because of their colour, because of their race, because of how they dress because of how they thingy you'd be a shit copper. We used to drive down the road and say he looks a dodgy c*** let's stop him. That is practical policing. It is mate. And nine times out of ten you are right. But in the training environment you can't be seen to do it because it's discrimination – it's against equal opportunities but when you are on the street you will fucking pick it up.

For him the 'police are racist mate, police are racist. They are, they fucking are'. He adds that if he was on patrol and encountered the Asian officer he would stop and search him ''cos he's black, 'cos he's Asian … because most Asians carry knives. And I'd fucking search him … plus he's a fucking, he's a Paki I'm searching him. It's fucking proactive policing yeah innit? He's a Paki and I'm stopping him – cause I'm fucking English. At the end of the day mate, we look after our own, you know that don't ya?'. Later on he declares that 'all Asians are lying bastards' and that the Metropolitan Police was probably the worst force for racism.

Daly confirms that the use of racialist language while recruits were socializing was relatively normal. PCs Jones, Turley, Salkeld, Lewin and Harrison all expressed equally extremist racist views and confirmed that they would have no problem with targeting Asians when they were posted to operational duties.

After passing out from Bruche, Daly had three weeks of further instruction at Sedgley Park, GMP's own training centre where there was further discussion of racist stereotyping. He was stationed at a white suburb in south Manchester where he continued with his covert investigations. He did not detect racism while on patrol with his tutor constables although one of his fellow officers did concede that he would pull over a car full of black people or Asians because they would be up to no good. Against the backdrop of the final passing out parade and a class photograph of Daly and his fellow probationers, Daly concludes:

> My time as a police officer demonstrated to me that there are policies now in place to combat discrimination and they are failing and *you can only find this out by going undercover*. The training had failed to root out the racists. If anything it made them aware that their views were seen as wrong. But this was driving their racism underground. They paraded their racism in different ways. Some used racially abusive language. Others went further and admitted they would put their racism into practice. All are setting back the police's efforts to cleanse the force of racism. I hope my investigation will help the process and allow the majority of officers to get on with their job of enforcing the law without prejudice.

After the closing credits, a BBC announcer informed viewers that programme makers would be handing over the recorded evidence they had collected in the course of their investigation to the police. He also read out an extended statement from the Greater Manchester Police confirming that the force would be unrelenting in its actions against racism.

Explaining Post-Macpherson racist culture

As was noted above, even before *The Secret Policeman* was broadcast, the documentary had provoked a major row between the BBC, the GMP and the Home Office that was fought out across the news media. The contents of this programme were explosive because in spite of decades of research findings to the contrary, it indicated that racist attitudes were transferring directly into discriminatory behaviour on the streets. The avalanche of news- media coverage of the 'race shame of police' programme in the following days contained commentary on the damage the racist-fascist views and actions shown in the programme would do to race relations; public confidence and trust in the police; internal staff relationships; and recruitment campaigns; and demands that all police forces take decisive action to tackle racism. There was also a chorus of editorial condemnation of the police and Home Office for trying to bully the BBC. *The Secret Policeman* attracted international news attention and respect from the broadcasting industry, with Mark Daly being awarded young journalist of the year for the quality of his reporting. In March 2005 Daly met with GMP senior officers to discuss the policies they had introduced in the light of his documentary.

The programme sent shockwaves through the police and the Home Office. David Blunkett, the then Home Secretary, quickly backtracked on his criticism of the BBC describing the programme as 'horrendous' and promising further action to eliminate racism and other forms of discrimination within the police. The chief officers in charge of the police forces implicated by the programme called press conferences to distance themselves from the rabid racist views and behaviour of their officers. Clive Wolfendale, the Assistant Chief Constable of North Wales, told reporters: 'I felt physically sick as I watched *The Secret Policeman* last night. Pulling has shamed his colleagues, his uniform and the service. He is a disgrace'. He disclosed that he would be writing to Doreen and Neville Lawrence to apologize about the attack upon them and their son. The Assistant Chief Constable of GPM, Alan Green, declared that: 'the programme has greatly shocked me and made me ashamed to be part of the British police service. It saddened me greatly as there still appears to be much work to be done, despite many of the efforts we have taken to tackle racism since the Stephen Lawrence inquiry'. Because one of the officers who had served with the Metropolitan Police and suggested that it was riven with racism and resentful of the Macpherson inquiry, Sir John Stevens was also forced to respond:

> It is small wonder that Stephen Lawrence's parents, Doreen and Neville Lawrence, have little faith in the police service and question our claims to progress and improvement regarding racial hatred when they see and hear officers behaving in such an abysmal manner. I have been a police officer for forty one years at the sharp end and I was absolutely astonished at that behaviour. I have never heard that type of conduct or behaviour and that type of racism. If I had I would have arrested them for it. (*London Evening Standard*, 22 October 2003)

The Commissioner also conceded that the words and actions of the police officers were 'not far away' from that displayed in the covert videos of the five white suspects in the Stephen Lawrence murder case. Chris Fox, the ACPO president, subsequently accepted that the racist attitudes and actions documented in the programme evidenced that the post-Macpherson work on race and cultural diversity issues had turned out to be a 'depressing failure'.

ACPO committed itself to working with the BPA, CRE, advisory groups, etc. to re-examine recruitment, selection, training and professional development practices as well as the cultural diversity strategy. It also authored a letter to the nation expressing its determination to eradicate racism within the police service:

> We regard the programme as providing an opportunity to reinforce the values and attitudes that we demand from our staff. We represent the leadership of the British Police service and are seized of the potential damage caused by the programme to the proud reputation of the service and the positive relationships that we enjoy with the diverse communities that we police. We have each worked hard to build and sustain this reputation and these positive relationships throughout our careers. Let us, therefore, make it absolutely clear: there is no room in the British police service for anyone with racist attitudes.
>
> Chief officers do have a significant power, provided by regulation 13 of the Police Act, to dispense with the services of any recruit within the first two

years of their career, so long as we are satisfied that they are unlikely to become a good and effective officer. We will now request Centrex – the body which oversees initial recruit training on our behalf – to take further steps to actively test the attitudes of recruits in the initial phase of training and to return to our police forces anyone whose attitude is questionable. We will then consider whether to dispense with the officer's services under regulation 13, or to undertake remedial development before allowing the would-be recruit to continue training.

We also agreed a six-point action plan to further develop our approach to this issue. In particular, we wish to guard preciously the following values of the police service: integrity, respect for diversity, compassion for others and commitment to public service. These are our core professional values and they are reflected in the attitudes and behaviour of the overwhelming majority of those we lead. We will not allow those values to be tarnished by any individual seeking to join our service who does not share them. (see *Guardian*, 23 October 2003)

A variety of explanations were put forward to explain the racist views expressed in the documentary. As Rowe (2004) has noted, PC Pulling and his colleagues were transformed into instant psycho-pathological racist 'folk devils', in a manner similar to the five white men held responsible for the murder of Stephen Lawrence. They became the 'natural born' personification of police racism. The dominant perspective articulated by ACPO, the Police Federation, politicians and commentators was that PC Rod Pulling and the other foul-mouthed 'racist recruits' were not in anyway representative of the post-Macpherson police service. To back this up it was emphasized that Daly found no evidence of racism when he took up operational duties with Greater Manchester Police officers. The Prime Minister Tony Blair attempted to reassure the nation with this latest version of the 'rotten apples' theory:

Anyone, including any police officer, with the best interests of the police service will have been appalled and shocked at some of the scenes we have witnessed. The vast bulk of police officers are thoroughly decent, committed people who are not in any shape or form racist but want to do the best for their local communities. Both in Manchester and elsewhere the police have made enormous strides forward in the past few years. It is just as important that when a shocking report, and it is shocking, comes forward like this that we keep a sense of perspective and balance (see *Times* 24 October 2003)

A subsidiary perspective concentrated attention on the blanket hostility displayed towards Asians. These officers were representative of deprived northern English localities that had fractured into racially hostile enclaves. The white population had rejected cosmopolitan multiculturalism and diversity and was increasingly intolerant of Asians as a result of 9/11. The recruits' selectively racist views were also linked with the racially motivated rioting of spring and summer 2001 when simmering tensions between Asian and white communities in Bradford, Oldham and Burnley erupted into violent street confrontations. The reporting of the threat posed to the nation by asylum seekers and refugees in the tabloid media was also blamed for fostering extremist attitudes among a generation of young whites. In a twist of this theme, the racist recruits were also paraded as evidence that far right extremist groups had managed to infiltrate the police force in order to ferment racial hatred and destroy its reputation. This was buttressed by a provocative BNP statement declaring that it did have card carrying members who worked as police officers and that 'most police sympathize with the BNP's view that a multicultural society is not a stable society'. A final perspective was that BBC reporter had acted as an irresponsible *agent provocateur* posing questions and issues that had tricked immature, unthinking young men into letting their guard down.

Trevor Phillips, the chair of the CRE, insisted that it was not just a matter of a few 'rotten apples' who could be screened out of the force or 'unthinking racists' who could be 'trained out' of their racist viewpoint. The documentary, for Phillips, revealed a pattern of behaviour which was pervasive, and though officially condemned, was 'tacitly condoned by their peers' and not restrained by senior officers. He developed his perspective in the following manner:

> It seems to me a racing certainty that these men could behave in the way they did, not because everyone else shared their views – I do not believe most police officers do – but because they knew that the *culture of their workplace* is not to grass up a colleague, no matter how repellent his behaviour. Let me return to what I said to you four years ago, which I now feel was perhaps prophetic.
>
> In the ethos of uniformed services, a few people may do wrong, but the pressure not to 'grass' is so strong that they are protected by a vow of silence; and all too often, their success at getting 'collars' can lead others, who start with no racial bias to emulate their ways. We have to draw a line here and make it possible for the vast majority of decent officers to feel comfortable speaking out against evil, and driving those who bring dishonour to the uniform out of the service. (Phillips, 2003, p. 9)

Six Greater Manchester Police officers, two North Wales officers and two Cheshire officers resigned and twelve officers were subsequently disciplined as a result of an official investigations. ACPO committed itself to introducing a standardized 'race and diversity proof' recruitment process which would involve candidates being evaluated on seven different competencies including 'respect for race and diversity'. This competency was defined as the 'golden thread' of the new assessment procedure. There would be additional psychological integrity tests to screen out applicants suspected of racism and to use covert monitoring and integrity tests to detect racists already in post and encourage officers to identify and marginalise colleagues displaying unacceptable attitudes and behaviour. This 'firewalling' was reinforced by banning police officers from membership of the BNP and other extremist political parties. In addition, and most alarming for the Home Office and chief officers, the police service found itself facing another round of external investigations into why its post-Macpherson race and diversity policies had failed in such a disquieting manner. Given who was likely to be in charge of the inquiries it was clear that they would move well beyond the updated version of the 'rotten apple' theory to a cultural de-contamination agenda.

Trevor Phillips argued that there would have to be deeper organizational transformation rather than yet more reform of race and diversity training:

> Police forces in the UK have spent according to HMIC 137,000 days on race and diversity training. Unfortunately no-one has taken the trouble to evaluate whether this training did any good. Insofar as we know anything, its quality has been variable and its impact dubious. I take the view that officers do need to know the law and they need to know what is acceptable professional conduct. There is a role for this kind of education. However, I do now doubt whether the many millions poured into trying to change attitudes in the course of one or few several days has been the best use of resources. Indeed, there is some evidence that what has been done may have even hardened some racist attitudes.
>
> The fact is that racism should not be different to other issues of professional misconduct. When police forces across the country are faced with corruption, they do not send officers to priests for guidance in not being greedy. They first use all the methods at their disposal to catch the bent officer, they prosecute him or her and they dismiss him or her. They tell everyone else that such conduct will earn the same treatment. Racism should be no different. Again here is what I said to you the last time: The point is that the first task will be to prevent police officers believing that their duty is simply to be more careful. They have to revolutionise their practice – and to achieve that we need new rules and new regulations. (Phillips, 2003. p. 12)

In the light of the disturbing evidence of racism reported in the HMIC report on GMP and the contents of *The Secret Policeman*, Phillips announced that he had written to all chief constables asking them to provide evidence that they had recruitment, vetting and training policies in place to prevent racists from joining their forces. In addition, the CRE activated the recently amended Race Relations Act 1976 to establish an independent inquiry to examine: the screening processes for candidates; the provision of race training for recruits; the extent of racial prejudice and discrimination; the mechanisms for the identification and management of racist behaviour among officers; the effectiveness of the race-related disciplinary process and grievance procedures; the sanctions that are used when inappropriate race related conduct is detected; the role of the various bodies involved in police governance in assessing how individual forces and the service in general were combating racial discrimination and complying with their race equality duty. This investigation, led by Sir David Calvert-Smith, the former Director of the CPS, started its deliberations in January 2004 (one month before the Morris inquiry) and published a final report in March 2005.

De-contaminating post-Macpherson racist culture

The implementation of the post-Macpherson diversity agenda of the Metropolitan Police had a central place in the deliberations of the Morris Inquiry which reported in December 2004. Evidence was taken from individual officers from all parts of the force and the staff associations in reviewing the high-profile disciplinary cases. The report provided an unprecedented insight into the functioning of the disciplinary and complaints procedures of the Metropolitan Police. It also painted, what the *Observer* (12 December 2004) described as a 'heart of darkness' picture of the force's management of race and diversity issues. The 'diversity' agenda, while correct in principle, was poorly understood, lacked coherence and was not embedded in the organizational culture. It was also dominated by race issues which were 'at worst, a source of fear and anxiety and at best, a process of ticking boxes'.

Senior managers lacked the confidence to deal with non-white officers fearing that they would be branded racist. This 'culture of fear' was responsible for the disproportionality in the number of internal investigations brought against ethnic minority officers compared to white officers (Morris, 2004, para: 5.65–7). Noting the number of white officers who had lodged employment tribunal claims alleging race discrimination, the inquiry verified that aspects of the cultural diversity agenda was counter-productive and in danger of fuelling a full-blown backlash. The report also found continuing evidence of a sexist, homophobic, racist and culturally insensitive rank-and-file 'canteen culture'.

The Morris report called for the elimination of discriminatory management practices, the replacement of antiquated disciplinary regulations and a review of how complaints are investigated. This fed into a separate review of police disciplinary arrangements (see Taylor, 2005). It also concluded that a cultural diversity training approach had to be devised and implemented which would engage 'all within the workforce of the MPS community which would overcome the cynicism and resistance we have seen. This approach would emphasize that diversity encompasses all aspects of difference including gender, faith disability, sexual orientation and transgender issues as well as race. It is applicable to the majority group as to minorities' (para 5.5.4).

At the time of the release of the Morris report there were warnings that the final Calvert-Smith inquiry report (2005) would be even more radical in its recommendations. The CRE inquiry focused on internal employment matters (recruitment, training and management) and racial discrimination rather than operational policing. The inquiry team had originally threatened to cross-examine the racist officers who had been outed by *The Secret Policeman* in public, much in the same way as the Lawrence five had been during the Macpherson inquiry. The report concluded that the police force was 'like a perma frost – thawing on the top, but still frozen solid at the core'. Despite the commitment of chief officers 'the fact remains that every time you drill down you find that ice, and unless more is done, it won't melt any time soon'. Forces were either not recording the data required by the ethnic monitoring duty or were not properly monitoring this data. Nor were they carrying out race impact assessments of their policies. As a consequence, very few police forces had produced a satisfactory race equality scheme as required by the Race Relations (Amendment) Act 2000.

It confirmed, in line with the Morris report, that middle managers were not properly supported or fully trained on how to handle race based grievances and complaints. There was also a fear of reporting racist incidents in case matters escalated out of control: 'such action as the service takes to deal with racist behaviour tends to concentrate on the superficial (for example, racist language) rather than the subtleties underlying racist behaviour' (Calvert-Smith 2005, p. 16). The report declared that the screening processes were rejecting proportionately more ethnic minority than white applicants on grounds of attitudes to race, gender, homophobic attitudes, etc. The initial race and diversity training was institutionalizing racial problems.

Ethnic minority recruits 'expressed concerns about the quality or commitment of the trainers, the superficial treatment of diversity issues, the "bar and alcohol" culture, the lack of proper evaluation' (p. 28). Trainers were 'unconfident, uncommitted or even hostile to "diversity"; institutional racism remained widely misunderstood after the training and was seen as smear on the police service' (p. 28). The training programme had alienated many white officers, who believed they were 'being coerced into a "politically correct" exercise of re-programming following the Lawrence report finding as-they-saw-it- that they were collectively racist. This gave the trainers the impossible task of dealing with resentments that arose from people who felt they were being processed rather than trained, and blamed rather then developed' (p. 36). This was driving racial discrimination underground and allowing what was defined as a new breed of 'stealth racist' to remain undetected.

The report concluded that if the police was to move beyond a crisis management approach to race relations, it would have to create a culture with an anti-racist ethos, in which racist behaviour would be eradicated. It recommended changes to be made at every level of police activity, from recruitment to training, complaints and governance, in order to inculcate forces with a commitment to racial equality. Resolving the issue of racial prejudice and discrimination would enable the police to undertake similar work across all diversity issues and make it an organization 'less and less attractive to recruits and serving officers of the kind so graphically displayed in *The Secret Policeman'*. Trevor Phillips issued a final warning to the police, 'we don't want to be heavy-handed – we want to work with all involved in the governance of the police service to melt this ice. But if no-one's prepared to hit the defrost button, we will simply have to turn up the heat' (CRE Press Release, 8 March 2005). Failure on behalf of police to improve their race equality and diversity schemes would lead to legal action and possibly a CRE enforcement order. If forces failed to act on such an order, it could lead to a fine or court case and even a prison sentence for the chief constable concerned.

Conclusion

Lord Scarman's report into the 1981 riots was intended to produce a radical culture shift on race relations and policing in the UK. However, as we have seen, more than two decades after a multitude of initiatives resultant from the Scarman report and the Macpherson report, the evidence unearthed in *The Secret Policeman,* combined with the findings of the Morris and Calvert-Smith reports, demonstrated that there was still a serious race problem embedded in police culture and identity formation. This has much to do with the defining characteristics of race-related reform programmes within the police. They are drafted in a panic environment that invariably disconnects them from the 'lived experience' of the crisis that triggered demands for reform in the first place. Little attention is paid to the social and cultural conditions that produced the crises. They are launched with a news-media fanfare with reassurances that the police and the public can look to the future with confidence. Internal organizational contestation and indeed confusion is downplayed or denied. The next crisis invariably exposes the failure of what turned out to be 'tick box' reforms and produces recrimination and disillusionment. And so it is left to another generation of reformers to pick up the 'we have never been reformed' mantle, ready to repeat much the same mistakes, safe in the knowledge that failure never matters. As a consequence, the burden of failed reform programmes liesh like a dead weight on the organisational structures and cultures of the force (see McLaughlin and Murji, 1999).

There is widespread acceptance within the police that it will be required to respond to a range of perplexing community tensions and conflicts and social problems; and ever-increasing public expectations, ranging from low level incivilities and anti-social behaviour through to violent crime, globally organized crime flows and new forms of terrorist threat. As Britain becomes ever more socially diverse and draws in more people from different cultures, religions and racial and ethnic backgrounds, the police need to be embedded within the 'multi-social' fabric to be able to understand and manage that volatile, insecure complexity. It must be in a position to be able to: legitimately gather information and intelligence; encourage the reporting of crime; identify developing crime trends, tensions and potential flashpoints; and intervene using coercive force if necessary. It is now widely accepted that recruiting people from a narrow set of backgrounds and then enculturing them to think and act in a particular 'tried and tested' organizational manner is of limited value. Diversity and pluralization of the police workforce is now defined by chief police officers and the government as an operational necessity (Blair, 2002b; HMIC, 2003, Ghaffur, 2004) – the twenty-first century police force requires a highly-skilled workforce capable of developing and working with new approaches, new tactics and new ways of thinking to pre-empt new criminal and anti-social threats and enhance public safety.

The recommendations contained in the latest set of reports are intended to produce a new organizational settlement on race and cultural diversity. There is, as we have seen, a focus on improved systems for identifying problem officers; intervening to challenge unacceptable attitudes and behaviour; disciplining and if necessary removing those officers who fail to conform; and equalizing opportunities. The crucial question is whether it is possible to imagine a differentiated, police identity that can also generate a sense of belonging, mutual obligation, inter-personal relations of trust, a sense of common purpose and special commitment. This contingent 'inside-out/outside-in' pluralist police identity would draw its strength, legitimacy and symbolism from its intersection and coherence with wider multi-cultural reference points. However, a series of highly sensitive matters remain to be addressed in the 'hollowing out' of traditional police culture and deconstruction of police identity.

First, little to no analytical attention has been paid to the unspoken but obviously pivotal role 'whiteness' has played in the nurturing and sustaining of both the formal and cultural identity of the constable. This reminds us of the need to continue to ground our analysis within the much broader and complicated canvas of emotional signification and ethno-cultural identification of 'Britishness' and 'Englishness' that the public police are part of. In order to diffuse potential conflict of racial divisions, the police will have to respond both to the cultural insecurities of white officers at the same time as meeting the needs of ethnic minority officers. And, to borrow Trevor Phillips' conceptualization, the police will have to develop the equivalent of a 'highway code' if officers are to successfully negotiate the multi-layered minefield of cultural diversity. It will also have to avoid an essentialisation process that further fragments workplace identities and relationships and precludes the possibility of cultural co-existence. An allied question is how the police can manage the 'institutional nostalgia' for the network of mutual support and camaraderie that was the hallmark of a hegemonic police culture that is now shredding itself on the unpredictable twitches and jerks of identity politics. Second, the force is now grappling with the idea of 'stealth racism', (and presumably 'stealth sexism', 'stealth classism' and 'stealth homophobia') that is supposedly being imported into the organization by recruits rather than produced, sustained and in certain instances amplified by it. This has been reaffirmed by the official reaction to *The Secret Policeman* documentary. i.e., contracting in yet more anti-racist training programmes and race monitoring and testing which run the risk of compounding an already paranoid work environment and reproducing an organizational discourse in which racism is very much a rank-and-file pathology. This conveniently absolves politically correct senior officers who are increasingly detached from the ground level realities that are racializing police work in complicated ways.

Third, the police are condemned not just to have to consider the present and future but to have to live with the ever-present racialized past. The police may never be in a position to get beyond the racial memories that will continue to haunt them. For example, in February 2005, files were released to the National Archive which revealed the true extent of prejudice Metropolitan Police officers felt towards the first generation of West Indian immigrants. Racist attitudes permeated all ranks of the force with officers making links between male immigrants and criminality and benefit fraud. Officers also expressed concerns about immigrants mixing with white women. The content of these files requires that further revisions be made to comforting post-war Dixonian histories of the police. Finally, there is the question of whether it is possible to realize a new overarching cultural identity in a radically unsettled multi-social context. A new generation of police officers inhabit a moment when we are witnessing multiple racializations of 'crime' along with new ethnic tensions associated with waves of immigration, asylum and settlement. And perhaps most significantly for the long term, these officers now have to live with the counter-terrorist repercussions of the attacks on London on the 17 July 2005 by homegrown Islamic suicide bombers as well as the failed attacks of 21 July 2005. The re-ignited debate on multi-culturalism and government arguments for a stronger sense of 'Britishness' to counter the threat to social cohesion and national security posed by 'Britishness' have wide-ranging implications for police practice, police community relations and of course a generationally contingent police culture and identity.

Police Governance

7

In liberal democratic societies, where the emphasis is on demonstrating the 'rule of law' and 'good governance', the term 'police accountability' is multi-faceted in meaning. Chan (1999, p. 267) has noted how 'the modern state is deeply ambivalent about the way in which the police should be held accountable'. Police accountability is, in theory, constituted through those mechanisms for ensuring that: police officers are answerable for how they handle individual citizens, particularly with regard to respect for due process, human rights and civil liberties and police forces are responsible for the quality of community safety, justice and security services they provide. And as police scholars routinely note, officer and organizational level accountabilities are intimately connected. Effective delivery of core policing services depends on how individual officers working the streets and neighbourhoods exercise their discretionary authority and powers, and the nature and quality of police-public interactions turns on what police forces do to inculcate ethical professional standards of behaviour.

The field of police accountability in the UK has distinct internal and external features. In theory, accountability inside the organization is ensured through internal corporate governance as exemplified by: organizational policies; reporting systems; codes of ethical standards; the cultural ethos; appraisal mechanisms; disciplinary regulations, and an inspection regime. External oversight is accomplished through the law courts; the tripartite constitutional structure; the police complaints system; pressure groups, and the news media. We also have to keep in mind that 'police accountability' in the UK is also expected to both represent and foster the legitimating philosophy of 'policing by consent' and safeguard the political neutrality of the 'office of constable' and the operational independence of the chief constable. Thus, police accountability is woven into a complicated web of bureau-legal rights, protections, obligations and responsibilities.

Much of the scholarship on police governance is concerned with understanding the functioning of one or more of these aspects of accountability. More recently, research in the UK has focused on how police accountability has been radically reconfigured as a result of human rights, equal opportunities and race relations legislation, micro-managerial scrutiny of operational effectiveness, and the recognition of the need to regulate the increasingly significant private security sector (see Newburn and Reiner, 2004). And, although it is beyond the scope of this chapter, discussion of police accountability in the twenty-first century must also attempt to comprehend the implications of policing that are connected to an emergent global security field. Particular concern has been expressed about the consequences of a dominant central government perspective that defines democratic scrutiny as a hindrance to effective policing and law enforcement as well as the interests of the post 9/11 and post 7/7 security state.

This chapter concentrates its analysis on thinking through the implications of the latest proposals to re-invigorate the structure of police governance and accountability in the UK so that it connects to the re-policing crime and disorder developments discussed in Chapter 5 (Home Office 2003a, 2004). The chapter is divided into three parts. In the first, I provide readers with a brief overview of managerialist inspired attempts to reform the structure of police governance and accountability. In the second part, I explore why and how the broader political discourse of 'new localism' came to inflect the unfolding debate about the need to revitalize police accountability. The concluding part offers a critical evaluation of the latest attempt to reorganize the structure of police governance. It needs to be noted from the outset that remarkably little research has been conducted on the UK's framework of police accountability during the past decade. This is extremely worrying given the radical changes that have taken place in this time period.

Officer level accountability

The handling of citizen complaints against abuse of police powers by officers is a 'wicked issue' for democratic governments. Put bluntly, how these complaints are responded to and resolved cuts to the heart of claims of democratic governance and human rights and sharpens the question of how to control the police. As has been established throughout this book, police officers hold a unique position in democratic societies. They are authorized with substantial original powers to intervene in the lives of citizens and can exercise considerable discretion in determining how to use these powers. This of course includes the power to coerce compliance and to use lethal force. Citizen complaints are almost inevitable given the variety of tasks police officers perform and the nature of police–citizen encounters. Indeed, police officers believe that this is an inevitable part of the job. However, as was noted in Chapter 3, this also means that policing is a 'high-risk' occupation. If citizens are to have confidence in the police as a whole, they must be assured that if they have to complain about an instance of improper, questionable, controversial or menacing behaviour their grievance will be investigated thoroughly and appropriate action taken. The police complaints process also has a duty to protect the honest officer who has been maliciously or mistakenly accused of an abuse of her or his powers.

The post-war history of police complaints is one of protracted struggle between the police and critics over the degree and nature of external involvement in the police complaints process. The default position was: police officers were accountable to the law and courts for their actions; malpractice was not a serious issue for the British police; and formalization of complaints procedures would make it impossible for policemen to do their job effectively because of the potential for malicious and unjustified complaints.

Regulation must come from within the force for several reasons. External or civilian investigators who would never be able to understand police work or be able to access real information about what happens among policemen. Internal investigation was more thorough and wide-ranging because it could draw upon both the formal and informal ethical codes that constitute the professional working lives of police officers. Externalization of regulation would: impinge on professional self-esteem; confirm the impression that the public and politicians did not trust or respect the police; and undermine both the authority of police leaders over the rank-and-file and internal quasi-military forms of self-discipline and self-regulation. Officers would erect or reinforce a 'blue wall of silence,' deny wrongdoing, cover up mistakes and put appearances before discipline. Police deviance would increase and the public would become even more sceptical. This would generate demands for stronger external control which would reinforce rather than break the downward spiral of distrust.

A series of high-profile controversies and scandals in the 1950s, compelled the government to establish a Royal Commission on the Police in 1960. As part of its deliberations about the constitutional structure of police accountability, this Commission considered the contentious issue of complaints against the police. A variety of interest groups submitted evidence concerning the state of policing in post-war Britain. Police representatives insisted that there was no evidence of serious deterioration in police–community relations whereas the National Council for Civil Liberties argued that one of the primary reasons for the decline in public confidence was the absence of any independent means of redress against the police. The Final Report (the Winnick report) of the Commission was published in 1962 and on the controversial issue of police complaints concluded that 'not enough has been given to the best arrangements for re-assuring the public that complaints are properly handled'. Particular concerns related to the fact that the existing provisions were geared to police discipline rather than complaints from members of the public; the recording of complaints in police forces throughout England and Wales was less strict than in the Metropolitan Police; and that minor complaints were not recorded (see Whittaker, 1964; Marshall, 1965; Bowes, 1966).

The Royal Commission sidestepped the issue of controlling individual police misconduct. An external police complaints process was rejected 'because the appearance of greater justice to the public is liable to be bought at the expense of the police' (quoted in Whittaker, 1964, p. 17). Instead, the final report made recommendations to clarify and tighten existing internal procedures 'to make its fairness more conspicuously apparent to the public'. The Police Act 1964 codified the legal right of the citizen to complain against the actions of a police officer and formalized the procedure. In addition, the Act conferred upon police authorities and Her Majesty's Inspectorate of Constabulary (HMIC) the statutory duty of keeping themselves informed as to the manner in which complaints were being dealt with by different police forces. However, to all intents and purposes, it remained an in-house 'police investigating police' model.

Various writers provide us with a picture of how the new complaints procedure worked in practice. Maguire and Corbett (1991) note an improvement in recording practices and a significant increase in the time and resources expended in dealing with complaints. In particular there was a nation-wide trend in establishing specialist Complaints and Discipline departments. However, in practice the police continued to delay or postpone investigations until counter allegations had been made by the police, and 'these delays effected the outcome of a complaint. It frequently led to both the evidence and the complainant being discredited' (see Box and Russell, 1973). The practice of 'police investigating police' was resulting in continued under-reporting, under recording and under investigation of complaints. In addition the police were not publishing full details of their investigations and refused to investigate established patterns of misconduct among certain police officers and stations.

Scandals, persistent demands for an independent police complaints body and resultant piecemeal reform of the existing system eventually resulted in the post-Scarman Police Complaints Authority (PCA) being operational from April 1985. Scarman accepted that a degree of external involvement in the handling of police complaints was necessary to keep police accountable as an organization and policemen as individuals. It was also important not to allow the police to investigate their own affairs because it gives the impression of procedures being biased in favour of the accused police officer and gives the impression to the public and to policemen themselves that they can act with impunity. At the level of improving the standard of policing, public confidence in the complaints procedures was seen as an important tool for improving police–community relations. The complaints procedures needed to be widely perceived as fair and impartial among the groups most likely to become the victims of police malpractice – typically marginal groups of society, poor people and ethnic minorities.

However, the police complaints system continued to be premised on the principle that the police would determine whether a complaint warranted investigation. Nor did the legislation tamper with the complicated police disciplinary regulations which were to be followed whenever a complaint included an allegation of a disciplinary offence. The proposals institutionalized a three-tiered system which would operate according to the seriousness of the complaint. Investigations into the most serious complaints would be supervised by outsiders. Medium serious complaints continued to be investigated in the traditional manner (with external scrutiny of the final report) and minor complaints would be dealt with informally. From its inception, the PCA, as an 'in-between' model of police complaints, found itself embroiled in considerable controversy. Police officers denounced it as a body that had too many powers, touted unscrupulously for business, and victimized 'good people doing a difficult' job. Civil liberties groups condemned it because it depended on serving police officers to carry out the actual investigations and had few real powers. Both civil libertarians and rank-and-file police officers were united in their demands for it to be replaced by a fully independent and impartial complaints investigation body.

The PCA acknowledged that it faced a number of problems in carrying out its work effectively. The low visibility of everyday police work meant that it had difficulties in gathering corroborative evidence to take any action over many complaints. In addition, very few officers were willing to give evidence against a fellow officer and officers exercised their right of silence when questioned over alleged misconduct. Internal disciplinary proceedings were difficult to pursue because, as a result of Police Federation campaigning, the standard of proof in police discipline cases was uniquely the same as that of a criminal trial; that is, proof beyond reasonable doubt as opposed to that of a civil trial, the balance of probabilities. Additionally, criminal lawyers could be engaged by officers to refute disciplinary allegations, though not to substantiate them. Furthermore the PCA found that officers under investigation could undermine the inquiry by leaving the force on medical grounds with full pension rights. This left a significant number of cases unresolved and pre-empted the outcome of disciplinary proceedings. Not surprisingly, given the obstacles that investigators faced, there were serious delays in bringing cases to court and important cases were thrown out by the courts. The PCA also complained about undue restrictions on the release of information to complainants and the public about the progress of cases.

But perhaps the most fundamental problem remained the reluctance of many people with grievances to activate the formal complaints procedure because of cynicism towards a 'police investigating police' system. The PCA's lack of success in bringing manifestly corrupt and criminal police officers to justice and lack of adequate explanation confirmed to many the pointlessness of using the formal complaints machinery. It is in this context that legal representatives advised clients that private prosecutions and civil proceedings were more effective ways of seeking redress and justice. As a consequence, during the 1990s the Metropolitan Police, for example, paid out millions of pounds in settled actions following claims for wrongful arrest, false imprisonment and assault. However, critics argued that this was unsatisfactory because in such cases police forces did not have to admit liability or guilt, did not have to apologize and were under no obligation to take further disciplinary actions against the officers involved (Smith, 2003).

Several important shifts in the investigation of police complaints took place from the late 1990s onwards. First, the police developed professional standards units and they became more conscious of the practical meaning of human rights for policework. International and national human rights protection mechanisms had been strengthened and the work of bodies such as the Council of Europe have communicated the message that respecting human rights is an integral part of police work. There has also been increasing recognition that human rights standards can provide clear objectives for policework, notably in respect of protecting citizens from violation of their rights by others and ensuring effective redress when such violations occur, as well as a framework within which the balance between liberty and the need for effective preventive and investigative policework. Consequently, certain forces began to conduct auditing activities to ensure that the commitment to human rights amounts to more than the publication of mission statements and 'know your rights' leaflets. There was also the development of an ethical policing training philosophy that sought to inculcate the idea that no other agency in civil society has the capacity to protect human rights as much as the police. Second, the police had to come to terms with losing a string of high-profile complaints cases that eroded public trust and undermined years of sustained work to repair relationships with alienated communities.

Third, the vitally important Police Ombudsman office for Northern Ireland was established by the Police (Northern Ireland) Act 1998 to provide an accessible, independent, impartial and robust system for investigating and resolving complaints against the police. A statement accompanying it's appointment acknowledged that in order to establish public confidence, it would have had to address the key issues that have de-railed previous reforms of the police complaints system, namely, independence; impartiality; remit; powers; resourcing; credibility; effectiveness; accessibility; transparency; equity. Building on global 'best practice' experience, the office was given an unprecedented degree of autonomy with its team of investigators being given arrest, search and seizure powers as well as the right to access and seize documentation or property and secure incident scenes. In order to ensure an appropriate degree of independence, it was also mandated to exercise the power to initiate investigations even if no formal complaint had been received; compile research data on trends and patterns in complaints against the police; and investigate and comment on police policies and practices, where these are perceived to give rise to policing difficulties. The Police Ombudsman's office which is part of a complicated regime of post-conflict police governance in Northern Ireland, effectively broke apart traditional police opposition to the idea of a fully independent police complaints system. It is also part of a network of 'Rolls Royce' international police complaints agencies that has yet to be researched.

Fourth, chief constables began to highlight the problem of networks of corrupt officers who were escaping justice because of the ineffectiveness of the discipline and complaints system. Finally, there were a series of official reports that raised more serious questions about the functioning of the PCA. Following the publication of a parliamentary committee report into police disciplines and complaints, moves were made to deal with unsatisfactory performance (as distinct from misconduct); use a civil rather than criminal standard of proof at discipline hearings; and fast track the dismissal of officers in cases of serious criminal misconduct where the evidence is overwhelming. In response to a Home Affairs Select Committee report, a highly critical report of the European Committee for the Prevention of Torture and Inhuman and Degrading Treatment or Punishment, the Macpherson report (1999) and the Patten Commission, the government commissioned management consultants KPMG and the civil liberties organization, Liberty to report on the viability of an independent complaints investigation process. The reports supported the establishment of an independent agency for complaints against the police for England and Wales (KPMG, 2000; Harrison and Cuneen, 2000). In June 2001, the Home Office announced that the police complaints system for England and Wales would be restructured. The new framework, which was established under the Police Reform Act 2002, became fully operational in April 2004, was anchored by an Independent Police Complaints Commission (IPCC) which recruited civilians to investigate allegations of serious police misconduct and corruption. The primary goal is to initiate, carry out and oversee investigations and monitor the way that complaints are handled by police forces. Most complaints will continue to be dealt with by the police as they have in the past by a 'local resolution' process. However, forces will have to adhere to new IPCC standards. The police must refer to it any case falling into specified categories, whether or not a complaint has been made, e.g., deaths in police care or custody, fatal road accidents, firearm incidents, serious corruption, miscarriages of justice, racist conduct, serious injuries, serious arrestable offences. It also has the 'call in' power to investigate or supervise other complaints and the discretion either to carry out its own investigation or to supervise an investigation by a police force. The IPCC decision to directly investigate or supervise is determined by: seriousness of the incident; issues of public confidence; and available resources. Police forces are required to co-operate with IPCC investigators, providing them with access to premises and documentation.

Figure 7.1   Stephen Lawrence memorial banner

The public's access to the IPCC controlled complaints system has been widened. A person other than the victim of the alleged police misconduct is allowed to make a complaint and complaints can be accepted without being submitted through the police. The complainant is entitled to: a full account of the investigation and an explanation as to how and why particular conclusions were reached. The complainant also has the right to appeal if he/she feels they have not received a satisfactory explanation. The key objective for the IPCC is to build a police complaints system which enjoys the confidence of all sections of the community and the police service. It seeks to do so by: raising public awareness of the complaints system; demonstrating its independence from the police; developing a greater sense of ownership of the system; seeking continuous improvement of the system; developing and promoting 'best professional practice'; identifying and remedying weaknesses; and helping to develop a culture in police forces which centres on complainant needs. An important feature of the new police complaints system is that as it develops, it will be possible to compare and contrast its functioning and effectiveness with that represented by the Police Ombudsman's office.

Force level accountability

Constitutional controls: explanatory and co-operative accountability

Police accountability in the UK is premised on a constitutional settlement which allocates statutory responsibilities and duties to chief constables, police authorities and the Home Office. The Police Act 1964 attempted to balance the operational autonomy of the chief constable in relation to the accountability needs of national and local government through what Marshall defined as an 'explanatory and co-operative' model of police governance (see Marshall 1978; Lustgarten 1986; Reiner 1993). Police authorities composed of two-thirds local councillors and one third magistrates were given the responsibility to secure and maintain adequate and efficient local forces. They had the powers to appoint chief constables and could require retirement on efficiency grounds. However, all major decisions made by the authorities were subject to the final approval of the Home Secretary who was also given the important fiscal responsibility for allocating a central grant, representing half of each forces annual budget. Police forces were placed under the 'direction and control' of the chief constable. To ensure political impartiality, the 1964 legislation enshrined the 'operational independence' of the chief constables from the police authorities and the Home Secretary, reiterating that they were not civil servants or local government employees and that they should be free from conventional processes of democratic accountability. Chief constables could be required to submit *ex post facto* reports on local policing matters, but could exercise discretion and refuse to do so if they considered the information not to be in the public interest or outside the authorities' remit. They could also appeal to the Home Secretary against such demands. Chief constables were also given responsibility for all appointments and promotions below assistant chief constable and the disciplinary authority for these ranks. The Home Secretary's supervisory powers spanned pay and regulations, the monitoring of force performance through Her Majesty's Inspectorate of Constabulary, and controversially to act as the police authority for the Metropolitan Police.

During the deliberations on the 1964 Act there were many angry protests from local government representatives that the powers of both the Home Secretary and the chief constables were being constitutionally clarified and enhanced at the expense of the local government police authorities. The legislation, it was claimed, was not sustaining a 'explanatory and co-operative' tripartite but creating a 'subordinate and passive' bipartite structure of police governance. The police authorities would in any constitutional dispute be squeezed between the Home Secretary's right of veto and the chief constables who were entitled to ignored them. Lord Denning legally confirmed the 'original not delegated' position of the chief constables, vis-a-vis the Home

Secretary and the police authorities, when he concluded that the chief constable:

> Is not the servant of anyone, save of the law itself. No minister of the Crown can tell him that he must or must not prosecute this man or than one. Nor can any police authority tell him so. The responsibility for law enforcement lies on him. He is answerable to the law and the law alone. (Lord Denning, RV Commissioner of Police for the Metropolis, *ex parte* Blackburn, 1968, 2, QB. 118. p. 136)

As Jefferson and Grimshaw (1984) noted, chief constables were no longer constrained by the authorities, their operational independence was constitutionally guaranteed, and their professional status and power enhanced as the result of the creation of fewer and larger police bureaucracies in the latter half of the 1960s. They could negotiate with the Home Office as equals. This professionalization augmented the power granted to both the Home Office and the chief constables by the 1964 Act.

This constitutional settlement has of course been subjected to relentless critique and demands for democratic reform. In the 1970s and 1980s, in response to increasing complaints about police racism, violence, corruption, and the paramilitarization of public order policing strategies, there was a sustained political campaign for police powers to be curbed, a general tightening of policework rules and procedures, and the establishment of effective independent institutions to investigate police malpractice.

The fact that every question posed to chief constables about a particular police action or indeed even policing style could be deflected by responding that it was an 'operational' matter also generated demands of democratic renewal to move the police authorities to an equal and proactive relationship with the other two parts of the tripartite arrangement. Some argued that police authorities should be legally able to require chief constables to account retrospectively for their decisions by explaining and justifying particular policies and actions. Others argued for the establishment of democratically constituted police committees which would have prospective control of policing policies. They would also have responsibility for all appointments, disciplinary proceedings and promotions and be able to require reports and to inspect files and records. In this division of duties and responsibilities, chief constables would be civil servants, responsible for operationalizing and enforcing, in accordance with the requirement of law, democratically agreed policies and decisions. The work of democratically constituted police authorities would also make it clear to the community that policing was political as well as legal in nature. Campaigners also pointed out that few democracies allowed police forces such organizational autonomy. Chief officers in the USA are subject to the formal electoral process while in Europe they are servants of Internal Ministers of Justice or municipal authorities, who are themselves democratically accountable. In an unfolding scenario of inner city rioting and industrial and social conflict, senior police officers and the Conservative government made it clear during the 1980s that they would not countenance moves towards what they defined as the political control of the police because this would undermine the sacred constitutional principles of independence and impartiality. Indeed, the most politically active metropolitan police authorities were abolished (see McLaughlin 1994).

Managerial controls: calculative and contractual accountability

In the first half of the 1990s the question of police accountability resurfaced. This time however it was what Reiner (1993) has defined as 'calculative and contractual', rather than democratic accountability that was foregrounded as the deeper impact of the 'new managerialism' became clearer in a host of areas in the public sector. From the 1980s onwards, it has become a key means through which the state sector is being reconstructed along 'business like' lines, so that management would be guided by objectives and organizations become customer focused. In the process the traditional distinction between 'public' and 'private' has been undermined as a set of essentially private sector values were injected into the centre of organizational and managerial thinking in the public sector. The traditional public sector model and its foundational assumption of being 'different' to the private sector creaked and buckled under successive governmental reform programmes. Over time a host of policy and legislative changes across the state sector destabilized it. Initially, the police appeared to stand alone and apart from all of the reform and reconfiguration around them. The police, it seemed, remained unique because of their 'double difference': First because of their place within the public sector, and secondly because they were also constitutionally different from the rest of the criminal justice system. The reasons for this state of affairs are fairly well established and do not need to be rehearsed here.

However, with the election of what turned out to be the last Conservative government, the new Home Secretary, Kenneth Clarke announced that 'root and branch' police reform would be necessary to win back the confidence of 'middle England'. In line with what was happening across the rest of the UK public sector, the principles of new managerialism were identified (NPM) as the pathway to a post-bureaucratic efficient and effective police service. This would be realized through: increased emphasis on achieving results rather than administrating processes; the setting of explicit targets and performance indicators to enable the auditing of efficiency and effectiveness; the publication of league tables illustrating comparative performance; the identification of core competencies; the costing and market testing of all activities to ensure value for money; the externalisation of non-essential responsibilities; the establishment of a purchaser-provider split; and the re-designation of clients as 'customers'. It is important to stress that the managerial template for reform did not just entail the importation and implementation of private sector management techniques and actuarial practices. Rather it signalled, in the short term, a fundamental assault on the professional cultures and discourses and power relations embedded in the police and, in the long term, indicated a shift to a mode of governmental co-ordination appropriate for an unfolding era of globalization (Clarke and Newman, 1998).

Reviews were established to evaluate: rank structure, remuneration framework and the terms and conditions service of police officers; the tripartite structure of police governance and what the core functions of policing should be. Overall, these reviews signalled the government's intention to subject the police, like the rest of the public sector, to the disciplines, rationales and discourses of new managerialism (Reiner 1993; Jones and Newburn 1997; McLaughlin and Murji 1995, 1998). The Police and Magistrates Courts Act 1994 contained less than the full reform package, because of the successful lobbying campaign by the police and, to a lesser extent, local authorities against the Sheehy and White Paper proposals. Nonetheless, the 'managerialist' provisions of the legislation, which were consolidated in the Police Act 1996, had a significant impact upon a constitutional settlement that had already empowered the Home Office and chief constables at the expense of police authorities. The police authorities were reformed as free-standing, precepting corporate entities that were separate from local councils. Depoliticized and managerialized, they were given responsibility for producing, in conjunction with the chief constable, a local policing plan laying down crime reduction targets, objectives and expenditure. The police authorities were also obligated to set a lawful budget for the year and to decide on the council tax contribution to costs of policing. They also had to discharge a statutory requirement to consult the public on policing matters. The Home Secretary's role in the managerialized constitutional structure was to determine national objectives and publish data relating to the effectiveness and efficiency of all forces and police authorities. The Home Secretary could also influence a variety of policy matters by issuing codes of practice and policy guidance and would have enhanced sanctions to give directions to police authorities in the case of an adverse report from the HMIC. The Home Secretary was also given the power to 'fast-track' force amalgamations on efficiency grounds. Finally, because police budgets were cash limited, chief constables, who retained overall charge of operational matters, were given a degree of autonomy in budget management (see, Jones and Newburn 1997; Loveday 1998; McLaughlin and Murji 2001; Reiner 2001; Jones, 2003).

This set of managerialist changes sparked a furious debate. On one side were those who argued that a final centralization of power was taking place to pave the way for a further regionalization or nationalization of police forces. The battery of powers and levers allocated to the Home Secretary would enable him/her to determine local police practices which would cut deeply into the operational independence of chief constables. The reconstituted police authorities would become increasingly accountable to central government. Because of their size and composition, these quango-like committees could not be said to represent local interests in a democratically accountable manner. The foregrounding of crude, over-simplistic, quantitative plans and targets, which highlighted crime control as being the core police task would be counter-productive and have an adverse effect on the overall quality of police–community relationships. Police forces would inevitably concentrate on those activities that could be easily identified and quantified and deliver immediate results. Officers would be forced to cut corners, bend the rules and twist the statistics to deliver their targets. Chief constables on fixed-term contracts and financial bonuses would collude with central government to protect their jobs. Overall, the 'calculative and contractual' mode of accountability would corrupt the unique ethos of British policing by gradually transforming the police from a public service into a crime control business. In the longer term, the 'value for money' discourses of managerialization would blur the distinction between the public police and private security sector thereby facilitating market-driven policing (see Reiner, 1995; Walker, 1996).

Others argue that it would be necessary to study carefully the workings of the new regime because the reforms would generate new organizational pressure points, contradictions and further reforms. Decentralization, devolution and localization as well as centralization and nationalization could happen, because in order to deliver on the local policing plan, responsibility for operational policework would have to be located as near as possible to actual service delivery. 'Balance sheet' accountability might be a crude starting point, but as a benchmark it would compel police authorities and police forces to begin to offer explanatory public accounts for differences in effectiveness in clearing up crime, efficiency, priorities and more significantly resourcing decisions. Sophisticated quantitative and qualitiative measures of local policework could be devised that avoided easy manipulation. In sum, new managerialism could unlock new much more localized forms of police governance and accountability and service delivery (McLaughlin and Murji, 1995; Loveday, 1998).

New Labour's commitment to modernizing the public sector as part of its broader governmental project, ensured that managerial centralisation remained central to the overall framework for improving police performance. The first New Labour administration (1997 to 2001) refined the centralizing logics of the existing legislative framework to ensure that police force and police authority efforts were directed to realizing both Whitehall defined 'best value' and crime reduction targets. As of April 2000, police authorities were charged with ensuring 'Best Value', a system of rolling audit to ensure that public services were delivering core services by the most economic, efficient and effective means available. To demonstrate this, the Home Office prescribed a suite of performance indicators against which the activities of each police force could be assessed. Because 'Best Value' was a statutory responsibility under the Local Government Act 1999, this regime institutionalized a performance framework that stressed continuous improvement. In the case of the police, one of the most significant developments was that under the guise of 'joined-up inspection' Her Majesty's Inspectorate of Constabulary was authorized to conduct inspections that would inculcate a 'culture of continuous improvement' at both force level and Basic Command Unit (BCU) level (see Leigh et al., 1999; Martin, 2003).

A further centralizing strand was to be found in New Labour's promotion of an evidence-based approach to crime control. Because traditional policing methods were viewed by the Home Office as having a relatively limited impact on core crime categories, there was a stress on more effective utilization of existing resources, a switch to focused police activity and exploring the possibility of outsourcing the patrol function (see Chapter 5). This discourse also supported the rolling out of pre-packaged, Home Office verified, 'what works in policing' strategies and practices to refine the organizational mission (Jordan, 1998, p.74). This linked across to New Labour's determination to direct resources to effective interventions. Equally significantly, the Home Office's establishment of statutory Crime and Disorder Reduction Partnerships (CDRPs), meant that local authorities had to set targets for reducing crime in a number of key performance areas. As a result, a series of public service agreement delivery target indicators were published, several of which also applied to policing. It was becoming increasingly clear that the Home Office would have to construct a performance management framework that spanned force, BCU and CDRP levels. The final, not really commented upon, tightening of central audit was achieved through requiring police forces to respond to the statutory race relations legislation requirements of the Macpherson report's core recommendations.

A number of notable significant shifts in the managerialization of policing took place during the early years of New Labour's (2001 to 2005) second administration. The appointment of David Blunkett as the Home Secretary was interpreted by political commentators that Downing Street wished to tackle the 'forces of conservativism' within the police. Blunkett stated that legislative reform was necessary because: the crime categories that were of public concern remained too high; the public's fear of crime was at a socially damaging level, particularly in disadvantaged neighbourhoods; there were significant variations in detection and conviction rates as well as response times; and there were low levels of public confidence in front-line policing services.

It was suggested that despite its modernization rhetoric, ACPO was determined to resist further Home Office encroachment on the doctrine of operational independence. Well-placed leaks hinted that the Home Secretary was determined to assert his authority over any chief constable who might be tempted to defend 'outdated' procedures and practices. To this end, David Blunkett laid down several markers as evidence that he was determined to succeed where Jack Straw, his predecessor, had failed. A Home Office Police Standards Unit (PSU) was set up in July 2001 to boost the operational effectiveness of BCUs as they had been identified as being the key to reducing crime, disorder and fear of crime. PSU was also authorized to identify problems which required the direct legislative intervention of the Home Secretary. The creation of PSU, with its explicit operational remit, also allowed the Home Office to press the HMIC to 'raise the bar' in terms of the inspection process.

Chief constables also found themselves on the receiving end of a series of 'red alert' interventions. In July 2001, Sussex Police Authority was pressurized by the Home Secretary to consider sacking its chief constable, Paul White-house, for his role in a disastrous police raid in which an unarmed man was shot dead. The chief constable retired, protesting that he had been unfairly stigmatized by the Home Secretary. Blunkett's response to the street crime crisis in London in February 2002, was to inform Sir John Stevens, the Commissioner, that he would send in a PSU 'hit squad' to run the Metropolitan Police. He subsequently let it be known during the 'SOS' visit of Mayor Giuliani, that he would consider appointing an American police chief as the next Scotland Yard Commissioner. And, as was noted in Chapter 5, to show that he was serious, the Home Secretary brought over William Bratton, the former Commissioner of the NYPD, to give chief constables a 'pep talk' about how to turn round the crime rate. In March 2002, in one of the most remarkable episodes in the history of post-war British policing, chief constables found themselves also having to respond directly to a Prime Ministerial Steering Group on their plans to cut soaring street crime in ten force areas. In the same period, the Home Secretary also demanded that chief constables 'face down' the Police Federation by taking managerial responsibility for the reform of pay and conditions, the eradication of 'Spanish practices' in the workplace and the introduction of the new tier of frontline police community support officers. This backfired spectacularly when the Police Federation mobilized its considerable resources and organized a demonstration of 10,000 police officers outside the Houses of Parliament. As a result of the damning Bichard Inquiry into the police handling of the high-profile Soham murders, the Home Secretary demanded the sacking of David Westwood, the Chief Constable of Humberside. This constitutional row was resolved in September 2004 when it was announced that the suspended chief constable had under immense pressure opted for early retirement.

One of the stated intentions of the controversial Police Reform Act 2002, was to provide the Home Office with the powers to ensure that effective policing practices were being used by all forces. The legislation confirmed the shift from the customary notion of a chief constable being 'operationally independent' to the notion of her/him being 'operationally responsible'. An annual National Policing Plan enabled the Home Office to set out strategic priorities, as well as to define how they would be delivered and the indicators by which performance would be measured. Police authorities would be required to produce a three-year strategy plan consistent with this plan. The Home Secretary was also empowered to ensure the consistent application of good practice through codes, regulations and 'guidance' governing policing practice and procedures. S/he was also given the authority to require a police force to take remedial action where it is judged to be inefficient or ineffective by the HMIC. Finally, the Home Secretary could instruct a police authority to compel the suspension or retirement of a chief constable in the interests of efficiency and effectiveness. Underpinning the legislative changes was a new Policing Performance Assessment Framework to identify strong and weak performance and identify good practice across a range of indicators. The Home Secretary was being constitutionally empowered by this legislation to micro-manage operational policing in an unprecedented manner (see Davies, 2003).

Local controls: democratic and participative accountability

What was notable by its absence during the first New Labour administration was any form of principled discussion about the forms of democratically constituted accountability and governance appropriate to the radically altered policing environment of twenty-first century Britain. The Police Federation's call for a Royal Commission on policing was rejected on the grounds that this would hinder rather than facilitate reform and modernization. Several police scholars presented the case for the UK equivalent of the Patten Commission's deliberations on the future policing in Northern Ireland. Johnston (2000), Loader (2000) and Shearing (2001) argued that there was an urgent need to replace state-centred with pluralized, multi-lateral or nodal conceptions of 'police governance' that were more appropriate to the unfolding network of policing and security arrangements. In addition, there was an urgent need to pay attention to an increasing number of criss-crossing 'beyond the-nation state' policing modalities and internal security developments.

From 2000 to 2002, the search began for the 'big idea' that would re-energize New Labour's 'Third Way' philosophy in preparation for the next term of government. This sparked a wide-ranging discussion about the need to articulate a value-based politics that would connect the state, civil society and citizenry. Critics linked New Labour's 'managerial mania' to declining levels of public confidence in governmental capacity and increasing levels of public dissatisfaction with public services. Performance indicators and targets stood accused of stifling diversity and creativity and dismantling local democratic checks and balances. This was compounded by the fact that New Labour's knee-jerk response to regulatory failure was to add yet more punitive targets. Consequently, valuable resources were being spent on inspection/audit bodies that were broadening and/or deepening their remit. As a result a new generation of public sector managers had been oriented towards Whitehall's 'box ticking' requirements rather than promoting public service values. This, in turn, was breeding cynicism among the public, who viewed professionals and practitioners as responding not to their needs but to the auditors and inspectors of the 'managerial state' (Bentley, 2001; Marquand, 2001). In a major intervention, the philosopher, Onora O'Neill (2002) used the BBC Reith Lectures to make the case for, the revalorization of all things 'public' and the promotion of a new ethos of public service.

Think tanks also argued that New Labour's managerial reforms could be transformed only by returning to the principle of locally delivered public services that were directly connected in governance terms to the communities they served. There was a difference of opinion on the scope of this 'new localism'. At the very least, a re-elected New Labour government would have to end a public sector reform programme premised on a top-down 'one size fits all' model. This could be achieved by slashing and burning central government red tape, 'lighter touch' Whitehall inspection of excellent performers and concentrating resources on poorly performing authorities. However, in its most radical interpretation, it was argued that the decentralization and devolution of decision making should be understood as the first steps towards the pluralization or mutualisation of democratic governance. New Labour's plans for neighbourhood regeneration, civic renewal, and the building of cohesive, inclusive communities, raised the prospect of empowering the 'localising state'. There was also the possibility, as part of plans for wider local government reform, of developing a tier of neighbourhood/community/parish level sub-councils to augment the existing machinery of local government. This raised the potential of transferring services from the County/Town/City Hall to self-governing/self-organizing or 'sovereign communities' (see Mayo and Moore, 2001; Bentley and Wilson, 2003; Corry and Stoker, 2003; Local Government Association, 2003, 2004b; Jenkins, 2004; Office of Deputy Prime Minister, 2005, 2006).

There were, of course, cautious voices warning that crazy quilt 'new localism' would undermine universalist social democratic principles of fairness, equality of treatment, consistency and national minimum standards. In a highly differentiated, increasingly atomized society the presence of a strong central state was vitally important to avoiding the Balkanization of policy making. There was also a suspicion that the populist 'new localism' agenda was a guise for one of two things. First, within the context of weak democratic engagement and tenuous communal attachments, that the neo-liberals within New Labour would bypass local government and push a 'choice' and 'consumer control' agenda as part of the move towards the next stage of offloading services to private and independent sector providers. More cynical commentators suggested that the plans for self-governing, 'sovereign communities' allowed central government to devolve, not real powers, but responsibility for a range of intractable 'wicked issues' (see Walker, 2002).

'New Localism' and police accountability

The implications of the 'new localism' debate for police reform surfaced in the countdown to the release of the Green Paper *Policing: Building Safer*

Communities Together in November 2003 (Home Office, 2003a). Echoing the sentiments of their colleagues in other government departments, Home Office Ministers conceded that police modernization had been over-directed and controlled by Whitehall and had produced audit overload. They also acknowledged that a decade of centrally-imposed managerial reforms had re-oriented the police authorities, in accountability terms, towards working with chief constables to manage the competing edicts of the Home Office, HMIC and the Audit Commission. The grip of the centre had in effect closed off the policy-making process to locally expressed policing priorities (see Jones and Newburn, 1997; Loveday, 1998; Loveday and Reid, 2003; McLaughlin and Murji, 2001; Neyroud, 2001, 2003; Jones, 2003; Newburn and Reiner, 2004). As a consequence, there was no way of constitutionally bridging the growing gulf between the police and the public as to the *nature* and *quality* as well as effectiveness of the local policing service being delivered.

A we saw in Chapter 5, there was considerable evidence of an overwhelming public desire, in the context of a full-blown crime panic, for a return to traditional order maintenance policing in the form of uniformed officers on foot patrol, working from local police stations, keeping the streets and neighbourhoods free of petty crime and anti-social and/or morally offensive behaviour. The disappearance of the 'local bobby' and the closure of police stations were symptomatic of how community concerns were of subsidiary importance to police chiefs and police authorities working to an increasingly detailed Home Office performance script. In addition 'Middle England' was incensed about the law and order consequences of using social class coding to re-distribute available policing resources to deprived neighbourhoods.

Docking (2003) confirmed that the public had little to no awareness or understanding of the function of the police authorities. To put it bluntly, the tripartite structure of police accountability had no meaning for the public. Myhill *et al.* (2003) concluded that there was an urgent need for police authorities to increase communication, information and citizen involvement in policing in order to strength both local accountability and police legitimacy. Newburn and Jones (2001) also discerned a real frustration on the part of many citizens about their inability 'to have some means through which officers could be held to account for failing to deliver policing services either as effectively, or in the style required' (p.x). They also posed serious questions about the ability of the police and police authorities to open up meaningful communication channels with hard-to-reach and vulnerable groups (see also Neyroud, 2001).

In a series of 'new localism' speeches Home office ministers (Blunkett, 2003; Blears, 2003) argued that the government recognized that effective solutions to crime and disorder must be formulated locally by beat officers. In addition, effective local policing was now viewed as central to the success or failure of the cross-governmental initiatives on neighbourhood regeneration, civil renewal, active citizenship, community cohesion and combatting political extremism.

Blunkett conceded that public confidence in the police was in sharp decline, communities had little meaningful information about local policing, the structure of local accountability was weak and there was limited community involvement in local policing decision-making processes. Equally significantly, this was confirmed by a report on citizen-focused policing produced by the Prime Minister's Office of Public Services Reform (2003).

Attention grabbing headlines in the national news media throughout 2002-4 suggested for the first time that direct democratic mechanisms must be employed to localize police accountability. The 'now *you* control the cops' spin put on policing proposals emanating from the main political parties during this period ranged from the democratic reconstitution of the police authorities, the establishment of elected neighbourhood policing boards, the introduction of US-style elected sheriffs or police commissioners and the handing over control of policing to New York or Chicago style elected mayors who would be required to present voters with a policing manifesto. The Conservative Party went so far as to declare that, in keeping with the US model, it would completely 'de-nationalize' policing by allowing chief constables to break free of Whitehall controls. ACPO representatives joined in the debate by arguing that sitting above local policing arrangements should be a small group of strategic regional police forces and a national law enforcement agency (see also HMIC, 2005).

Defining the 'New Local' Police accountability

The Home Office launched its consultation exercise on the next stage of police reform in November 2003 with the publication of *Policing: Building Safer Communities Together* (Home Office, 2003a). The Home Secretary's preface to what he described as a 'very green edged' text was constructed around a set of discourses that revalued local policing in terms of active citizenship and cohesive communities. Police–community relations would be at the heart of the reforms with the traditional notion of 'policing by consent' being replaced by 'policing by active co-operation'. The proposals were structured around: reform of the constitutional structure to enhance operational effectiveness; structural re-organization to distinguish between local and national/international serious crime functions; empowerment of local Basic Command Units police commanders; strengthening relationships between the police and local Crime and Disorder Reduction Partnerships (CDRPs) agencies; concentration of new funding on dedicated neighbourhood policing teams; and community engagement in local priority setting and performance evaluation.

Active community engagement necessitated improving the ways in which the public could access readily understood, meaningful information about the state of local policing and crime control activities. It also required a 'reassurance' policing style that would increase the visibility, accessibility, responsiveness and impact of police officers (Innes 2004a; b). This policing style would also need to harness the knowledge, skills and experience of voluntary, community and residents groups as well as the local authority and business sector who in turn could become actively involved in co-funding crime control projects. The Green Paper also raised the possibility of police authority appointed Community Advocates who would monitor local policing, crime reduction and community safety matters, offer independent advice to the public and take up complaints about quality of service issues and minor disputes. This would complement the work of the newly established Independent Police Complaints Commission (IPCC).

The Green Paper accepted the need to clarify the roles and responsibilities of the constitutional structure and strengthen accountability arrangements at neighbourhood, Basic Command Unit and police force levels. First, 'Neighbourhood Panels' could provide the forum for discussions between communities and police officers and other local agencies responsible for crime reduction and community safety. Second, following Northern Ireland, 'Policing Partnership Boards' or 'Community Safety Boards' could manage the post-1998 statutory crime reduction and community safety partnership work being undertaken at BCU and CDRP level. Finally, options were laid out for the future composition and role of police authorities. They could continue to concentrate on police management but become either more mixed in membership or be re-constituted as directly elected 'Police Boards'. They could also be replaced by broader strategic 'Policing Boards' which would be composed of elected members and representatives from all of those agencies involved in the statutory co-production and co-management of policing, crime control and community safety activities.

During the next year a variety of speeches and interviews supported the idea that radical localization of police accountability remained high on the political agenda. David Blunkett supported the idea of communities being allowed to hold mini-referendums on whether to pay for more police officers, community support officers and street/estate wardens. This, it was argued, would strengthen local ownership of policing arrangements. He subsequently argued that local communities should have the power to sack senior police officers if they did not tackle anti-social behaviour and fix 'broken windows':

> The broken windows theory about the way in which neighbourhoods disintegrate and the way in which once that is allowed to take shape, other forces of criminality and disintegration are reinforced, is just simple common sense. We all know it is true. The moment that things start to slip, the moment that self-belief in the community disappears, is the moment that those who can afford to do so get out of these neighbourhoods. And when they do they leave less capacity. They reduce the community and local asset base. They actually reduce therefore, the capability of the community to be part of the solution. (Blunkett, 2004)

The Home Secretary's colleague, Hazel Blears, reinforced the case for the radical localization and democratization of policing, noting that in terms of community involvement there should be risk-taking and democratic experimentation (Blears, 2003).

Re-defining the 'new local' policing

The disparate headlines that accompanied the launch of the White Paper *Building Communities: Beating Crime* in November 2004 confirmed that a shift in government thinking had taken place. The Home Office press releases and briefings were constructed through a consumerist rather than democratic discourse, and public attention was concentrated on plans to ensure that informed 'customers' would be able to call officers on their mobile phones as part of a new ten-point 'copper's contract'. The 'new localism' debate had been re-oriented by government ministers to address the question of how to provide more 'choice' as well as 'voice' for 'citizen–customers' in a developing market place of competing public service providers (see Needham, 2003; Clarke, 2004).

The cornerstone of the White Paper was to democratize police practice through shifting from the traditional doctrine of 'policing by consent' to 'policing by active co-operation'. By 2008, every local community would be policed by multi-functional Neighbourhood Policing Teams (NPTs). As was noted in Chapter 5, the mixed nature of the NPTs is viewed to be vitally important because it not only allows for maximum high visibility street presence, flexibility in staffing and working practices, but it also makes the local police more representative of the diverse communities in which they are working. In theory, therefore, it allows for direct 'community on patrol' (COP) participation in local policing as well as ensuring, for example, that some members of the NPT will be living in and having strong understandings of the locality.

To make NPT a reality, chief constables will be required to devolve more resources and operational decision-making powers to BCU commanders. The commanders, are, in turn, charged with ensuring that the NPTs are 'embedded' in the localities for which they are responsible. In order to do so, NPTs are being tasked to provide a visible, locally known, knowledgeable beat presence. As was discussed in Chapter 5, the logic of NPT work is that if police sovereignty is visibly restored on the streets and communities are provided with a sense of local security, this will also contribute to long-term efforts to build crime resistant cohesive communities. The NPTs are working on the premise that active consent and legitimacy can be constructed and maintained from a multitude of positive everyday interactions between officers and citizens (for further details, see O'Connor, 2003).

As was indicated previously, the police will also be required to improve 'customer service' and responsiveness. For example, they will have to develop a range of ways to allow the public to access policing services more easily. A new non-emergency police number will be used to ensure residents get a personal response to calls that might otherwise be ranked as a low priority by the police control room. Reflecting the 'bobby on the end of a mobile phone' idea, will be 'service contracts' setting out the minimum quality of service customers can expect to receive when they contact the police or the police get in touch with them. In addition, each household will receive an annual jargon-free statement providing details of the staffing structure and focus of local police, crime reduction and community safety agencies, how resources were allocated, how effective local policing is, how to participate in local policing matters and, if necessary, how to complain.

Improved 'customer service' will be augmented with greater community involvement in determining local policing priorities. The 'voice', rather than 'choice', of the community will be strengthened in various ways. The Home Office dropped the idea of both Neighbourhood Panels and an independent Community Advocate Service in favour of giving local councillors an explicit remit to act as a focal point for the community in terms of dealing with those agencies and departments responsible for policing and crime reduction. Councillors will ensure effective democratic representation of people's concerns and empower people to work with the police and other agencies. They will also ensure that local people's views were represented on the quality of service provided by the police and other community safety agencies. This could lead to developing and/or extending the capacity building and liaison role of local community safety officers to work with community organizations and networks and communicate local concerns to ward councillors. This will be an extension of the role many are playing as part of the CDRPs.

If the quality of policing service provided fails to meet the standards set out in the policing contract, or if there is a particular problem associated with crime or anti-social behaviour, councillors will in theory be able to 'trigger' action at a number of levels. At the first level, the councillor can access all available information on the handling of an issue. Councillors can require attendance by the police or relevant local authority agency at a public meeting to discuss the issues and spell out what action they are going to take. It can also lead to a specific request that agencies take action to address the problem. If the agencies decided that no action was to be taken they would have to provide an explanation as to why. To ensure that the neighbourhood policing initiative is effective, at the district level, there will be a new accountability framework covering the work of BCU, CDRPs and 'partner agencies'. However, what is notable is the absence of reference to the suggestion of establishing Local Policing Partnership/Community Safety Boards to govern at this level.

Substantive reform of the police authorities was dropped. Instead they have been told to raise their visibility and be more actively involved with local councils and local communities. They have also been given responsibility for including the local policing priorities identified at CDRP level in their deliberations about policing plans and strategies and providing information about policing performance to local communities. In addition, authorities would: oversee the relationship between CDRPs and neighbourhood bodies and ensuring community consultation, engagement and involvement; co-operate with neighbouring authorities to help tackle non-local serious crime; conduct the chief constables' performance appraisal; and be able to request an inspection by HMIC or direct intervention by the PSU. The focus regarding composition/ membership was not on democratization but on 'strengthening' the professional calibre and representative status of police authority members. The local authority councillor with portfolio responsibility for community safety should be a representative member of the police authority to strengthen democratic accountability. The White Paper also recommended that the magistrates' membership category should be merged with that of the independents.

Finally, the inspection and regulation role of Whitehall will become more obvious via the National Policing Plan, the National Intelligence Model, the National Policing Improvement Agency, HMIC and HOPSU. The centre, supported by the National Police Improvement Agency, will establish priorities, offer support and intervene as and where necessary. High performing police forces and BCUs will be rewarded with less inspection, more resources and a greater degree of operational autonomy. Equally importantly for debates about democratic accountability there has been the confirmation of proposals for the rationalization of the number of forces, as well as institutionalizing the idea of the 'lead force' model. Sitting alongside the new generation of strategic 'super forces' is a new 'complementary' national FBI-style law enforcement agency, the Serious Organized Crime Agency (SOCA). This new organized crime agency which became operational in April 2006 brings together police, customs and excise, and immigration functions into an integrated body.

Conclusion

Ulrich Beck (1997) has argued that Western societies increasingly find themselves in a situation where prevailing governmental institutions and discourses can neither comprehend nor respond to new challenges. He also talks about 'zombie institutions' – 'which have been dead for a long time but are unable to die' (p.140). The preceding discussion has analysed the development of the latest government plans to revitalize the 'zombie' framework of police accountability. There are, of course, some intriguing and potentially radical ideas signalled by both the new independent police complaints structure and the 'new local' policing framework. The government has been forced to acknowledge the need to activate innovative, transparent and relevant ways of ensuring that those tasked with policing are held primarily to professional and democratic account.

The shift to a neighbourhood policing philosophy foregrounds the possibility of more direct face-to-face forms of accountability, or indeed deliberative, trust-based policing and the development of highly localized multi-functional, mixed models of policing and security. For 'public facing' neighbourhood policing to work the logic of police decision-making will have to be reversed as communities will have to be increasingly involved in the design, delivery and review of a preferred portfolio of tailor-made services and maybe even providers. In addition, the broader long-term shifts associated with the 'new localism' agenda offer interesting possibilities regarding the leadership role to be played by local police commanders and local councils. And, in response to the threat of radical reform, the police authorities have been forced to accept more oversight powers and responsibilities, articulate how they will improve their public visibility and credibility and commit themselves to strengthening their relationships with local government and communities in a proactive manner.

However, serious questions have to be posed about whether there is genuine central government commitment to support localized, post-managerial forms of police accountability. Stuart Hall (2003) reminds us that we always need to be aware of New Labour's 'double shuffle' in policy matters. There is the strong impression that underneath the new 'going local' rhetoric, the forma-tion of a much stronger centrally controlled governmental matrix is taking place. As a result, what will be observed is not the passing of real power from the political centre to local citizens and communities, nor the relaxation of central controls. Instead, there will be further functional clarification, consol-idation and rationalization of the existing managerial performance regime; a tightening of key Home Office controls over local policing units, CDRPs, coun-cils, police authorities and chief constables; the ongoing nationalization of force structure; the managerialization of the 'office of constable' and chief constable; and the surreptitious post 9/11, post 7/7 rationalization and strengthening of political policing and national security services well beyond the gaze of democratic accountability.

I have indicated how the radical democratic imaginary that framed the national newspaper headlines accompanying the initial political debate was removed from the White Paper. Direct democratic forms of control were ruled out by the Home Office because of: the threat posed by extremist, populist right-wing groups in working-class constituencies; Muslim radicals in minority communities; the potential for policing to be hijacked by populist US style zero tolerance 'crime-busting' politicians; the need to protect unpopular minorities from the local pol-itics of law and order; the risk of policy gridlock; and the unpredictable outcomes of news-media driven 'law and order' local elections. The point was also made that for all the talk of 'localism', the public and newsmedia were quick to demand central government intervention when locally formulated crime policies failed. Underpinning this climb down seems to have been increasing government concerns about the volatile, segregated state of many multi-ethnic neighbour-hoods, as demonstrated by the official reports into serious public disorder in Bradford, Oldham and Burnley and confidential assessments of the state of com-munity relations post 9/11 and 7/7. It is worth noting that concerns were also raised by ACPO about the ability of micro-locally organized policing arrange-ments to respond to forms of serious criminal threat that flow and or/locate between the local and national level.

However, this retreat on the democratic reformation of local policing leaves us with a series of unresolved problems. First, the police authorities are committing themselves to act as the strategic hub for local police matters. However, because of their non-democratic constitution, serious questions will continue to be posed both about their legitimacy and policy orientation. In addition, despite the proposed changes, they remain powerless to challenge both the Home Office's performance regime and police headquarter's control of core operational policing matters. Second, we are no further forward in developing democratic structures of local-level accountability. This is something noticeably absent from government considerations.

The 'new localists' emphasize that local councils, for all their faults, remain the only democratically constituted institutions that can construct a regulatory framework for integrating and delivering neighbourhood policing and multi-agency policing/security/safety/surveillance services. They are in a geo-political position to ensure that different and indeed changing needs and interests are identified and ensure the relevant infrastructure is in place to enable agencies to work together and promote and facilitate active community participation. More broadly, this would highlight the choices re: taxation and expenditure. The key trigger in all this is clarifying the electoral accountability of local politicians for the delivery of a portfolio of local policing/security/safety/surveillance services. Hence, it needs to be realized that focusing on the 'local council' rather than the 'police authority' offers the possibility of moving to democratically constituted policing. To reinforce this focus, local councils could be mandated to establish 'Policing Committees' that take co-responsibility with local police commanders for co-ordinating, regulating and commissioning all policing/ security/safety/ surveillance activities and negotiating with police authorities. In addition, they could be resourced to set up 'Neighbourhood Policing Panels' which would have the vital role of enabling service users to take on a more proactive role in identifying and addressing local policing needs and concerns. This new 'democratic localism' would have to establish principles and procedures about how to make the difficult choices that are the hallmark of policing culturally diverse communities. However, numerous studies have already identified appropriate deliberative principles and procedures. And as local policing is further localized and democratized, mistakes will be made that will require explanation and action. However, 'democratic localism' provides us with the intriguing possibility that policing will be radicalized, politicized and particularized in unpredictable and very possibly uncomfortable 'raw in tooth and claw' ways with the conceptualization of 'accountability' becoming a micro-polis matter of political debate, negotiation and provisional settlement.

Policing the New Terrorism

As we have seen throughout this book, there have been many notable attempts by police scholars to delineate the future organisational formation, purpose and composition of the police after policing. For understandable reasons there are those who question whether the 'public police', as traditionally understood, have any future as the global market society and the 'war on terror' unfolds relentlessly in the course of the twenty-first century. And there are those who urge caution in the rush to judgement arguing that transformative forces continue to be understood, mediated, reworked and in certain instance resisted in localized policing contexts. In the last chapters we have also examined how the Metropolitan Police has attempted to respond to new realities by attempting to: police not only crime but disorder, incivility and anti-social behaviour; re-culture the organization so that it's workforce not only reflects but is capable of engaging with the multi-cultural metropolis it is responsible for and re-structure modes of accountability so that it is capable of negotiating the security needs of myriad neighbourhoods and communities.

In this last chapter I will focus on some of the unpredictable challenges facing the Metropolitan Police through a discussion of the long term consequences of the suicide bomb attacks on London's transport system on 7 July 2005. There is now the distinct possibility that the responsibility for prosecuting the 'long war' against what has been defined as the 'new terrorism' will bring to the fore a national security consciousness that sets down thicker internal security parameters for discussions about twenty-first century policing infrastructure, operational priorities, preferred culture and modes of accountability.

The darkening skies over the metropolis

On a cold and damp November 2005 night I made my way to the historic church of St. Leonards in Shoreditch, East London to hear Sir Ian Blair, the Commissioner of the Metropolitan Police, deliver the BBC's prestigious annual Richard Dimbleby Lecture. After successfully negotiating the various security checks, I joined the pre-lecture reception that consciously attempted to reflect the multi-ethnic, multi-cultural, multi-faith metropolis. The audience was then ushered downstairs to our seats where the BBC production team informed us that no time had been allocated for post-lecture questions. The sound check manager also tutored us on how to applause enthusiastically at the end of Sir Ian's lecture.

This was an extremely important occasion for seasoned police watchers for many reasons. First, as everyone involved was only too aware, Sir Ian Blair was the first chief police officer to be given the opportunity to deliver this esteemed televised lecture since Sir Robert Mark had done so in November 1973. And as was noted previously, allowing a chief police officer with strong political views the space to address the nation had proved to be an extremely controversial decision. Second, this was a media-event seemingly tailor-made for a chief police officer whose career was defined by having his finger on the political *zeitgeist*. Before becoming Deputy Commissioner of the Metropolitan Police in 2000, Ian Blair was chief constable of Surrey and prior to that assistant chief constable of Thames Valley. He received his knighthood in 2003 for services to policing. Blair had earned a reputation as the most progressive, reform oriented senior officer in the UK and his appointment as Commissioner was seen to be in line with New Labour's 'modernization' agenda. There were high expectations of this sophisticated police officer with the Oxford degree in English and impeccable liberal credentials. One profile noted his resemblance to Adam Dalglish, the fictional 'philosopher-poet' detective in the novels of P.D. James. Throughout his career Blair was part of a generation of media conscious senior officers within the force who used interviews, speeches and lectures to articulate a policing philosophy suited to postmodern complexities (see Blair, 1998; 1999; 2000a;b; 2003;2005).

As Deputy Commissioner of Scotland Yard, in 2002 he had issued a 'wake up call' to politicians concerning the long term implications of allowing the private sector to become an increasingly central part of the policing and security portfolio. He warned that if the police were not allowed to adapt to new circumstances, British cities would see US style Balkanization of policing and security. He was particularly concerned about the signs that London's upper middle class neighbourhoods were being transformed into US-style 'gated communities' and/or employing private security services for neighbourhood patrol. If a line was not drawn, the public police would face a residualized future. His robust defence of a 'full spectrum' public service model of policing stood in stark contrast to his previous views on a much narrower professional model where the private sector and municipal authorities would be allowed to establish street and neighbourhood patrols to discharge the traditional role of the beat constable (see Chapter 5). Blair's rediscovery of the reassurance value of 'feet on the street' was timed to coincide with parliamentary debates concerning his plans to introduce the second tier of Police Community Support Officers to form the basis for the much vaunted neighbourhood policing experiment.

It is no exaggeration to say that Blair's commissionership, when it was confirmed to the news media in October 2004, was expected to inaugurate the equivalent of a mini-Camelot. It was accepted that he would gather around him a progressive senior management team who, having learned from the mistakes of their predecessors, would operationalize the long overdue cultural revolution at Scotland Yard. The days of the quick coat of (reform) varnish were at an end. When Sir Ian Blair took over as Commissioner at the beginning of February 2005 much was made of his determination – and ability – to engage the news media in a proactive manner. In a series of interviews he identified the pressing policing issues facing London. However, sections of the conservative news media were instinctively alarmed that the most powerful police officer in the UK was not just a liberal but 'dusted with the sparkle' of New Labour. The new commissioner made headlines for his declaration that he would have no hesitation in deploying police resources to target the capital's celebrity class and elites who assumed that there was nothing wrong with taking cocaine at dinner parties and private clubs. This story eventually coalesced around the Metropolitan Police investigation of supermodel Kate Moss after tabloid newspapers published front page photographs in September 2005 seeming to showing her cutting and snorting cocaine in her boyfriend's recording studio. This resurrected memories of highly embarrassing police actions relating to London's permissive art and fashion world.

A particular cause for concern for the conservative press was the role that Blair had played in championing political correctness and his public criticism of the racist, sexist and homophobic 'canteen culture'. His decision to spend thousands of pounds changing the Scotland Yard strapline from 'Working for a Safer London' to 'Working *together* for a Safer London' and changing the type face so that it conformed with the disability discrimination act was also criticised as 'political correctness gone mad'. In June 2005 three white officers who claimed at an industrial tribunal that they had been 'hung out to dry' by Sir Ian Blair in a racism case won £90,000 in compensation. He stood accused of interfering in an internal disciplinary case in an attempt to prove the antiracist, politically correct credentials of the force to the public and media. Blair was always going to be compared unfavourably to the traditional leadership qualities of his predecessor, Sir John Stevens. This highly experienced 'coppers copper' was lauded for: rebuilding officer morale in the aftermath of the devastating findings of the Macpherson report; standing up to the managerialist demands of the Home Office; successfully pressing for NYPD levels of front-line resources; and keeping the capital safe from terrorist attack (see Westmarland, 2002; Stevens, 2005). In March 2002, in a speech reminiscent of that of Sir Robert Mark, Stevens had mobilised the conservative news media behind his commissionership by declaring that criminals were above the law; the judiciary and legal profession were ignoring the needs of victims and witnesses and an 'appalling' criminal justice system was handcuffing the police and contributing to the rise in violent street crime.

The final and perhaps most significant reason why the Dimbleby Lecture mattered was Sir Ian Blair's responsibility for keeping the capital safe from the 'new terrorism' threat. In the post 9/11 era, senior police officers and security representatives had stressed that the terrorist threat facing the UK, was fundamentally different to that posed by the Provisional IRA. The terrorism collectively designated as Al Qaeda was a dispersed globalized 'network of networks' or franchise rather than a territorially based organisation. Its potency lay in its ability to exploit freedom of movement and information and theological willingness to sanction acts of spectacular mass violence that were intended to provoke western retaliation as justification for further violence.

There was general police and security services acceptance that post 9/11, Al Qaeda would authorize a spectacular mass casualty attack in London. In November 2002 the country was put on full scale alert with heightened security surrounding a variety of vulnerable targets and locations. Sir John Stevens, the previous commissioner, had cautioned that a London bombing was 'inevitable' given how active extremist Islamic networks were in parts of the UK. He had also confirmed, just before he retired in December 2004, that the police had already disrupted several major terrorist plots, including one on the scale of the March 2004 Madrid train bombing in which 191 people had died. This had been backed up by a warning in November 2004 by both David Blunkett, the then Home Secretary and Eliza Manningham, the then head of MI5, that there was a 'serious and sustained' terrorist threat against Britain. A detailed analysis of how London would respond to a comparable event was undertaken and the emergency services rehearsed a simulated terrorist incident on the London underground to ensure an effective emergency services response to a major chemical, biological or radioactive attack. Key references in the warnings during this time period were Richard Reid, the British 'shoe bomber' who tried to blow up a transatlantic flight and the suicide bomb attacks by British born Omar Sharif and Asif Hanif in Tel Aviv. This pointed to Britain being part of a global 'production line' of suicide bombers being recruited by Al Qaeda. In 2003 there were attacks on British interests in Instanbul and Special Branch Detective Constable Stephen Oake was murdered during a Greater Manchester Police raid on a suspected terrorist cell involved in a chemical poison plot. In January 2005, Sir David Veness, head of Metropolitan Police anti-terrorism operations, reiterated that the levels of 'background noise' from a range of 'indeterminate groupings' and 'networks' confirmed that Britain remained in the global frontline of potential terrorist targets. This was supplemented by Scotland Yard concerns about the possibility of a Bali-style nightclub bomb in London's West End.

The rules have changed: policing the post 7/7 terrorist crisis

In April 2005, Sir Ian Blair intervened in the general election campaign, using BBC's *Breakfast with Frost* programme to call for new laws to tackle loose knit terrorist conspiracies and to support government plans for compulsory identification cards and legislation to enable the police to tackle terrorist conspiracies (*Times*, 20 April 2005). His demands came in the wake of the jailing of Kamel Bourgass for life for the murder of Detective Constable Stephen Oake and plotting to manufacture chemical poison for terrorist purposes. The Commissioner's comments on the gravity of the terrorist threat facing London were amplified globally as a result of the attack by four suicide bombers on the transport network at the end of the morning rush hour on 7th July 2005.

The main newstory that morning was how London had celebrated winning the competition to host the 2012 Olympics. Sir Ian Blair had assured *BBC Radio 4* news listeners that London was a safe city to hold the Olympics in and that the counter-terrorism capability of the Metropolitan Police was 'the envy of the world'. After 9 a.m local radio stations noted that there were serious problems on the underground due to power problems. Because of a lack of information they appealed to listeners to phone or text in any information. As a result it became clear that the system was in shut down mode due to a series of 'critical incidents'. Bombs had exploded on three underground trains within fifty seconds of each other at 8.50a.m and another exploded on a bus at 9.47 a.m. Fifty six people, including the bombers, died and seven hundred were injured. Amidst images of the emergency services rushing across London and blood splattered survivors emerged from the underground stations, Sir Ian Blair pledged that his officers would 'strain every sinew' to identify those responsible for the attacks and bring them to justice. This message was reinforced by Tony Blair, the Prime Minister, who told Parliament: 'we will pursue those responsible not just the perpetrators but the planners of this outrage, wherever they are and will not rest until they are identified, and as far as humanly possible, brought to justice' (*The Times*, 11 July 2005).

Scotland Yard had, in the words of the Prime Minister, earned the 'heartfelt thanks and admiration' of the nation for: managing the largest criminal investigation in the history of British policing; reassuring Londoners with a massive deployment of officers; employing high definition policing tactics at key locations; calming community tensions; responding to the backlash fears of Muslim communities; and evaluating the public relations impact of inevitable anti-terrorist operations.

Figure 8.1   Memorial for 7/7 bomb victims

Full credit must go to the police and emergency services. London did not need a Rudy Giuliani. The crisis was managed by bobbies in the black uniform and silver insignia of the Metropolitan Police. By taking control of the situation they robbed terror of one of its most powerful psychological weapons: the sense that no-one is in charge (*Financial Times*, July 9/10, 2005)

By 13 July the police had established that three of the suicide bombers, Hasib Hussain, Mohammed Sidique Khan and Shehzad Tanweer were from Pakistani families in the north of England and the fourth Germain Lindsay was a Jamaican convert to Islam. There was remarkable CCTV footage of the four bombers making their way from Luton to London where they split up and entered the transport system. The shock of the no-warning bombings was reinforced by global news media commentary on the fact that the United Kingdom had become the first Western society to be attacked by 'home grown' Islamic human bombers (Home Office, 2006; House of Commons Intelligence and Security Committee, 2006).

The 'enemy within' nature of the attacks and the fear that those who had masterminded the bombings was still at large, led police to warn that there was no choice but to roll out a robust counter-terrorist policing strategy. After 7/7 Sir Ian Blair and Chief Constable Ken Jones, chair of ACPO's terrorism sub-committee, presented government ministers and officials with a package of counter terrorism proposals. These included everything from the introduction of new offences of preparing, training for and inciting acts of terror through to the extension of maximum pre-charge detention up to three months and the removal of legal obstacles to the fight against terrorism. They also argued the case for extra resources to upgrade the national counter-terrorism capabilities (Jones, 2005). The police had already drawn up operational guidelines that had been gleaned from consultations with international police and security forces on how to respond to terrorists who were willing to carry out no-warning mass casualty attacks. Under 'Operation Kratos' the rules of engagement shifted from a police to a military mentality: armed officers would be permitted to deliver a 'critical headshot' to ensure that a suspected suicide bomber could not detonate an explosive device. In the words of Sir John Stevens, the former commissioner of the Metropolitan Police, the task was to destroy the brain of the suicide bomber 'instantly, utterly'. Under the new protocol, it would not be necessary for armed police officers to issue a verbal warning before using their weapons (*London Evening Standard*, 13 July 2005). A new command structure was put in place to oversee 'Operation Kratos' (Metropolitan Police Authority, 2005).

Counter-terrorist protocol: shoot-to-kill-to-protect

Exactly two weeks later, London's commuters were caught up in the midst of what turned out to be an unsuccessful lunchtime attempt to replicate the 7/7 attacks on the transport system. Amidst the chaos, rumours spread of nail bomb attacks on the underground. The sense of panic was palpable not least because the attempted bombings contradicted intelligence speculation that Western capital cities were being targeted for symbolic one-off strikes. And of course those responsible for attempting to detonate explosives were on the run. The following afternoon the Metropolitan Police held a news conference for the world's news media to provide an update on city wide raids and arrests by armed police and to issue remarkable CCTV images of the four suspects. Sir Ian Blair also informed journalists that:

> as part of the operations linked to yesterday's events, Metropolitan police officers have shot a man outside Stockwell underground station at approximately 10 a.m. this morning. London ambulance service and the air ambulance both attended and the man was pronounced dead at the scene. I understand Stockwell tube station remains closed. The information I have available is that this shooting is directly linked to the ongoing and expanding anti-terrorist operation. Any death is deeply regrettable. As I understand the situation, the man was challenged and refused to obey police instructions. I can't go any further than that at this stage. (Sir Ian Blair, Metropolitan Police Press Conference, *BBC News*, 23 July 2005)

According to journalists as soon as the Stockwell shooting in south London was confirmed and before the official press conference, a senior police source had provided an off-the-record briefing in which it was stated that police officers had killed one of the would be suicide bombers (*Sunday Times*, 31 July 2005).

The news media provided a graphic second-by-second picture of the sequence of extraordinary events that had led to a suspected suicide bomber being shot by police marksmen operating within new 'shoot-to-kill' guidelines. The suspect had emerged from a residential property in Tulse Hill that was under police observation because of alleged links to the failed bombings. He was under constant surveillance as he travelled by foot and then bus towards Stockwell tube station, one stop away from the scene of the failed attack on the Oval tube station. Police suspicions were raised because the man was wearing a bulky coat and it was feared that this could be concealing a bomb. The man, who at least one eyewitness defined as 'Asian', entered Stockwell tube station, ignoring the challenge by officers who ordered him to stop. According to eyewitness accounts, he vaulted over the ticket barriers, raced down an escalator pushing past passengers and jumped onto a crowded tube train where he tripped and was shot multiple times at point blank range by plainclothes marksmen who had overpowered him. The terrorist suspect died at the scene of the shooting. As further details of this dramatic event emerged, Scotland Yard sources added to the impression that the dead man's 'clothing and behaviour' indicated to officers that they were dealing with someone closely connected with the previous days events.

The Stockwell shooting turned into a public relations disaster for the Metropolitan Police, casting doubt on the leadership of the new Commissioner and the operational competency of key members of his senior command team and undermining legitimacy for its newly minted counter-terrorism policies. It also signalled another major setback for the Metropolitan Police in its post-Macpherson attempts to establish public trust and confidence. The shooting managed to alienate one of London's globalized communities and produced an international incident. Within a matter of hours, Scotland Yard had established that the dead man, Jean Charles de Menezes, a 27 year old Brazilian electrician, was not carrying a bomb and was not linked to the failed bomb attacks of the previous day. Sir Ian Blair acknowledged that an innocent man had been shot dead by his officers:

> This is a tragedy. The Metropolitan Police service accepts full responsibility for this. To the family, I can only express my deep regrets. This is a terrifying set of circumstances for individuals to make decisions. We have to recognise that people are taking difficult decisions in life-threatening situations. It wasn't just a random event. There's nothing gratuitous going on here, no conspiracy to shoot people. There are still officers out there having to make these calls as we speak. We have to take this tragedy, deeply regret it and move on to the investigation which is proceeding at extraordinary pace. What would have happened if these officers had not shot, and that man had been as bomber and got on the tube? It would have been absolutely dreadful. (*BBC News*, 24 July 2005)

He reiterated that there could be no softening of the Metropolitan Police response to suspected suicide bombers. What was now defined as a 'shoot-to-kill-to-protect' operational protocol was not open to debate and would remain in place. The armed officers who had rushed towards and incapacitated the suspected suicide bomber at Stockwell tube station had acted with 'extreme bravery' and had the 'unequivocal support' of the Commissioner. On the following Monday, 3,000 armed police officers were deployed across London in what was described as 'an unprecedented display of firepower' (*London Evening Standard*, 25 July 2005). Scotland Yard must have been only too conscious, however, of the internal organizational ramifications of yet another 'shoot-to-kill' controversy. In November 2004, armed officers had threatened to strike unofficially in protest at the suspension of two colleagues who were involved in the Harry Stanley case. Stanley was shot dead in 1999 by armed officers who were under the impression that he was carrying a sawn off shotgun wrapped in a plastic bag. It subsequently transpired that he had in fact been carrying the leg of a coffee table. Sir John Stevens subsequently called for the Home Office to provide robust legal protection from prosecution for officers who had one of the most difficult and exposed jobs in policing.

There was public appreciation of the near impossible crisis circumstances the Metropolitan Police found themselves in. The general tenor of initial news media reporting was that – at a moment of extreme threat and heightened insecurity – the Stockwell shooting could not be allowed to undermine police morale or hinder the manhunt for terrorists who cared little for human rights and were intent on committing mass murder. Police and security service personnel were operating under intense public pressure and putting themselves at personal risk as they responded to sightings of the four or possibly five failed suicide bombers who were on the run in the capital. In such a fast-time high stakes multi-operational environment, despite all precautions, it was inevitable that firearms officers ran the risk of making mistakes. There was also understanding of the degree to which it was viable for the police to keep the public informed about new operational strategies that had been formulated to deal with such a lethal threat. Jean Charles de Menezes was the unfortunate victim of the fall-out from the unparalleled terrorist campaign that had been launched on London. He would not have been identified, tracked and shot by police officers otherwise. In addition, the post 7/7 policing context was all-important: this shooting had happened as it dawned on the police that they were facing the possibility of a prolonged campaign of terror against the nation's capital. The Prime Minister gave his full support to the regrettable police action as did Ken Livingstone, the Mayor of London and representatives of the Metropolitan Police Authority (*Guardian*, 26 July 2005).

The removal of the police marksmen from operational duties and the establishment of an IPCC investigation should have calmed public debate about the de Menezes shooting. It did not and the Metropolitan Police faced a storm of criticism relating to the specifics of what was turning into a rolling global news story. The clinical nature of the SAS-style killing and police rationalization of the need to 'test' the new counter-terrorism protocol touched a raw nerve. The news media carried extensive interviews with the de Menezes family, friends of the dead man and members of London's Brazilian community where they expressed incredulity that the Metropolitan Police could have profiled Jean Charles de Menezes as a Muslim suicide bomber. Family members also drew a direct comparison between the nature of the shooting and the ruthless actions of police death squads in Brazil. Ever multiplying photographs and personal accounts circulated in the news media and internet of a hard working young man who had come to London in 2002 from an extremely poor part of Brazil to forge a new life and support his family. A corner of the entrance to Stockwell Underground Station quickly became an improvised shrine to 'the boy from Brazil'. The family was also angry that in the immediate aftermath of the killing, senior Metropolitan Police officers had given damaging off-the-record briefings to journalists confirming the idea that although Mr de Menezes was innocent he was, through his actions of fleeing from the police, somehow responsible for his own death. The official version of what had happened and why was reinforced by innuendo and a Home Office announcement that the dead man may have run from police officers because his student visa had expired and he was working in London illegally. Sir Ian Blair stood accused of not correcting the misleading representations Scotland Yard briefings had caused. Human rights groups warned that providing the police with an SAS style 'license to kill' was adding to the climate of public fear rather than providing public reassurance. They also located this latest shooting within the failure of the Metropolitan Police to learn the lessons of previous controversial firearm actions of its officers, including of course the Harry Stanley case. And the broader point was made that counter terrorism would define the future trajectory of the Metropolitan Police's much vaunted neighbourhood policing initiative.

Scotland Yard's press directorate continued with its efforts to re-focus news-media and public attention on the nature of the dilemma facing officers conducting Britain's biggest counter-terrorist operation. On 29 July, the day that Jean Charles de Menezes was buried in his home town of Gonzaga in Brazil and a memorial mass took place at Westminster Cathedral, armed police and members of the special services seized the fugitives wanted for the failed 21 July bombings in a series of dramatic 'live television' raids across London. This operation was praised by all sections of the news media, not least because unlike in Madrid, the Metropolitan Police had managed to make arrests without casualties. On the same day *Police Review* carried an exclusive interview with Sir Ian Blair in which he reiterated that his officers had 'done a fantastic job and have been told it', that the investigation into the attacks was 'close to genius' and that the force enjoyed support from such a large swathe of the public. The Commissioner also disclosed that there had been 250 separate

Figure 8.2   Jean Charles de Menezes shrine

occasions when his officers thought they might be dealing with a suicide bomber. Marksmen had been on the verge of opening fire on seven occasions.

The Metropolitan Police received implicit support from the Prime Minister at the beginning of August in a speech that signalled a major shift in the terms in which the fight against domestic terrorism would be conducted. Tony Blair declared 'Let no one be in any doubt. The rules of the game are changed'. To address accusations that the government had allowed Britain to become a logistics centre for Islamic militants, he unveiled plans to: deport non-UK nationals who advocated or condoned terrorism; proscribe extremist organizations and to push forward with the counter–terrorism strategy that ACPO had recommended in the immediate aftermath of the 7/7 attacks (*The Times*, 8 August, 2005). This was followed by a powerful image of heavily armed police officers in flak jackets guarding the subsequent court appearance of the four 21 July suspects.

The controversy surrounding the Metropolitan Police's SAS style 'shoot-to-kill' policy refused to subside. Disclosures from a multitude of sources to a news media alert to the possibility that Scotland Yard's version of events was flawed, eventually generated a starkly different account of the Stockwell shooting. The *Daily Mail* and the *Observer* newspapers, for example, ran investigative features which queried key aspects of the police account of what happened on the morning of 22 July and suggested that there were multiple mistakes in the process by which Jean Charles de Menezes was identified as a prime suspect. On 16 August ITN news sensationally led with documents leaked by an IPCC employee, including statements from witnesses and police officers, the pathology report and photographs relating to the shooting. These revealed that a catastrophic series of mistakes and intelligence and communication confusion had led to Jean Charles de Menezes being positively targeted and shot dead. They also confirmed previous news reports that there were noteworthy inconsistencies in Metropolitan Police accounts of what had happened. The documents verified that Mr de Menezes had 'dressed, and behaved, with startlingly normality' (*Independent*, 18 August 2005). Officers were not sure which flat the suspect had emerged from. Due to a lapse in concentration, a surveillance officer, on secondment from the army, had failed to take video footage which would have helped positively identify the suspect to colleagues. This meant that the available intelligence was vague and not properly filtered. The suspect was not wearing a suspicious bulky jacket or carrying a bag, did not know that he was being followed, was not challenged, did not run away from the police and did not jump over the ticket barrier. Oblivious to the fact that he was being followed by the police, he picked up *The Metro* a free newspaper and made his way through the underground ticket barrier as normal. He ran only briefly, when he spotted a Northern Line train with its doors open at the platform. Jean Charles de Menezes sat in the carriage unaware that he was in the company of surveillance officers who were waiting for armed officers to arrive. By the time this unit arrived there was confusion about the nature of the threat posed by de Menezes. Armed officers entered the carriage and, believing they were confronting a suicide bomber, shot him repeatedly in the head as he was being restrained by at least one surveillance officer. He was not given the opportunity to surrender. Of the 11 shots fired at point blank range by the two marksmen, seven hit the suspect in the head and one hit him in the upper body.

Key elements of the news media who had been willing to give Scotland Yard and Sir Ian Blair the benefit of the doubt, front-paged the dreadful blunder with a leaked colour photograph of Jean Charles de Menezes lying dead on the floor of the tube train in a pool of blood. The de Menezes family called for officers to face murder charges and for Sir Ian Blair to resign, claiming that he had ultimate responsibility for what they viewed as the execution of their son.

Reports that Commander Cressida Dick, one of the senior officers in charge of the operation to stop de Menezes, had ordered colleagues to 'detain' him shortly before he was shot cast new doubts over the way that the incident had been handled.

During the following week the crisis deepened as questions mounted about why Mr de Menezes had been mistaken for a suicide bomber, what was the chain of command that had authorized the use of lethal force and how the suspect had died. First, ITN news, making the most of the leaked IPCC documents, prime timed its own investigations into the Metropolitan Police mistakes surrounding the fatal shooting. The news agency also gave considerable airtime to the views of the family of Mr de Menezes. Second, the IPCC confirmed the rumour that Sir Ian Blair had initially attempted to block its investigation, claiming that the 'national security' priority was hunting down the bombers. Although the Home Office had rejected his request, the IPCC investigation had been delayed by several days as a result. Third, further leaks suggested that a Metropolitan Police report submitted to the pathologist about the shooting of de Menezes contained erroneous claims. Fourth, there was confirmation that officers directly involved in the shooting had not been questioned by IPCC investigators. Fifth, the de Menezes family said that the Metropolitan Police had insulted them by making an interim compensation payment offer. Sixth, the Brazilian government decided to send justice officials to London to meet with representatives of Scotland Yard, the IPCC, the CPS, the coroner and government officials. Seventh, Scotland Yard broke ranks with rival factions providing insider briefings for and against both Sir Ian Blair and Commander Cressida Dick. There were also rumours of a serious difference of opinion between the surveillance and armed police units involved in the shooting. Eighth, there was renewed speculation as to what had happened to the recordings removed from the underground station's CCTV cameras. Finally, the legal team representing the de Menezes family demanded that the Home Secretary establish a public inquiry as they had no faith in the IPCC investigation. They wanted this inquiry to investigate two main concerns: the operational decision making process that had culminated in the targeting and killing of an innocent man; and why and how Scotland Yard misinformation had been allowed to circulate in the news media.

The Commissioner denied allegations of a deliberate cover up and rejected renewed calls for him to step down (*London Evening Standard*, 19 August 2005). The depth of Scotland Yard's public relations crisis became apparent in the following Sunday's press coverage of the week's developments. The overwhelmingly critical press commentary accorded to the Commissioner was reminiscent of that experienced by Sir Paul Condon in the aftermath of the publication of the Macpherson report. The *News of the World* carried an exclusive interview with Sir Ian Blair in which he was given the opportunity to defend his officers, stand firm against calls for his resignation and rebut the news media's undue focus on the Stockwell shooting:

> I have apologised in public, in private and we have taken full responsibility for this death. We are very concerned for the family and their loss. But what concerns me is that this part of the story is concentrating on the death of one individual when we have fifty two dead people from all faiths and communities in London and from abroad. We still have double figures of people whose lives have been completely transformed in a very bad way, through loss of limbs and eyes and everything else. We have four dead bombers and we have to concentrate on how we find people who are helping or thinking about planning further atrocities. It seems the balance of reporting is in the wrong place. (*News of the World*, 21 August 2005)

In the course of the interview Blair had admitted that he had only found out 24 hours after the shooting that Jean Charles de Menezes was not a suicide bomber: 'Somebody came in at 10.30 am and said the equivalent of "Houston, we have a problem". I thought "That's dreadful. What are we going to do about that?"'

Although the *News of the World* editorial was broadly sympathetic, it did express concern about the Commissioner's 'Houston we have a problem' insensitivity to the de Menezes family and the damage that had been done to the reputation of the Metropolitan Police. The rest of the Sunday newspapers not only carried comprehensive investigative reports on the contents of the leaked IPCC documents but also devoted commentary pieces and editorials to the crisis at Scotland Yard and the Commissioner's remarkable 'Houston, we have a problem' interview. Most were careful to say that there should be no rush to judgment before the findings of the IPCC inquiry and coroners inquest were published and most were reluctant to countenance the Commissioner's resignation at a moment of national crisis. While there was support for frontline police officers, the press expressed grave concerns about police tactics and the quality of Sir Ian Blair's handling of the controversy and his refusal to accept responsibility. There was also considerable sympathy for the de Menezes family campaign to find out why this policing operation had gone so wrong.

A significant turn around in fortune for the embattled Commissioner occurred during the following week despite the fact that the de Menezes family support group staged a vigil outside Downing Street and a memorial service was held in a church used by the Brazilian community. First, government ministers, the Mayor of London, ACPO and London politicians rallied to give unqualified support to Sir Ian Blair and to quell demands for an independent public inquiry. Second, the conservative news media focus widened to: profile the hard line anti-war groups who stood accused of hijacking the death of Jean Charles de Menezes and using it as a news media opportunity to undermine public support for Britain's 'war on terror'; highlight the complaints of families of those who died in the 7/7 bombings whose loss was being overshadowed by the storm surrounding the accidental shooting of one man; and criticize the increasing involvement of the Brazilian government, on the grounds that given the human rights record of its police force, it had no right to condemn Britain for the killing.

Prior to the arrival in London of the parents of Jean Charles de Menezes, Sir Ian Blair once again apologized for the death and conceded that more could have been done to rectify the misleading rumours that had circulated in the news media in the aftermath of the shooting. However, he reiterated that there could be no change to the 'shoot-to-kill' policy: 'I accept that a watershed has been passed. I think that we now have to find a process for debating these issues without necessarily revealing the absolute details of the tactics'.

The family visit was also accompanied by leaked evidence to the *London Evening Standard* that painted a picture of 'utter confusion' at Scotland Yard and the almost immediate realization among the firearms officers that they had shot the wrong man. The parents of Jean Charles de Menezes once more demanded that Sir Ian Blair resign, the officers who shot their son be prosecuted and a public inquiry be established. Extra publicity was gained as a result of Bianca Jagger lending her support to the family, Vivian Westwood releasing a 'I am not a terrorist – please don't arrest me' T-shirt and an art installation of the de Menezes shooting in the front window of Selfridges department store. Subsequently, various home made 'Don't shoot' T-Shirts could be seen on the streets of London.

In November 2005 as the government's embattled counter-terrorist bill entered its Commons Committee stage, the Metropolitan Police was at the forefront of government efforts to persuade wavering MPs to support measures to extend the detention period for terrorist suspects from 14 to 90 days without trial and outlaw the 'encouragement' or 'glorification' of terrorism. Sir Ian Blair addressed the nation directly in a 'Trust Us to Beat the Bombers' letter published in *The Sun* newspaper, the day after a memorial service had been held for the 7 July victims at St Paul's cathedral. This newspaper had already taken the lead in campaigning for much tougher counter-terrorism police powers. The Commissioner warned that the terrorist threat was still high and that the police and the security forces had recently prevented further attacks. He then laid out the reasons why MPs should support police demands for new detention powers:

> The sky is dark. Intelligence exists to suggest that other groups will attempt to attack Britain in the coming months. In the House of Common's today, MPs will debate how long police can detain people in terrorist cases. This is a matter in which the professional opinion of the police, including my most senior and experienced anti-terrorist officers – backed up by senior people in the security service – is clear: We need to detain terrorist suspects for far longer than we have ever had to do before ... The reasons are simple. These people present a threat so profound that as soon as we begin to understand they are planning an attack we must disrupt them by arrest. There is no choice. (*The Sun*, 2 November 2005)

Blair was supported in his efforts by Andy Hayman, head of anti-terrorism at Scotland Yard and Chief Constable Michael Todd to persuade the public to trust the professional judgement and operational requirements of those charged with fighting terrorism. The police needed the extra time to prepare for increasingly complex and multi-facetted terrorist prosecutions. Behind the scenes, the Home Office and ACPO campaigned to persuade MPs to vote for the new powers. The Commissioner also provided a briefing for Westminster journalists and reporters.

Despite the intervention of Sir Ian Blair and other senior police officers and enormous pressure being exercised by Downing Street and *The Sun* newspaper, Tony Blair's first Common's defeat since coming to power in 1997 was a heavy one and provoked speculation about his Prime Ministerial authority. There were a variety of complicated party political reasons why the anti-terrorism legislation had suffered parliamentary defeat. The breakdown in the post 7/7 party political consensus on countering terrorism was joined by a notable mobilization of human rights and civil liberties activists to oppose the 'draconian' legislation. A key concern was that although the police had failed to substantiate the case for what amounted to 'internment by the back door', and despite warnings from senior lawyers that the proposals were unnecessary, unworkable and unconstitutional, the government had refused to compromise on its ninety days stance. It was also clear that certain Labour MPs resented the unprecedented police–*Sun* newspaper–Downing Street alliance to place illiberal proposals on the statute book (*Independent*, 10 November 2005).

The *Financial Times* noted that the vote represented a major set back for the credibility of both Sir Ian Blair and the hard sell tactics of ACPO. Simon Jenkins berated the Commissioner for stepping over the constitutional line and acting as if he were the Minister of Police rather than the commissioner of a democratically accountable police force (*Sunday Times*, 13 November 2005).

'What kind of police force do we want'?: The 2012 vision

On the day of the Dimbleby Lecture, a summary of its main arguments was provided in a special interview with the *Guardian* newspaper in which Sir Ian Blair emphasized that it was time to ignite a public debate about the kind of police force Britain wanted and the hard choices that would be required to achieve it. The traumatic events of July 2005 would form the background to his lecture with commentary on both his aspirations for policing in the countdown to the 2012 London Olympics and the watershed implications of the suicide attacks and the fatal shooting of Jean Charles de Menezes. This was the Commissioner's first news media interview since the parliamentary defeat of the 90 days detention law.

After a context setting introduction by David Dimbleby, Sir Ian Blair walked onto a podium bathed in soft blue/green light to deliver his public address. It seemed fitting that Sir Ian was positioned between a split image of the Metropolitan police badge. After an opening joke at his own expense, he reminded the audience of the evolution of the 'uniquely mild' British model of policing:

quite remarkably, despite scandals and challenges ... a rather benign and, in rural areas, somewhat bucolic model of policing developed and worked well, perhaps particularly in the first half of the twentieth century. By then, the bobby had become an icon of Britishness, an image of the golden age of social cohesion, to which more dangerous modern times are frequently compared. Much like 'Dr Findlay' for general medical practice, 'Dixon of Dock Green' has the twin advantages of perfectly representing the ideal and, of course of being completely fictional.

The Commissioner went on to identify a major flaw in the British model. The constitutional emphasis on 'gradual compromise and evolution' had produced a police service 'which has always been separate and silent, which successive governments – until recently – and nearly all of you, your parents and grand-parents have broadly left alone to get on with the job you have given it'. This had separated the police from society.

Because of the hostile response to Sir Robert Mark's 'brilliant' Dimbleby lecture 'the waters closed, the silence continued' and the police had fallen behind 'the curve of modern Britain'. He detailed how he and a new generation of police leaders had learned to quietly exercise their professional judgement to manage contradictory public demands and government expectations. They had also been left, for example, to formulate the rules of engagement governing the use of lethal force in private. While this quiet professionalism and aloofness may have worked well in the past, times had changed. Chief police officers were now in a 'lose-lose' situation: they had reached the limits of what they could achieve reform wise on their own and they increasingly found themselves in an impossible position if policing operations went wrong. He declared:

The silence can no longer continue. The citizens of Britain now have to articulate what kind of police service they want. For this reason: after the atrocities in New York, Madrid and London, after Bali, Casablanca, Istanbul, Delhi and Jordan, fears for personal and communal safety are inextricably part of contemporary life ... This is not the time for a Royal Commission but for open thought. It is time for politicians and commentators of every stripe and opinion actively to consider how citizens can be involved in a debate about what kind of police service we want.

An improvement in the quality of public discussion and the re-establishment of public legitimacy could be achieved through the establishment of a national police forum. A significant percentage of the public was 'undertaking a permanent NVQ on policing – its called 'The Bill' – and the British have loved detective stories since Sherlock Holmes – and newspapers and news programmes would be empty without us – informed commentary on policing is piecemeal'. Public discussion about policing tended to be crisis-led and contradictory and as a result 'little dispassionate thought through public examination of just what it is we are here to do in the twenty-first century – to fight crime or to fight its causes, to help build stronger communities or to undertake zero tolerance; nor of how these things should be done or what priority each should have or what we should stop doing'.

Blair maintained that the need for active public engagement and informed deliberation was urgent. For him, the five great evils identified by the architects of the British welfare state – want, idleness, ignorance, squalor and disease had now been joined by 'personal insecurity' – 'based on fear of anti-social behaviour, of crime and of terrorism'. As a result the police had been increasingly drawn into the political arena where choices had to be made because society was demanding actions 'to deal with feral children, hoodies and yobs: to the curse of drugs, to date rape and gun crime: to the smuggling of women for sexual slavery: to street robbery: to truancy, graffiti and drunken aggressiveness: to paedophilia, identity theft, organised crime and murder'.

He expressed particular concern about how increasing anti-social behaviour was degrading the quality of communal life in London. The police were being required to manage the damaging consequences of the declining influence of structures of social cohesion, the disappearance of the agencies of social control and the closure of long term mental institutions:

> At the same time, those choices must [also] reflect what kind of police service is needed after July. Terror has changed its methods – or, more accurately, brought some existing methods to Britain for the first time. And while 6th July represents an aspiration, 7th July represents a fact. Britain remains a target of the highest possible priority to al-Qaeda and its affiliates; we are in a new reality. The sky is dark. The terrorists seek mass casualties and are entirely indiscriminate: every community is at risk ...

Given this context, he argued that the public needed to make its mind up on sensitive issues such as the rules governing the use of lethal force by police officers.

Blair insisted, however that in spite of the unprecedented terrorist threat, the preferred model for policing an 'open, diverse society, with equality of opportunity and freedom of movement' would be the neighbourhood policing team model: 'local, visible, accessible, familiar, accountable and friendly ... unarmed ... a unified police service, engaged with and accountable to the community and being shaped by the needs of citizens, capable of dealing with every requirement from truancy to terror, from graffiti to gunmen'.

The cherished ideals of the British model meant, for the Commissioner, that there was a natural affinity towards the Chicago rather than NYPD policing model. However, the omni-competent police mission – in the post-7/7 context – would have radical implications for the organizational structures, workforce composition, regulations, operational practices and partnership arrangements of the police force as well as governance and accountability and the overall relationship between the police and society.

Blair made a particular point of addressing the issue of the representativeness of the police workforce. He noted that Sir Robert Peel had insisted that the new Metropolitan Police force 'was not to be an occupation for gentlemen'. This had the detrimental effect of separating the police 'from the established currents of British life, so that those who join the police are a bit of a puzzle to others'. Blair noted how, despite the disappearance of traditional class divides and eroding social barriers, there was a tendency in British society for certain classes and social groups to view themselves as too superior to consider the police as a career choice. The result was that the police service became the preserve of the 'striving lower-middle class, predominantly white, predominantly male'. This was no longer viable: 'It can't work this way any longer. I need your brothers and your sisters, your mothers, your fathers, your sons, your daughters, from every race and creed to be in the police ... Only through the widest possible recruitment will you all begin to know who we are and will we be able to create the police service you want'.

Towards the end of the lecture, the Commissioner noted the need to move from a passive notion of 'policing by consent' to an active notion of 'policing by direct collaboration'. He concluded:

> As the Bobbies named after him prove, Robert Peel created policing in Britain and in the free world. I will leave you with perhaps his most important yet enigmatic statement, 'the police are the public and the public are the police'. You and we are one. A new giant has arisen. You all now – we all now – need to make some decisions.

Because no space was allocated for questions at the end of Sir Ian's lecture, it was left to members of the audience to discuss his vision of policing among themselves as they slowly made their way out of the church into the Shoreditch night and to wonder what would capture the news headlines.

'What kind of police service do we want?': The Response

Despite the best efforts of the BBC to amplify the importance of Sir Ian Blair's lecture, it did not generate much public debate. There was general acceptance across the press of the Commissioner's basic premises that there was both a growing gulf between the police and the public; the police perspective deserved to be heard; policing was too important to be left to the police; there was a need to foster rational debate to clarify priorities. The liberal press was broadly supportive of Sir Ian Blair's attempt to galvanise public attention and offer a leadership role in a much needed post 7/7 debate on the future direction of policing. There was nothing particularly controversial in what had been said. This was not so much a radical policing blueprint as a bricolage of the Commissioner's previous pronouncements. The *Guardian* editorial did express concern about the Commissioner's willingness to inhabit the political arena. Sir Ian's cause was not helped in liberal quarters by the revelation in the *London Evening Standard* just before the lecture that Jean Charles de Menezes had been shot dead with 'dum-dum' bullets. If correct this represented a drastic departure from conventional police practice.

There were, however, serious points of disagreement with Sir Ian Blair's attempted re-authorization of policing in editorials and commentary pieces in the conservative press. They were more than willing to provide the Commissioner with an answer to his 'tell-us-what-you-think' lecture. Many of the newspapers anchored their views around Blair's critical comments on the lack of support for the police among the middle classes. Police chiefs were castigated for their willingness to ally themselves with the New Labour government and the unrepresentative liberal elite. This had left them out of touch with 'Middle England's' desire for a return to Dixonian policing. The Commissioner was criticized for a seeming inability to recognise that the first principles contract between police and law abiding public required officers to symbolize order and enforce the law in a philosophizing free manner. Minette Marrin's piece 'I'd rather PC Plod than PC Clever Clogs' summed up many of the points that can be found in the conservative commentary:

> The police are not there to 'fight the causes of crime', the police are not social workers or teachers or foster parents or psychiatrists, nor should they be, even if they had the time or the money or the manpower. The police are not there to build communities of any sort: a monstrous idea.

> What the police can do is remove the obstacles to community, such as violence and disorder and public nuisances. What they can do – could do much more – is stay so close to the community they police that they can anticipate crime and deter it by their close knowledge of who's who and what's going on. Failing that, they are there to catch criminals. You do not need a public debate to discover that, that's what most people think. (*Sunday Times*, 20 November 2005)

The conservative press was also incredulous about the Commissioner's description of the police as a marginalised 'silent service' and his frustrations at the lack of informed public debate. Heather Brook writing responded as follows:

> If he's frustrated how does he think the public feel? How are we meant to have an informed opinion when the police surround and shroud their routine activities with such secrecy? How are we supposed to join the debate when the police and politicians continue to foist their decisions ready-made on us in feudal fashion.

> There was no debate about the shoot-to-kill policy. The first the public knew about it was the killing of Jean Charles de Menezes. Yesterday it emerged – through leaks of course – that he was shot with hollow-point bullets; ammunition

selected in total secrecy three years ago. Even now the police refuse to justify such decisions, hiding behind the excuse of 'national security.'

The Association of Chief Police Officers increasingly controls many aspects of policing. It receives substantial sums of public money, yet is not accountable to us. It is not even considered a public body under the Freedom of Information Act. ACPO lobbied hard for 90-day detention, yet it failed to provide any compelling reason why the police need to hold terror suspects without charge longer than any other democratic society ... For too long the authorities have demanded that we trust them while giving nothing in return. If the commissioner really wants a mature debate he can kick off by trusting the public enough to give us a full and frank account of what his officers do. (*Sunday Times*, 20 November 2005)

Ex-police officers also joined in the criticism of the Commissioner. For example, John Stalker, the former deputy chief constable of Greater Manchester, denounced the lecture as a cynical public relations stunt designed to limit the damage of the Stockwell shooting. However, as far as Stalker was concerned, the authority and credibility of the Commissioner had been fatally compromised (*Independent on Sunday,* 20 November 2005). Sir Ian Blair was compromised further with the IPCC announcement just over one week later that it had decided to set up a separate investigation to examine the allegations of the family of Jean Charles de Menezes that Scotland Yard had misled the public over the circumstances of the Stockwell shooting.

Conclusion

There seems little possibility that Sir Ian Blair's search for post 7/7 solid ground and his plea for calm and reasoned public deliberation about the future of British policing can be realised. The volatility and heavily mediated nature of the twenty-first century policing debate in Britain was demonstrated by the fact that the Commissioner's views were quickly overtaken by the shooting of two unarmed police officers less than 48 hours after he had given his lecture. On 19 November, WPC Sharon Beshevisky was shot dead and her colleague WPC Teresa Milburn seriously injured when they confronted an armed gang fleeing the robbery of a travel agency in Bradford in the north of England. She was the first women officer to be shot dead in the line of duty since WPC Yvonne Fletcher was killed outside the Libyan embassy in 1984. The shootings were taken as a reminder of the high routine risks police officers face in protecting the British public from gun-wielding foreign criminals. They also reignited a furious media debate over whether to arm all front-line police officers. Opinion remained divided between those who demanded routine armament because police officers were being outgunned on the streets and those who still held onto the ideal of the unarmed Dixonian police force. There was general acceptance of course that the 7/7 bombings had to a degree already normalized the presence of heavily armed officers on Britain's city streets. There were also calls from within the police to bring back capital punishment for the murder of police officers. Sir John Stevens', Sir Ian Blair's predecessor, declared in the *News of the World*, that officers were entitled to maximum judicial protection:

> Hard though it may seem, murdering someone you know is a police officer IS different. You are not just killing an individual, you are attacking everything they represent. A police officer is someone you and I have chosen to defend and uphold the very basics of our society, or state. We appoint them guardians of what we have decided is right and wrong. That's why if they abuse that privilege, we rightly punish that breach of trust heavily. But it is also right that their position of trust be safeguarded ... The truth is plain about the beasts who commit such awful crimes – they care about nothing, respect nothing and are deterred by nothing. Even if they are caught and convicted, how can we punish or deter such people who care about so little? What I now realize is there's only one way – the death penalty. It is the only deterrent or punishment that will warn monsters this is the price they'll pay. (20 November 2005)

He was supported in his call by Steven Green, the chief constable of Nottinghamshire. The *Daily Telegraph* illustrated its letters page debate on capital punishment with *The Blue Lamp* still of PC George Dixon confronting Tom Riley outside the cinema.

In addition, many of the core issues raised in the aftermath of the terrorist attacks of July 2005 and the Stockwell shooting remain unresolved. The police and security services continue to caution about the threat posed to London by Islamic terrorists. An official update in February 2006 acknowledged that there were up to 500 terrorist suspects in Britain and that the nation could be at psychological war with indigenous Islamic terrorism for the next fifty years. And the devastation caused by suicide bomb attacks in other parts of the world do serve as vivid reminder of the potency of this threat. In addition, the government continues with its attempts to push through its anti-terrorist legislation and to redefine the terms of public debate about the balance between human rights and civil liberties on the one hand and personal safety and internal security on the other. Conspiracy theories abound about just how much the police and security services knew about those responsible for the 7/7 bombings, why they had been willing to sign up to a 'non-aggression pact' with British based militant Islamic groups and why they had lowered the terrorist threat level three weeks before the attacks. And, of course, although the IPCC reports into the Stockwell shooting have not been officially published, numerous leaks have further destabilised the internal dynamics of the Metropolitan Police and the authority of its Commissioner.

In July 2006 the CPS revealed that there was insufficient evidence to provide a realistic prospect of conviction against any individual police officer implicated in the Stockwell shooting. The IPCC report confirmed that planning and communication mistakes had resulted in the death of Jean Charles de Menezes. However, no senior commanding officer was culpable to the degree necessary for a criminal prosecution and the marksmen had opened fire because they 'genuinely believed' that they were confronting a suicide bomber. Instead, the CPS was satisfied that the operational errors were serious enough to warrant prosecution of the Office of Commissioner of Police for 'failing to provide for the health, safety and welfare' of Mr de Menezes. It was stressed that this would not result in the prosecution of Sir Ian Blair in a personal capacity (CPS Press Release, 17 July 2006). This decision satisfied neither the Metropolitan Police nor the legal team representing the de Menezes family. Scotland Yard entered a 'not guilty' plea to the CPS charges in September 2006 arguing that it was 'a test case not only for policing in London but for the police service nationally. It also has implications for the general public in that it concerns the ability of the police service to protect the public at large when carrying out armed operations'. The legal representatives of the de Menezes family declared that, irrespective of the outcome of the case, they would continue to demand that the IPCC publish its report and the criminal prosecution of those police officers who presided over the Stockwell shooting. The stakes are extremely high in the ongoing de Menezes case and its looks like key aspects of the new framework of police accountability, discussed in Chapter 7, are going to be tested to the legal and political limit.

In the aftermath of the Dimbleby Lecture, Sir Ian Blair continued to feature prominently often for the wrong reasons in the news headlines. There was saturation coverage on Blair's allegations that the press was institutionally biased in its coverage of murder cases and the inexplicable focus on the Soham murders. Such was the intensity of the commentary, the majority of it highly negative, across all the news media formats, that Sir Ian Blair found it necessary to go on BBC Radio 4's 'Today' programme the following morning to explain his comments and to issue an 'unreserved apology' to the parents of Holly Wells and Jessica Chapman. He did attempt to hold the line on his insistence that the press was institutionally racist in its coverage of murder cases. Blair's apology only fuelled the news media's coverage of the story which carried through to the Sunday newspapers. There was also reflection on whether the Commissioner was using the Soham example subconsciously to work through why the news media had decided to concentrate on the Stockwell shooting.

Sir Ian Blair had to issue another apology in March 2006 when one of his aides disclosed that he had secretly taped his telephone conversations with the Attorney General, members of the IPCC and a *Guardian* journalist. In June 2006 a further apology was forthcoming from Scotland Yard as a result of the most high profile anti-terrorist operation in London since the previous July. Intelligence that suggested that a house in Forest Gate, East London contained a chemical bomb led to a raid by 250 officers. In the course of the operation a suspected bomb maker was shot in the shoulder. The two suspects – Abul Koyir and

Mohammed Abdul Kahar Kalam were detained under anti-terrorism legislation for more than a week before being released without charge. The Forest Gate raid generated another IPCC inquiry, a well-organized campaign for Sir Ian Blair to resign his Commissionership, and warnings that the police actions were widening the sense of alienation and victimization amongst Muslim youth.

A sense of the escalating internal turmoil within the Metropolitan Police was revealed in various leaks and declarations which claimed that officers of all ranks supported Sir Ian Blair's resignation. Equally significantly, in early 2006 the Metropolitan Police began to roll out its neighbourhood policing teams in earnest. Scotland Yard and the Mayor's office felt it necessary to draft in William Bratton, the LAPD commissioner, and Philip Cline, a senior representative of the Chicago Police Department, presumably to provide extra authority. This perhaps more than anything else indicates the degree to which British police forces are now having to come to terms with a dislocated future in which they have seemingly exhausted the possibilities of generating an indigenous philosophy of routine policing that the public can believe in. Consequently, they seem fated to be increasingly dependent on pre-packaged, media-validated US crime control initiatives.

There are two concluding points that need to be made. First, Sir Ian Blair, despite his call for public debate, did not refer to the work of police scholars in the course of his Dimbleby lecture. The nearest he came to doing so was a passing reference to what he referred as one of the first books to examine the working culture of the British police officer. I was wondering whether he would refer to Michael Banton's seminal text, or Maureen Cain's meticulously crafted study of 'beatwork' or the work of Maurice Punch, Simon Holdaway or 'Tank' Waddington? Maybe he would bypass the UK literature and mention one of the US classics such as Westley, Skolnick or Manning. No, the book he cited was *A Man Apart*, an insider account by an ex-policeman Tony Judge which was published in 1972. Perhaps Sir Ian thought that the mountain of monographs, handbooks, readers, journal articles, chapters and research reports produced by police scholars were of little real relevance to the multiple organizational pressure points he is grappling with. Maybe it was impossible to refer to the new policing and security governance literature because the alternative pluralist futures of policing are little more than a distraction given the chaotic complexities of the post 7/7 world. And when one re-reads this literature, one is confronted with the intense strangeness of trying to make sense of the voided narratives of policing futures. Second, to my knowledge, police scholars, including myself, did not respond in public to the subject matter of Sir Ian Blair's Dimbelby lecture. Indeed this has been a notable absence and is quite remarkable given that there is the pressing need for a vigorous debate about whether it is possible to piece together a policing and security philosophy that can protect human rights, democratic values and cosmopolitan citizenship.

References

Ackroyd, C., Rosenhead, J., and Shallice, T. (1980) *The Technology of Political Control*, London: Pluto Press.

ACPO (2001) *Reassurance – Civility First: A Proposal for Police Reform*, London: ACPO.

Adam, H.L. (1931) *CID: Behind the Scenes at Scotland Yard*, London: Sampson and Co.

Albrow, M. (1989) 'Sociology in the United Kingdom after the Second World War' in N. Genov (eds.) *National Traditions in Sociology*, London: Sage.

Aldgate, A. (1992) *Cinema and Society: Britain in the 1950s and 1960s*, Milton Keynes: Open University Study Guide.

Aldgate, A. and Richards. J. (1999) 'The thin blue line: the Blue Lamp' in A. Aldgate and J. Richards (eds.) *Best of British: Cinema and Society from 1930 to Present*, London: I.B. Taurus.

Arthur, P. (2001) 'Murderers tongue: identity, death and the city in the *film noir*' in Slocum, J.D. (ed.) *Violence and the American Cinema*, London: Routledge.

Ascoli, D. (1979) *The Queen's Peace: The Origin and Development of the Metropolitan Police, 1829–1979*, London: Hamish Hamilton.

Ashley, R.P. (1951) 'Wilkie Collins and the detective story' in *Nineteenth Century Fiction*, 1: 47–61.

Attinger, J. (1989) 'The decline of New York', *Time Magazine*, 7 September: 36–44.

'Aytee' (1942) 'The police and public', *Howard Journal* 6 (2): 112–5.

BBC (2000) 'The Right Stuff: the making of a chief constable', *Analysis*, BBC Radio 4, 31 January 2000.

BBC (2001a) 'Raw Blues', BBC1, February.

BBC (2001b) 'The Black Police Association', *Analysis*, BBC Radio 4, Autumn.

BBC (2002) 'Ealing Studios', BBC Radio 4, 8 and 15 January.

BBC (2001c) 'Racism in the Police Force', *File on Four*, Radio 4, 25 September.

BBC (2003) 'The Secret Policeman', BBC1, 23 October.

BBC (2006) 'Jack of All Trades', BBC Radio 4, 20 July.

Bahn, C. (1974) 'The reassurance factor in police patrols', *Criminology*, 12: 338–45.

Balcon, Sir M. (1969) *Michael Balcon Presents: A Lifetime of Films,* London: Hutchinson.

Baldwin, R. and Kinsey, R. (1982) *Police Powers and Politics*, London: Quartet Books.

Banton, M. (1955) *The Coloured Quarter: Negro Immigrants in an English City*, London: Jonathan Cape.

Banton, M. (1957) *The West African City; A Study of Tribal Life in Freetown*, Oxford: Oxford University Press.

Banton, M. (1959) *White and Coloured: the Behaviour of British People towards Coloured Immigrants*, London: Jonathan Cape.

Banton, M. (1963a) 'Police discretion' *New Society*. 48, 29 August: 6–8.

Banton, M. (1963b) 'Social Integration and police authority', *The Police Chief*, 30(4): 8–21.

Banton, M. (1964a) *The Policeman in the Community*, London: Tavistock.

Banton, M. (1964b) 'A Policeman's Lot', *Listener,* 9 January: 68.

Banton, M. (1971) 'Report to the Nuffield Foundation on a seminar on the sociology of the police', *Police Journal*, 18: 227–243.

Banton, M. (2005) 'Finding and correcting my mistakes', *Sociology*, 39(3): 463–79.

Barot, R. (2006) 'Reflections on Michael Banton's contribution to race and ethnic relations', *Ethnic and Racial Studies*, 29(5): 785–96.

Barr, C. (1980) *Ealing Studios*, London, Cameron and Tayleur.

Barrett, W. (2000) *Rudy! An investigative biography of Rudolph Giuliani*, New York: Basic Books.

Bass, S. (2001) 'Policing space, policing race: social control implications and police discretionary decisions', *Social Justice*, 28(1): 156–76.

Baudrillard, J. (1990) *Fatal Strategies*, London: Pluto.

Baudrillard, J. (1994) *Simulcra and Simulation*, Ann Arbor: University of Michigan Press.

Baudrillard, J. (1995) *The Illusion of the End*, Cambridge: Polity Press.

Bauman, Z. (2001) *Liquid Modernity*, Cambridge: Polity Press.

Bayley, D. (1988) 'Community policing: a report from the Devil's Advocate' in J.R. Greene and S.D. Mastrofski (eds.) *Community Policing: Rhetoric or Reality?*, New York: Praeger.

Bayley, D. and Shearing, C.D. (1996) 'The future of policing', *Law and Society Review*, 30 (3): 585–606.

Bayley, D. and Shearing, C.D. (2001) *The New Structure of Policing: Description, Conceptualisation and Research Agenda*, Washington: National Institute of Justice.

Beattie, J. (2002) *Policing and Punishment in London, 1660–1750*, Oxford: Oxford University Press

Beck, U. (1997) *The Reinvention of Politics: Rethinking Modernity in the Global Social Order*, Cambridge: Polity.

Becker, H. (1963) *Outsiders: Studies in the Sociology of Deviance*, New York: Free Press.

Decker, T. (1974) 'The place of private police in society: an area of research for the social sciences', *Social Problems,* 21(3): 438–453.

Bentley, T. (2001) *It's Democracy Stupid*, London: Demos.

Bentley, T. and Wilson, J. (2003) *The Adaptive State: Strategies for Personalising the Public Realm*, London: Demos.

Best, S. and Kellner, D. (1991) *Postmodern Theory: Critical Interrogations*, Basingstoke: MacMillan.

Bhavnani, R., Mirza, H.S., and Meeto, V. (2005) *Tackling the Roots of Racism*, Bristol: Policy Press.

Bittner, E. (1970) *The Functions of the Police in Modern Society: A Review of Background Factors, Current Practices, and Possible Role Models*, Rockville, MD: National Institute of Mental Health.

Blair, I. (1998) 'The police has lost its monopoly of crime patrols. Here is how it should respond', *Financial Times*, 17 July: 20.s

Blair, I. (1999) 'The modernisation of the police', Speech to *Social Market Foundation*, London, 18 February.

Blair, I. (2002a) 'The policing revolution: back to the beat', *New Statesman*, 23 September: 21–22.

Blair, I. (2002b) 'Policing a multi-ethnic society', Runnymede Trust (ed), *Developing Community Cohesion: Understanding the Issues, Delivering the Solutions*, London: Runnymede Trust.

Blair, I. (2003) 'Leading towards the future', *Future of Policing Conference*, LSE, 10 October, http://www.padpolice.com/futureofpolicing.php.

Blair, I. (2005) 'What kind of police service do we want?', The Dimbleby Lecture, BBC 1, 16 November, http://news.bbc.co.uk/1/hi/uk/4443386.stm.

Blair, T. (1993) 'Why crime is a socialist issue', *New Statesman*, 29(12): 27–8.

Blakely, E.J. and Snyder, M. (1997) *Fortress America: Gated Communities in the United States*, Washington: Brookings Institute.

Blears, H. (2003) *Communities in Control*, London: Fabian Society.

Blunkett, D. (2003) *Towards a Civil Society,* London: IPPR.

Bogarde, D. (1978) *Snakes and Ladders*, London: Chatto and Windus.

Bowden, T. (1978) *Beyond the Limits of the Law*, Harmondsworth: Penguin Books.

Bowes, S. (1966) *The Police and Civil Liberties*, London: Lawrence and Wishart.

Bowling, B. and Phillips, C. (2002) *Racism, Crime and Justice*, Harlow: Pearson Education.

Bowling, B. and Phillips, C. (2003) 'Policing ethnic minority communities' in T. Newburn (ed.), *Handbook of Policing*, Cullompton: Willan Books.

Box, S. and Russell, K. (1983) 'The politics of discredibility', *Sociological Review*: 23(2): 315–46.

Bratton, W. (1995) 'The New York City Police Department's civil enforcement of quality of life crimes', *Journal of Law and Police*, 3: 477–464.

Bratton, W. (1996) *Cutting crime and restoring order: What America can learn from New York's finest*, Lecture at the Heritage Foundation, 15 October, www.heritage.org.

Bratton, W. (2002) 'How you can win back the streets of Britain by the man who tamed New York', *The Sun*, 25 March: 14–15.

Bratton, W. (with Knobler, P.) (1998) *Turnaround: How America's top cop reversed the crime epidemic,* New York: Random House.

Brett, D.T. (1979) *The Police of England and Wales: a Bibliography*, 3rd edition, Bramshill: Police Staff College.

Bridges, L. (1983) 'Policing the urban wasteland', *Race and Class*, 25 (2):31–47.

Brodeur, J.P. (1983) 'High and low policing: remarks about the policing of political activities' *Social Problems*, 3 (5): 507–20.

Brogden, M. (1982) *The Police: Autonomy and Consent*, London: Academic Books

Brogden, M., Jefferson, T. and Walklate, S. (1988) *Introducing Policework*, London: Unwin Hyman.

Brooks, D. (2003) *Steve And Me: My Friendship with Stephen Lawrence and the Search for Justice*, London: Abacus Books.

Brunsdon, C. (2000) 'The structure of anxiety: recent British crime drama' in E. Buscombe (ed.), *British Television: A Reader*, Oxford: Oxford University Press.

Bunyan, T. (1977) *The Political Police in Britain*, London: Quartet Books.

Button, M. (2002) *Private Policing*, Cullompton: Willan Publishing.

Cain, M. (1977) 'An ironical departure: the dilemma of contemporary policing' in K. Jones (ed.) *Yearbook of Social Policy in Britain,* London: Routledge and Kegan Paul.

Cain, M. (1979) 'Trends in the sociology of policework', *International Journal of Sociology of Law*, 7: 143–67.

Cain M. (1993) 'Some go back, some go forward', *Contemporary Sociology*, 22(3): 319–24.

Caldeira, T. (2000) *City of Walls: Crime, Segregation and Citizenship in Sao Paulo*, Berkeley: University of California Press.

Calvino. I. (2002) *Why Read the Classics?*, New York: Vintage Books.

Calvert-Smith, D. (2005) *The Police Service in England and Wales: Final Report of a Formal Investigation by the Commission for Racial Equality*, London: Commission for Racial Equality.

Cantell, T. (2001) *Community Cohesion: A Report of the Independent Review Team*, London: Home Office.

Cashmore. E. (2001) 'The experiences of ethnic minority police officers in Britain: under-recruitment and racial profiling in performance culture', *Ethnic and Racial Studies*, 24 (4): 642–659.

Cashmore, E. (2002) 'Behind the window dressing: ethnic minority police perspectives on cultural diversity', *Journal of Ethnic and Migration Studies,* 28 (8): 327–341.

Cashmore, E. and McLaughlin, E. (eds) (1991) *Out of Order? Policing Black People*, London: Routledge.

Cathcart, B. (1999) *The Case of Stephen Lawrence*, London: Viking Press.

Centre for Research on Criminal Justice (1975) *The Iron Fist and the Velvet Glove; an Analysis of the US Police*, San Francisco: Garrett Press.

Chan, J. (1997) *Changing Police Culture: Policing in a Multicultural Society*, Cambridge: Cambridge University Press.

Chan, J. (1999) 'Governing police practice: the limits of the new accountability', *British Journal of Criminology*, 50, 251–70.

Channel 4 (1999) *Siege of Scotland Yard*, Films of Record, February 17.

Chapman, A.J. (1998) *The British at War: Cinema, State and Propaganda, 1939–1945*, London: I.B. Taurus.

Chevigny, P. (1969) *Police Power: Police Abuses in New York City*, New York: Panthean Books.

Chibnall, S. (1977) *Law and Order News*, London: Tavistock.

Chibnall, S. (1997) 'The teenage trilogy. The Blue lamp, I Believe In You and Violent Playground' in A. Burton, T. O'Sullivan and P. Wells (eds), *Liberal Directions: Basil Dearden and Postwar British Film Culture*, Trowbridge, Wilts: Flick Books.

Christian, L. (1983) *Policing by Coercion*, London: GLC Police Support Unit.

Christoph, J.B. (1962) *Capital Punishment and British Politics*, London: Allen and Unwin.

Clarke, A. (1983) 'Holding the "Blue Lamp"', *Crime and Social Justice*, 19(2): 44–51.

Clarke, D.B. (2003) *The Consumer Society and Postmodern City*, London, Routledge.

Clarke, J. and Newman, J. (1998) *The Managerial State*, London: Sage.

Clarke, J.P. (1965) Review of *The Policeman in the Community*, American Sociological Review, 30: 954–5.

Clarke, R.V.G. (1980) '"Situational" crime prevention: theory and practice', *British Journal of Criminology,* 20 (2): 136–47.

Clarke, T.E.B. (1974) *This Is Where I Came In*. London: Joseph.

Clay, A. (1998) 'When the gangs came to Britain: the post-war crime film', *Journal of Popular British Cinema*, 1: 76–86.

Coetze, J.M. (1993) 'What is a classic?', *Current Writing*, 5 (2): 7–24.

Cohen, N. (2003) 'Why the Met faces a crisis over race', *New Statesman*, 25 November: 16–18.

Cohen, P. (1979) 'Policing the working class city' in B. Fine, R. Kinsey, J. Lea. S. Picciotto and J. Young (eds.), *Capitalism and the Rule of Law,* London: Hutchinson.

Cohen, S. (1995) *Visions of Social Control*, Oxford: Blackwell.

Coldstream, J. (2004) *Dirk Bogarde: The Authorised Biography*, London: Weidenfeld and Nicolson.

Colley, L. (1994) *Britons: Forging A Nation, 1707–1837*, London: Pimlico.

Collins, P. (1964) *Dickens and Crime*, London: MacMillan.

Colls R. and Dodd, P. (1986) *'Englishness': Politics and Culture, 1880–1920,* London: Croom Helm.

Commission for Racial Equality (1996) *Race and Equal Opportunities in the Police Service: A Programme of Action*, London: Commission for Racial Equality.

Compton, S. (2002) 'Why we love the best TV detectives', *The Times,* 13 November: 25.

Condon, Sir P. (1998) *Working Together For an Anti-Racist Police Service*, London, Metropolitan Police.

Cooke, L. (2003) *British Television Drama: A History*, London: BFI.

Cornish, G.W. (1935) *Cornish of the Yard*, London: Victor Golantz.

Corry, D. and Stoker, G. (2003) *New Localism: Refashioning the Central-Local Relationship*, London: New Local Government Network.

Cosgrove, S. (1996) 'Real cops never had it so good', *Independent*, 26 January: 23.

Coultras, A. (1989) *Images for Battle: British Film and the Second World War*, Newark, New Jersey: University of Delaware Press.

Cowell, D., Jones, T., and Young, J. (1982) *Policing the Riots*, London: Junction Books.

Crank, J. (2004) *Understanding Police Culture*, 2nd edition, Cincinnati: Anderson and Co.

Crawford, A. (2005) 'Policing and Security as 'Club Goods': The New Enclosures?', in J. Wood and B. Dupont (eds), *Democracy, Society and the Governance of Security*, Cambridge: Cambridge University Press.

Crawford, A. (2006) 'Reassurance policing: seeing is believing', in D. Smith and A. Henry (eds.), *Police and Public*, Cullompton: Willan Publishing.

Critchley, T.A. (1967) *A History of the Police in England and Wales. 1900–1966*, London: Constable.

Crompton, S. (2002) 'Why we love the best TV tecs', *Times 2*, 10 September: 10.

Davies, N. (2003) 'How politics put policing in the dock', *The Guardian*, 11 July: 1–4.

Davis, M. (1993) *City of Quartz*, London: Fontana.

Davis, M. (1994) 'Beyond Blade Runner' *Open Magazine Pamphlet Series,* Westfield, New Jersey: Open Magazine.

Deacon, A. (1980) 'Spivs, drones and other scroungers' *New Society*, 51 (908): 28 February: 446–7.

Dean, M. (199) *Governmentality: Power and Rule in Modern Society*, London: Sage.

Dennis, N., Erdos, G. and Al-Shahi, A. (2000) *Racist Murder and Pressure Group Politics: The Macpherson Report and the Police*, London: Institute for the Study of Civil Society.

Dickens, C. (1870) *The Mystery of Edwin Drood*, Harmondsworth: Penguin.

Didion, J. (2003) *Fixed Ideas: America Since 9/11*, New York: New York Review of Books.

Dilnot, G. (1930) *The Story of Scotland Yard*, London: Bles Books.

Disher, M.W. (1955) *Victorian Song*, London: Phoenix House Publishers.

Docking, M. (2003) *Public Perceptions of Police Accountability and Decision Making*, Home Office Online Report 38/03 (http://www.homeoffice.gov.uk./rds).

Doherty, T. (1988) *Teenagers and Teenpics: the Juvenilization of American Movies in the 1950s*, Philadelphia: Temple University Press.

Downes, D. (1965) 'Review of *The Policeman in the Community*', *Sociological Review*, 13: 215–6.

Downes, D. and Rock, P. (1983) *Sociology of Deviance*, Oxford: Blackwell.

Doyle, A. and Ericson, R. (2003) 'Two realities of police communication', in C. Sumner (ed), *Blackwell Companion to Crime*, Oxford: Oxford University Press.

Drazin, C. (1998) *The Finest Years: British Cinema of the 1940s*, London: Andrea and Deutsch.

Duffield, M. (2005) *Global Governance and New Wars*, London: Zed Books.

Durgnat, R. (1970) *A Mirror for England: from Austerity to Affluence*, London: Faber and Faber.

Eagar, C. (2004)'The boys are back in town', *Observer Magazine*, 9 October: 29–34.

Eck, J.E. (2004) 'Why don't problems get solved?' in W.G. Skogan (ed), *Community Policing: Can it Work?*, Belmont CA: Wadsworth/Thompson.

Eck, J.E. and Spelman, W. (1987) *Problem Solving: Problem-Oriented Policing in Newport*, Washington DC: Police Executive Research Forum.

Edwards, R. (1974) *Dixon of Dock Green*, London: Pan Books.

Ellison, G. and Smyth, J. (2000) *The Crowned Harp: Policing Northern Ireland*, London: Pluto Press.

Emsley, C. (1991) *The English Police: A Political and Cultural History*, London: Longman.

Emsley, C. (1992) 'The English Bobby: An Indulgent Tradition' in R. Porter (ed), *Myths of the English*, Cambridge: Polity Press.

Enley, F. (1950) 'The Blue Lamp', *Sight and Sound*, 19(2): 3.

Ericson, R. (1989) 'Patrolling the facts: policing and publicity in policework', *British Journal of Sociology*, 40 (2): 205–26.

Ericson, R. (1991) 'Mass media, crime, law and justice', *British Journal of Criminology*, 31: 219–26.

Ericson, R. and Haggerty, K. (1997) *Policing the Risk Society*, Oxford: Clarendon.

Felson, M. (1998) *Crime and Everyday Life*, Thousand Oaks, CA: Pine Forge Press.

Fitzgerald, M. (1999) *Stop and Search*, London: New Scotland Yard.

Fitzgerald, M. (2000) *Final Report into Stop and Search*, New Scotland Yard, Metropolitan Police.

Fitzgerald, M., Hough, M., Joseph, I. and Querish, T. (2002) *Policing for London*, Cullompton: Willan.

Ford, C. and Harrison, B. (1983) *A Hundred Years Ago*, London: Allen Lane.

Fox, C. (2003) 'A test of leadership', *Policing Today*, 9(4): 5.

Fukuyama, F. (2005) *State Building: Governance and World Order in the Twenty-First Century*, London: Profile Books.

Furhammar L. and Isaksson, F. (1971) *Politics and Film*, London: Studio Vista.

Fyvel, T.R. (1963) *The Insecure Offenders: Rebellious Youth in the Welfare State*, Harmondsworth: Penguin.

Galliher, J.F. (1971) 'Explanations of police behaviour: a critical review', *Sociological Quarterly*, 12: 308–318.

Gammond, P. (1956) *Music Hall Song Book*, Newton Abbott: David Charles.

Garland, J., Rowe, M., and Johnson, S. (2003) *Police Community and Race Relations Training*, Leicester: Scarman Centre.

Gatrell, V.A.C. (1990) 'Crime, authority and the policeman-state' in F.M.L. Thompson (ed.), *Cambridge Social History of Britain, 1750–1950*, Cambridge: Cambridge University Press.

Ghaffur, T. (2004) *Thematic Review of Race and Diversity in the Metropolitan Police Service*, London: Metropolitan Police.

Giddens, A. (1999) *Runaway World*, Cambridge: Polity.

Gilroy, P. and Sim, J. (1985) 'Law and Order and the state of the left', *Capital and Class*, 25: 15–55.

Gittings, C. (1998) 'Imaging Canada: the singing Mountie and other commodifications of the nation', *Canadian Journal of Communication*, 12: 507–22.

Giuliani, R.W. (2002) *Leadership*, New York: Talk Mirimax Books.

Glazer, N. (1979) 'On subway graffiti in New York', *The Public Interest*, 4: 549–46.

Goldstein, H. (1963) 'Police discretion: the ideal versus the real', *Public Administration Review*, 63: 140–148.

Goldstein, H. (1977) *Policing a Free Society*, Cambridge Mass: Ballinger.

Goldstein, H. (1990) *Problem-Oriented Policing*, New York: McGraw-Hill.

Goldstein, J. (1960) 'Police discretion not to invoke the criminal process. Low visibility decisions in the administration of justice', *Yale Law Journal*, 69(4): 543–588.

Gollomb, J. (1938) *Scotland Yard*, London: Hutchinson and Co.

Gorer, G. (1955) *Exploring English Character*, London: Cresset.

Gould, R.W. and Waldren, M.J. (1986) *London's Armed Police*, London: Arms and Armour Press.

Graef, R. (1989) *Talking Blues: The Police in their Own Words*, London: Collins Harvill.

Green, D.G. (ed) (2000) *Institutionalized Racism and the Police; Fact or Fiction?*, London: CIVITAS.

Greer, C and McLaughlin, E. (2006) 'Making Murder News', Paper Presented to British Criminology Conference, Glasgow Caledonian University, July 2006.

Haining, P. (1996) *Hunted Down: the Detective Stories of Charles Dickens*, London: Peter Owen Publishers.

Hall, S. (1980) *Drifting into a Law and Order Society*, London: Cobden Trust.

Hall, S. (1985) 'Cold comfort farm', *New Socialist*, 32: 10–12.

Hall, S. (1999) 'From Scarman to Stephen Lawrence', *History Workshop*, 48, pp.187–97.

Hall, S. (2003) 'New Labour's "double shuffle"', *Soundings*, 24: 10–24.

Hall, S., Critcher, C., Jefferson, T., Clarke, J. and Roberts, B. (1978) *Policing the Crisis: Mugging, the State and Law and Order*, London: Macmillan.

Halsey, A.H. (1992) *Decline of Donnish Dominion: the British Academic Professions in the 20th Century*, Oxford: Clarendon Press.

Harper, S. (1994) *Picturing the Past: the Rise and Fall of British Costume Drama*, London: BFI Publishing.

Harris, A.T. (2004) *Policing the City: Crime and Legal Authority in London, 1780–1840*, Columbus: Ohio State University Press.

Harrison, J. and Cuneen, M (2000) *An Independent Police Complaints Commission*, London: Liberty.

Harvey, D. (1991) *The Condition of Postmodernity: an Enquiry into the Origins of Cultural Change*, Oxford: Blackwell.

Hay, D. and Snyder, F. (eds.) (1989) *Policing and Prosecution in Britain, 1750–1850*, Oxford: Clarendon Press.

Hebdige, D. (1988) *Hiding in the Light: On Images and Other Things*, London: Routledge.

Henry, V. (2002) *The Compstat Paradigm*, New York: Looseleaf Law Publications.

Hicks, J. (1997) 'Dispelling the Dixonian myth', *Police Review*, 6 June: 16–17.

Hirst, P.Q. (1975) 'Marx and Engles on crime, law and morality' in I. Taylor, P. Walton and J. Young (eds), *Critical Criminology*, London: Routledge.

HMIC (1996) *Developing Diversity in the Police Service*, London: Home Office.

HMIC (1997) *Winning the Race: Policing Plural Communities*, London: Home Office.

HMIC (1999a) *Keeping The Peace: Policing Disorder*, London: Home Office.

HMIC (1999b) *Winning the Race: Policing Plural Communities Revisited*, London: Home Office.

HMIC (2000) *Policing London, Winning Consent*, London: Home Office.

HMIC (2001a) *Open all Hours: A Thematic Inspection on the Role of Polcie Visibility and Accessibility in Public Reassurance*, London: HMIC.

HMIC (2001b) *Winning the Race: Embracing Diversity*, London: Home Office.

HMIC (2003) *Diversity Matters*, London: Home Office.

HMIC (2005) *Closing the Gap*, London, Home Office.

Hobsbawm, E. and Ranger, T. (1983) *The Invention of Tradition*, Cambridge: Cambridge University Press.

Hodgkin, E.C. (1948) 'Crime marches on', *Spectator*, April 23: 488–9.

Hodgkinson, A.W. and Sheratsky, R.E. (1982) *Humphrey Jennings: More than a Film Maker Clarke*, New England: University Press of New England.

Holdaway, S. (1983) *Inside the British Police*, Oxford: Basil Blackwell.

Holdaway, S. (1995) 'Culture, race and policy; some themes of the sociology of the police' *Policing and Society*, 5: 109–120.

Holdaway, S. (1996) *The Racialisation of British Policing*, Basingstoke: Macmillan.

Holdaway, S. (2003) 'Police race relations in England and Wales: *Police and Society*, 7: 49–74.

Holdaway, S. and O'Neill, M. (2004) 'The development of the Black Police Associations: changing articulations of race within the police', *British Journal of Criminology*, 44: 854–865.

Holder, K.A., Nee, C., Ellis, T. (2000) '"Triple jeopardy"? Black and Asian women police officers experiences of discrimination', *International Journal of Police Science and Management*, 3(1): 68–87.

Home Office (1999) *Stephen Lawrence Inquiry: Home Secretary's Action Plan*, London: Home Office.

Home Office (2001) *Policing a New Century; A Blueprint for Reform*, London: HMSO.

Home Office (2001) *Secure Borders, Safe Havens: Integration with Diversity in Modern Britain*, London: Home Office.

Home Office (2003a) *Policing: Building Safer Communities Together*, London: HMSO.

Home Office (2003b) *Respect and Responsibility: Taking a Stand Against Anti-Social Behaviour*, London: Home Office.

Home Office (2004) *Building Communities, Beating Crime*, Cm 6360, London: Home Office.

Home Office (2005) *Guidance on Publicising Anti-Social Behaviour Orders,* London: Home Office.

Home Office (2006) *Report of the Official Account of the Bombings in London on 7July 2005,* HC 1087, London, Stationary Office

Hopkins, H. (1964) *The New Look: a Social History of the '40s and '50s in Britain,* London: Secker and Warburg.

Hough, M., R.V.G. Clarke and Mayhew, P. (1980) *Designing Out Crime.* London: Home Office

House of Commons Intelligence and Security Commitee (2006) *Report into the London Terrorist Attacks on 7 July 2005,* CM 6785, London, Houose of Commons.

Hubbard, P. and Hall, T. (eds.) (1998) *The Entrepreneurial City,* Chichester: John Wiley and Sons.

Hughes, D. (1986) 'The spivs' in M. Sissons and P. French (eds), *Age of Austerity, 1945–51,* Oxford: Oxford University Press.

Humphrey, J. (2000) 'So farewell Morse. Now you've finally forced me to confess my secret addiction', *Daily Mail,* 13 November: 13.

Humphries, S. (1981) *Hooligans or Rebels: An Oral History of Working Class Childhood and Youth, 1889 and 1939,* Oxford: Oxford University Press.

Hurd, G. (1984) *National Fictions,* London: Cassen

Innes, M. (2004a) 'Reinventing tradition? reassurance, neighbourhood security and policing', *Criminal Justice,* 4 (2): 151–71.

Innes, M. (2004b) 'Signal crimes and signal disorders: notes on deviance as communicative action', *British Journal of Sociology,* 55 (3): 335–353.

Ionann Management Consultants Limited (2000) *Community and Race Relations Workshop for Police Personnel,* London: Ionann Management Consultants Limited.

Jacobs, J. (1961) *The Death and Life of Great American Cities,* Harmondsworth: Penguin.

Jameson, F. and Miyoshi, M. (eds) (1998) *The Cultures of Globalisation,* Durham NC: Duke University Press.

Jefferson, T. and Grimshaw, R. (1984) *Controlling the Constable: Police Accountability in England and Wales,* London: Muller.

Jenkins, C. (1999) 'Race conscious', *Police Review,* 15 October: 16–17.

Jenkins, S. (2004) *Big Bang, New Localism,* London: Policy Exchange.

Johnston, L. (1992) *The Rebirth of Private Policing,* London: Routledge

Johnston, L. (2000) *Policing Britain: Risk, Security and Governance,* London: Longman.

Johnston, L. and Shearing, C. (2003) *Governing Security,* London: Routledge.

Jones, K. (2005) 'After 7/7: reflections on a new policing world', *Policing Today,* 11: 3: 17–18.

Jones, T. (2003) 'Police accountability', in: T. Newburn (ed.), *The Handbook of Policing*: Cullompton: Willan.

Jones, T. and Newburn, T. (1997) *Policing After the Act: Police Governance after the Police and Magistrates' Court Act 1994,* London: Policy Studies Institute.

Jones, T. and Newburn, T. (2002) 'The Transformation of Policing: Understanding current trends in police systems?', *British Journal of Criminology,* 42 (1): 129–46.

Jordan, P. (1998) 'Effective strategies for reducing crime' in Home Office (ed.), *Reducing Offending: An Assessment of Research Evidence on Ways of Dealing with Offending Behaviour,* London: Home Office Research Study No. 187.

Kardish, L. (ed) (1984) *Michael Balcon: The Pursuit of British Cinema,* New York: Museum of Modern Art.

Karmen, A. (2001) *New York Murder Mystery: The true story behind the crime crash of the 1990s,* New York: New York University Press.

Kayman, M.A. (1992) *From Bow Street to Baker Street: Mystery, Detection and Narrative,* London: Macmillan.

Keith, M. (1993) *Race, Riots and Policing: Lore and Disorder in a Multi-Racist Society,* London: UCL Press.

Kelling, G. and Coles, C. (1996) *Fixing Broken Windows,* New York: Touchstone Books.

Kelling, G. and Sousa, W.H. (2001) *Do Police Matter? An analysis of the impact of New York City's police reforms,* Civic Report No. 22, New York: Manhattan Institute.

Kempa, M. and Johnston, L. (2005) 'Challenges and Prospects for the Development of Inclusive Plural Policing in Britain', *Australian and New Zealand Journal of Criminology,* 38(2): 181–91.

Kent, R.A. (1981) *A History of British Empirical Sociology,* Aldershot: Gower.

Kettle, M. (1984) 'The police and the left', *New Society,* 70: 366–367.

Kift, D. (1996) *The Victorian Music Hall,* Cambridge: Cambridge University Press.

Kim, C.W. and Mauborgne, R. (2003) 'Tipping point leadership', *Harvard Business Review,* April: 61–69.

Kinsey, R., Lea, J. and Young, J. (1986) *Losing the Fight Against Crime,* Oxford: Blackwell.

Klockars, C.B. (1988) 'The rhetoric of community policing', in Green, J.R. and Mastrofski, S.D. (eds), *Community Policing: Rhetoric or Reality?,* New York: Praeger.

Kohn, M. (1992) *Dope Girls: The Birth of the British Drug Underground,* London: Granta Publications.

KPMG (2000) *Feasibility of an Independent System for Investigating Complaints against the Police,* London: Home Office, Home Office Research Services Paper, 122.

Krauthammer, C. (1993) 'Defining deviancy up', *The New Republic,* 22 November: 20–25.

Kumar, K. (2001) 'Sociology and the Englishness of English social theory', *Sociological Theory* 19 (1): 41–64.

La Fave, W. (1962) 'The police and non-enforcement of the law', *Wisconsin Law Review,* I: 104–37 & II: 179–239.

Landy, M (1991) *British Genres: Cinema and Society 1930 and 1960,* Princeton, New Jersey: Princeton University Press.

Lardner, J. and Reppetto, T. (2000) *NYPD: A city and its police,* New York: Henry Holt.

Lawrence, R.G. (2000) *The Politics of Force: Media and the Construction of Police Brutality,* Berkeley: University of California Press.

Lea, J. and Young, J. (1984) *What is to be Done about Law and Order,* London: Pluto Press.

Lee, W.L.M. (1901) *A History of the Police of England,* London: Metheun.

Leishman, F. and Mason, P. (2003) *Policing and the Media: Facts, Fictions and Factions,* Cullompton: Willan Publishing.

Lennon, J. (1967) Review of 'The Policeman in the Community', *Sociological Quarterly,* 8: 2, pp.280–1.

Loader, I. (1997a) 'Private security and the demand for protection in contemporary Britain', *Policing and Society,* 7: 143–162.

Loader, I. (1997b) 'Policing and the social: questions of symbolic power', *British Journal of Sociology,* 48: 1–18.

Loader, I. (1999) 'Consumer culture and the commodification of policing and security', *Sociology,* 33(2): 373–92.

Loader, I. (2000) 'Plural policing and democratic governance', *Social and Legal Studies*, 9(3): 323–45.

Loader, I. and Mulcahy A. (2003) *Policing and the Condition of England: Memory, Politics and Culture*, Oxford: Oxford University Press.

Loader, I. and Walker, N. (2001) 'Policing as a public good: reconstructing the connections between policing and the state', *Theoretical Criminology*, 5 (1): 9–35.

Loader, I. and Walker, N. (2004) 'State of denial? Rethinking the governance of security', *Punishment and Society*, 6 (2): 221–8

Loader, I. and Walker N. (2005) 'Necessary virtues: the legitimate place of the state in the production of security' in J. Wood and B. Dupont (eds.) *Democracy, Security and the Governance of Security*, Cambridge: Cambridge University Press.

Local Government Association (2003) *Designs on Democracy: Case Studies on Democratic Participation*, London: Local Government Association.

Local Government Association (2004b) *Towards Self-Governing Communities*, London: Local Government Association.

Lofland, L. (1973) *A World of Strangers*, New York: Basic Books.

Loveday, B. (1998) 'Waving not drowning: chief constables and the new configuration of accountability in the provinces', *International Journal of Police Science and Management*, 1, 2, pp. 133–147.

Loveday, B. and Reid, A. (2003) *Going Local: Who Should Run Britain's Police?*, London: Policy Exchange/Localis.

Lustgarten, L. (1986) *The Governance of the Police*, London: Sweet and Maxwell.

Lyman, J.L. (1964) 'The Metropolitan Police Act of 1829', *Journal of Criminal Law, Criminology and Police Science*, 55: 141–54.

Manning, P. (2005) 'The study of policing', *Police Quarterly*, 8(1): 23–43

McArdle, A. and Erzen, T. (eds) *Zero tolerance: Quality of Life and the New police Brutality in New York City,* New York: New York University Press.

McClintock, F.H. and Wiles, P. (1972) *The Security Industry in the United Kingdom*, Cropwood Conference, Cambridge: Institute of Criminology.

McCrystal, C. (1988) 'The "Big Apple" turns sour', *Sunday Times Magazine*, 12 February: 24–37.

McDonald, P. (2004) *Managing Police Operations: Implementing the NYPD Crime Control Model*, Belmont CA: Wadsworth.

McInnes, C. (1957) *City of Spades*, London: Alison and Busby.

McInnes, C. (1963) 'An unrewarded virtue: Britain 1945–51', *Queen*, 25 September: 13–15.

McLaughlin, E. (1994) *Community, Policing and Accountability*, Aldershot: Avebury.

McLaughlin, E. (2001) 'Key issues in policework' in E. McLaughlin and J. Muncie (eds), *Controlling Crime*, London: Sage.

McLaughlin, E. (2005) 'Recovering blackness and repudiating whiteness: the *Daily Mail's* construction of the five white suspects accused of the murder of Stephen Lawrence' in K. Murji and J. Solomos (2005) *Racialization*, Oxford: Oxford University Press.

McLaughlin, E. and Murji, K. (1995) 'The End of Public Policing?', in Noaks, L. Levi, M. and Maguire, M (eds), *Contemporary Issues in Criminology*, Cardiff: University of Wales Press.

McLaughlin, E. and Murji, K. (1996) 'Times change: new formations and representations of police accountability' in C. Critcher and D.Waddington (eds), *Policing Public Disorder: Theoretical and Practical Issues*, Aldershot: Avebury.

McLaughlin, E. and Murji, K. (1997) 'The future lasts along time: public policework and the managerialist paradox' in P. Francis et al. (eds), *Policing Futures*, Basingstoke, Macmillan.

McLaughlin, E. and Murji, K. (1998) 'Resistance through representation: storylines, advertising and Police Federation Campaigns', *Policing and Society*, 8: 367–399.

McLaughlin, E. and Murji, K. (1999) 'After Stephen Lawrence', *Critical Social Policy*, 19 (3): 371–385.

McLaughlin, E. and Murji, K. (2001) 'Lost connections and new directions: neo-liberalism, new public managerialism and the modernization of the British police', in K. Stenson and R.R. Sullivan (eds), *Crime, Risk and Justice: The Politics of Crime Control in Liberal Democracies*, Cullompton: Willan.

McLaughlin, E. and Neal, S. (2004) 'Misrepresenting the multi-cultural nation: the policy making process, news media management and the Parekh Report', *Policy Studies*, 25(3): 155–74.

Mack, J.A. (1964) 'Dock Green or Z Cars?, *New Society*, 91, June, p.25.

Macpherson, Sir, W. (1999) *Stephen Lawrence Inquiry*, CM4262–I: London: TSO.

Maguire, M. and Corbett, C. (1991) *A Study of the Police Complaints System*, London: Home Office.

Mannheim, H. (1946) *Criminal Justice and Reconstruction*, London: Routledge.

Manning, P.K. (1977) *Police Work*, Cambridge, MA: MIT Press.

Manning, P.K. (1978) 'Police mandate: strategies and appearances' in P.K. Manning and J. Van Maanen (eds), *Policing: A View from the Street*, New York: Random House.

Manning. P.K. (1995) 'The police occupational culture' in W. Bailey, *The Encyclopedia of Police Science*, New York: Garland.

Manning, P.K. (1999) 'A dramaturgical perspective' in B. Forst and P. Manning, *The Privatization of Policing: Two Views*, Washington DC: Georgetown University Press.

Manning, P.K. (2001) 'Theorizing policing: The drama and myth of crime control in the NYPD', *Theoretical Criminology*, 5, 3, 315–344.

Manning, P.K. (2003) 'The dynamics of police reflection' in P.K. Manning, *Policing Contingencies*, Chicago: Chicago University Press.

Manning, P. (2005) 'The study of policing', *Police Quarterly*, 8(1)23–43.

Manning, P.K. and Van Maanen, J. (eds) (1978) *Policing: A View from the Street*, Santa Monica, California: Goodyear.

Maple, J. (1999) *The Crime Fighter: How You Can Make Your Community Crime Free*, New York: Broadway Books.

Marenin, O. (1983) 'Parking tickets and class repression: the concept of policing in critical theories of criminal justice', *Contemporary Crises*, 6:(2): 241–266.

Mark, R. (1977) *Policing a Perplexed Society*, London: Allen and Unwin.

Mark, R. (1979) *In the Office of Constable*, London: Collins.

Marquand, D. (2001) 'The breath of renewal', *The Guardian*, 20 March, 19.

Marshall, G. (1965) *Police and Government*, London: Methuen.

Marshall, G. (1978) 'Police accountability revisited', in: D. Butler and A.H. Halsey (eds.), *Policy and Politics*, London: Macmillan.

Martin, D. (2003) 'The politics of policing: managerialism, modernisation and performance', in: R. Matthews and J. Young (eds), *The New Politics of Crime and Punishment*, Cullompton: Willan.

Massing, M. (1998) 'The Blue Revolution', *New York Review of Books*, November 19, pp. 32–34.

Mayo, E. and Moore, H. (2001) *The Mutual State: How Local Communities can run Public Services*, London: New Economic Foundation.

Mays, J.B. (1965) Review of *The Policeman in the Community*, *British Journal of Criminology*, 5 (2): 217–8.

Mazerolle, L.G. and Ransley, J. (2005) *Third Party Policing*, Cambridge: Cambridge University Press.

Medhurst, A. (1986) 'Dirk Bogarde' in C. Barr (ed.), *All Our Yesterdays: 90 Years of British Cinema*, London: BFI Publications.

Medhurst, A. (1995) 'Myths of consensus and fables of escape: British cinema 1945 and 1951' in J. Fyrth (ed.), *Labour's Promised Land: Culture and Society in Labour Britain 1945-1951*, London: Lawrence and Wishart.

Metropolitan Police (1998) *Working Together Towards an Anti-Racist Police Service: Report of a Conference 18 December 1998*, London: Metropolitan Police.

Metropolitan Police (1999a) *A Police Service for all the People: Report of the MPS Ethnic Minority (Recruitment and Advancement) Working Party*, London: New Scotland Yard.

Metropolitan Police (1999b) *Protect and Respect: The Met's Diversity Strategy*, London: Metropolitan Police.

Metropolitan Police (2000) *Policing Diversity: The Metropolitan Police Service Handbook on London's Religions, Cultures and Communities*, London: New Scotland Yard.

Metropolitan police (2005) *Counter Terrorism Suicide: Memo to Members*, London: Metropolitan Police.

Miller, D.A. (1981) 'The novel and the police' in G. Most and W. Stowe (eds), *The Poetics of Murder*, New York: Harcourt Brace.

Miller, W.R. (1977) *Cops and Bobbies: Police Authority in New York and London, 1830–1870*, Chicago: Chicago University Press.

Millie, A. and Herrington, V. (2005) 'Bridging the gap: understanding reassurance policing', *The Howard Journal*, 44: 41–56.

Millie, A., Jacobson, J. McDonald, E. and Hough, M. (2005) *Anti-Social Behaviour: Finding a Balance*, Bristol: Policy Press.

Minns, R. (1980) *Bombers and Mash: the domestic front 1939–1945*, London: Virago.

Montgomery-Hyde, H. (1954) *The Trial of Christopher Craig and Derek Bentley*, London: Hodge and Co Ltd.

Morley, S. (1999) *Dirk Bogarde: Rank Outsider*, London: Bloomsbury Books.

Morris, T. (1989) *Crime and Criminal Justice Since 1945*, Oxford: Oxford University Press.

Morris, W. Sir (2004) *The Report of the Morris Inquiry – the Case for Change, People in the Metropolitan Police Service*, London: Metropolitan Police Authority.

Moylan, J. F. (1929) *Scotland Yard and the Metropolitan Police*, London: Putnam.

Muir, R.D. (2001) *The Virdi Inquiry Report*, London: Metropolitan Police Authority.

Murphy, R. (1989) 'The spiv cycle' in R.Murphy, *Realism and Tinsel: Cinema and Society in Britain, 1939-1948*, London: Routledge.

Murphy, R. (1993) *Smash and Grab: Gangsters in the London Underworld 1920 and 1960*, London: Faber and Faber.

Murphy, R. (1999) *British Film Noir: Shadows are my Friends*, London: I.B. Taurus.

Murray, C. (1995) 'The Underclass: the crisis deepens', *Sunday Times*, 22 May: 10–11.

Murray, C. (2000) 'Baby beware', *Sunday Times News Review,* 13 February: 1–2.

Myhill, A., Yarrow, S., Dalgleish, D. and Docking, M. (2003) *The Role of Police Authorities in Public Engagement,* Home Office Online Report 37/03 (http://www.homeoffice. gov./uk.rds).

Neiderhoffer, A. (1967) *Behind the Shield,* New York: Doubleday.

Nelson, J. (2000) *Police Brutality: An Anthology,* New York: W.W. Norton.

New Local Government Network (2003) *New Localism in Action,* London: New Local Government Network.

Newburn, T. (2003) 'Policing since 1945' in T. Newburn (ed.), *Handbook of Policing,* Cullompton: Willan Publishing.

Newburn, T. and Jones, T. (2001) *Widening Access: Improving Police Relations with Hard to Reach Groups* (Home Office Police Research Series 138), London: Home Office.

Newburn, T. and Reiner, R. (2004) 'From PC Dixon to Dixon PLC: policing and police powers since 1954', *Criminal Law Review,* 30: 101–118.

Newburn, T. and Sparks, R. (2004) 'Introduction: criminal justice and political cultures' in T. Newburn and R. Sparks (eds.), *Criminal Justice and Political Cultures,* Cullompton: Willan Publishing.

Newman, G. (1987) *The Rise of English Nationalism: A Cultural History,* New York: St Martins Press.

Neyroud, P. (2001) *Public Participation in Policing,* London: IPPR.

Neyroud, P. (2003) 'Restoring confidence after crime', Speech to Howard League Conference, Oxford, 17 September 2003.

O'Connor, D. (2002) 'After Dixon: the realities of reassurance and neighbourhood control' *Policing Today,* 8 (2): 13–16.

O'Connor, D. (2003) 'Reassurance, security and order', *Policing Today,* 10 (3): 15–17.

O'Neill, O. (2002) *A Question of Trust: The Reith Lectures,* Cambridge: Cambridge University Press.

Oakley, R. (1989) 'Community and race relations training for the police: a review of developments', *New Community,* 16 (1): 61–79.

Oakely, R. (1993) 'Race relations training in the police', in Gelsthorpe, L. (ed), *Minority Ethnic Groups in the Criminal Justice System,* Cambridge: Cambridge Institute of Criminology.

Office of Deputy Prime Minister (2005) *Citizen Engagement and Public Services: Why Neighbourhoods Matter,* London: Office of Deputy Prime Minister.

Office of Deputy Prime Minister (2006) *All Our Futures,* London: Office of Deputy Prime Minister.

Ousby, I. (1976) *Bloodhound from Heaven: the Detective in English Fiction from Godwin to Doyle,* Cambridge, Mass: Harvard University Press.

Ousley, H. (2000) *The Diversity Strategy: A Review,* London: Metropolitan Police Service.

Palmer, S.H. (1988) *Police and Protest in England and Ireland, 1780–1850,* Cambridge: Cambridge University Press.

Paoline, E.A. (2003) 'Taking stock: toward a richer understanding of police culture', *Journal of Criminal Justice,* 31 (03): 199–214.

Parekh Report (2000) *The Future of Multi-Ethnic Britain,* London: Profile Books.

Parenti, C. (1999) *Lockdown America: Police and Prisons in the Age of Crisis,* London: Verso Books.

Parker, T. (1963) 'From the other side of the fence', *New Society,* 29 August: 7–8.

Paterseon, R. (1980) 'The Sweeney', *Screen Education*, 20: 79–86.

Patten Commission (1999) *A New Beginning: Policing in Northern Ireland: A Report of the Independent Commission on Policing in Northern Ireland*, Belfast: HMSO.

Perlmutter, D.D. (2000) *Policing the Media: Street Cops and Public Perceptions of Law Enforcement*, Thousand Oaks: Sage.

Phillips, D. and Storch, R.J. (1999) *Policing Provincial England 1829–1856: The Politics of Reform*, London: Leicester University Press.

Phillips, T. (2003) 'Opening Address to Metropolitan Police Association', 30 November, London: Commission for Racial Equality.

Platt, A. M. (ed.) (1971) *The Politics of Riot Commissions*, New York: Collier.

Platt, A. and Cooper, L. (eds) (1974) *Policing America*, Engelwood Cliffs, NJ: Prentice-Hall.

Pollard, C. (1997) 'Zero tolerance: short term fix, long term liability' in N. Dennis (ed.), *Zero Tolerance: Policing a Free Society*, London: Institute of Economic Affairs.

Pratt, J. (2000) 'Emotive and ostentatious punishment: its decline and resurgence in modern society', *Punishment and Society*, 2 (4): 417–39.

Prime Minister's Office of Public Services Reform (2003) *Citizen Focused Policing,* London: Prime Minister's Office of Public Services Reform.

Pulling, C. (1964) *Mr Punch and The Police*, London: Butterworth.

Punch, M. (1979) *Policing the Inner City: A Study of Amsterdam's Warmoesstraal,* London: Macmillan.

Punch, M. (1993) 'Observation and the police: the research experience' in M. Hammersley (ed.), *Social Research: Philosophy, Politics and Practice*, London: Sage.

Quinney, R. (1977) *Class, State and Crime*, New York: Longman.

Radzinowicz, Sir L. (1955) *A History of English Criminal Law*, Vol 3, London: Stevens.

Radzinowicz, Sir L. (1971) 'Opening Address' in P. Wiles and F.H. McClintock (eds), *The Security Industry in the United Kingdom*, Cambridge: Institute of Criminology.

Ramsden, J. (1987) 'Refocusing "the peoples' war": British war films of the 1950's', *Journal of Contemporary History,* 31 (1):35–63.

Reiner, R. (1991) *Chief Constables*, Oxford: Oxford University Press.

Reiner, R. (1992a) 'Policing a postmodern society', *Modern Law Review*, 55: 761–81.

Reiner, R. (1992b) *'Fin de siecle* blues: the police face the millennium', *Political Quarterly*, 63 (1): 37–49.

Reiner, R. (1993) 'Police accountability: principles, patterns and practices', in Reiner, R. and Spencer, S. (eds), *Accountable Policing*, London: IPPR.

Reiner, R. (1994) 'The dialectics of Dixon: the changing image of the TV cop' in M. Stephens and S. Becker (eds), *Police Force: Police Service*, Básingstoke: MacMillan.

Reiner, R. (1995) 'From the sacred to the profane: the thirty years war of the British police', *Policing and Society*, 5: 121–28.

Reiner, R. (1997a) 'Policing and the police' in M. Maguire, R. Morgan and R. Reiner (eds), *The Oxford Handbook of Criminology*, 2nd Edition, Oxford: Oxford University Press.

Reiner, R. (1997b) 'Media made criminality' in M. Maguire, R. Morgan and R. Reiner (eds), *The Oxford Handbook of Criminology*, 2nd Edition, Oxford: Oxford University Press.

Reiner, R. (2001) 'The organisation and accountability of the police', in M. McConville and G. Wilson (eds.), *Handbook of Criminal Justice Process*, Oxford: Oxford University Press.

Reiner, R. (2003) 'Police and the media' in T. Newburn (ed.), *Handbook of Policing*, Cullompton: Willan Publishing.

Reiss, A. (1972) *The Police and the Public*, New Haven, Conn: Yale University Press.

Reith, C. (1938) *The Police Idea*, Oxford: Oxford University Press.

Reith, C. (1943) *British Police and the Democratic Idea*, Oxford: Oxford University Press.

Reynolds, E.A. (1998) *Before the Bobbies: The Night Watch and Police Reform in Metropolitan London, 1720–1830*, Stanford: Stanford University Press.

Richards, J. (1997) *Films and British National Identity: From Dickens to Dad's Army*, Manchester: Manchester University Press.

Richards, J. (2001) 'British film censorship' in R. Murphy (ed.), *British Cinema Book*, London: BFI Publishing.

Richards, J. and Aldgate, A. (1983) *Best of British: Cinema and Society 1930–1970*, Oxford: Oxford University Press.

Roberts, J.A. (1974) 'Laughter and the law: Shakespeare's comic constables' in E.C. Viano and J.H. Reiman (eds), *The Police in Society*, Lexington, Mass: DC Heath.

Roberts, J.C. (1988) *The Hidden Cinema: British Film Censorship in Action 1913–1972*, London: Routledge

Roberts, R. (1971) *The Classic Slum: Salford Life in the First Quarter of the Century*, Manchester: Manchester University Press.

Robertson, J.C. (1985) *British Board of Film Censors,* London: Croom Helm.

Rock, P. and Cohen, S. (1976) 'The teddy boy' in V. Bogdanor and R. Skidelsky (eds), *The Age of Affluence, 1951–64*, London: MacMillan.

Rose, N. (1996) 'The death of the social? Refiguring the territory of government', *Economy and Society,* 25:3: 327–356.

Rose, N. (1999) *Powers of Freedom: Reframing Political Thought*, Cambridge: Cambridge University Press.

Rose, N. (2000) 'Government and Control', *British Journal of Criminology*, 40: 321–339.

Ross, J.I. (2000) *Making News of Police Violence: a Comparative Case Study of Toronto and New York City*, Westport, Conn: Praeger Press.

Rowe, M. (2004) *Policing, Race and Racism*, Cullompton: Willan Publishing.

Rumbelow, D. (1988) *The Houndsditch Murders and the Siege of Sydney Street*, London: W.H. Allen.

Rumney, J. (1945) 'British sociology' in G. Gurvitch and W.E. Moore (eds.) *Twentieth Century Sociology*, New York: The Phiosophical Library.

Sarre, R. (2005) 'Researching private policing: challenges and agendas for researchers', *Security Journal,* 18 (3): 57–70.

Sarto, B. (1949) *Soho Spivs*, London: Modern Fiction Books.

Savage, S., Charman. S. and Cope, S. (2000) *Policing and the Power of Persuasion*, London: Blackstone.

Scarman, Lord (1981) *The Brixton Disorders 10–12 April 1981: Report of an Inquiry*, Cmnd 8427, London: HMSO.

Scott, Sir H. (1957) *Scotland Yard*, London: Mayflour.

Scott, M.S. (2000) *POP: Reflections on the First Twenty Years*, Washington DC: US Department of Justice.

Scott, T.M. and Macpherson, M. (1971) 'The development of the private sector of the criminal justice system', *Law and Society Review*, 6 (2): 267–288.

Scraton, P. (1985) *The State of the Police*, London: Pluto.

Scraton, P. (2002) 'Defining 'power' and challenging 'knowledge': critical analysis as resistance in the UK' in K. Carrington and R. Hogg (eds), *Critical Criminology: Issues, Debates, Challenges*, Cullompton: Willan Publishing.

Selwyn, F. (1988) *Gangland: The Case of Bentley and Craig*, London: Routledge.

Sennett, R. (2006) *The Culture of the New Capitalism*, New Haven: Yale University Press.

Sewell, B. (2003) 'Why I love trash TV', *London Evening Standard*, 5 December: 11.

Shearing, C. (1992) 'Policing: relationships between public and private forms' in M. Tonry and N. Morris (eds), *Modern Policing*, Chicago: Chicago University Press.

Shearing, C. (2001) 'A nodal conception of governance: thoughts on a police commission', *Police and Society*, 11: 259–72.

Shearing, C. (2006) 'Policing our Future', in A. Henry and D.J. Smith (eds), *Reflections Twenty Years After Police and People in London*, Aldershot: Ashgate.

Shearing, C.D. and Stenning, P.C. (1980) The quiet revolution: the nature, development and general legal implications of private security in Canada', *Criminal Law Quarterly*, 22: 220–48.

Shearing, C.D. and Stenning, P.C. (1981) 'Modern private security: its growth and implications', M. Tonry and N. Morris (eds), *Crime and Justice: An Annual Review of Research*, Vol. 3, Chicago: University of Chicago Press.

Shearing, C.D. and Stenning, P.C. (1983) 'Private security: implications for social control', *Social Problems*, 30 (5):493–506.

Shearing, C. & Wood, J. (2003) 'Nodal Governance, Democracy and the New 'Denizens', *Journal of Law and Society,* 30 (3): 400–19).

Sheptycki, J. (1995) 'Transnational policing and the making of a postmodern state'. *British Journal of Criminology*, 35: 613–31.

Sheptycki, J.W.E. (1998) 'Policing, postmodernism and transnationalism', *British Journal of Criminology*, 38 (3): 485–503.

Shepycki, J. (2000) *Transnational Policing*, London: Routledge.

Sherman, L. (1974) 'The sociology and the social reform of the American police: 1950–1973', *Journal of Police Science and Administration*, 2:2, 255–62.

Sherman, L., Gottfredson, D.C., Bushway, P., Eck, J. and McKenzie, D.L. (1997) *Preventing Crime: What Works, What Doesn't, What's Promising*, Washington DC: US Department of Justice.

Sherman, L. and Eck, J. (2002) 'Policing for crime prevention', in L. Sherman, D.P. Farrington, B.C. Welsh and D.L. Mckenzie (eds) *Evidence Based Crime Prevention*, London: Routledge.

Shils, E. (1949) *The Present State of American Sociology*, Glencoe, III, Free Press.

Shils, E. and Young, M. (1953) 'The meaning of the Coronation', *Sociological Review*, 1: 63–81.

Siegal, F. (1992) 'Reclaiming our public spaces', in P. Kasnitz (ed.) *Metropolis: Centre and Symbol*, New York: New York University Press.

Silverman, E.B. (1999) *NYPD Battles Crime*, Boston: North Eastern University Press.

Singer, P.W. (2003) *Corporate Warriors: the Rise of the Privatized Military*, Ithaca: Cornell University Press.

Skogan, W. (2006) *Police and Community in Chicago*, New York: Oxford University Press.

Skogan, W. and Frydl, K. (eds) (2004) *Fairness and Effectiveness in Policing: The Evidence*, Washington DC: National Academies Press.

Skolnick, J. (1964) 'Review of *The Policeman in the Community*', *Jewish Journal of Sociology*, 6 (2): 277–8.

Skolnick, J.H. (1966) *Justice Without Trial: Law Enforcement in a Democratic Society*, New York: Wiley.

Skolnick, J. and Bayley, D. (1986) *The New Blue Line*, New York: Free Press.

Smith, D.J. and Gray, J. (1985) *Police and People in London: The PSI Report*, London: Gower.

Smith, G. 'Actions for damages against the police', *Policing and Society*, 13(4): 413–22.

Smithies, E. (1982) *Crime in Wartime: A Social History of Crime in World War 2*, London: Allen and Unwin.

Soja, E. (1995) 'Postmodern urbanization: the restructuring of Los Angeles' in S. Watson and A. Gibson (eds.) *Postmodern Cities*, Oxford: Blackwell.

Soja, E. (2000) *PostMetropolis: Critical Studies of Cities and Regions*, Oxford: Blackwell.

Spicer, A. (1997) 'Male stars, masculinity and British cinema, 1945–1960' in R. Murphy (ed.), *The British Cinema Book*, London: BFI Publishing.

Spitzer, S. and Scull, A.T. (1977) 'Privatization and capitalist development: the case of the private police', *Social Problems*, 25, pp.18–29.

Sprott, W.J.H. (1957) 'Sociology in Britain: preoccupations' in H. Becker and A. Boskoff (eds), *Modern Sociological Theory in Continuity and Change*, New York: Dryden Press.

State Research (1980) *Policing The Eighties: The Iron Fist,* London: State Research.

Stenson, K. (1999) 'Crime control, governmentality, and sovereignty' in R. Smardyeh (ed.), *Governable Places: Readings on Governmentality and Crime Control*, Aldershot: Ashgate

Stevens, J. (2005) *Not for the Foolhearted: My Life Fighting Crime*, London: Weidenfeld and Nicolson.

Stevenson, S. and Bottoms, A. (1989) 'The politics of the police 1955–64: A Royal commission in a decade of transition' in D. Downes (ed.), *Unravelling Criminal Justice*, Basingstoke: MacMillan.

Storch, R.D. (1975) '"The plague of blue locusts": police reform and popular resistance in Northern England 1840–57', *International review of Social History*, 20: 61–90;

Storch, R. D. (1976) 'The policeman as domestic missionary: urban discipline and popular culture in northern England 1850–1888, *Journal of Social History,* 9: 481–509.

Straw, J. (1997) 'I have a dream – and I don't want it to be mugged', *Guardian*, 8 June: 19.

Straw, J. and Michael, A. (1996) *Tackling the Causes of Crime: Labour's Proposals to Prevent Crime and Criminality*, London, Labour Party.

Sumner, C. (1981) 'Race, crime and hegemony: a review essay', *Contemporary Crises* 5: 277–291.

Sydney-Smith, S. (2002) *Beyond Dixon of Dock Green: Early British Police Series*, London: I.B. Taurus.

Symons, J. (1992) *Bloody Murder: From the Detective Story to the Crime Novel*, London: Pan Books.

Takagi, P. (1974) 'A Garrison state in a "democratic" society', *Crime and Social Justice*, 1: 27–33.

Taylor, I. (1981) *Law and Order: Arguments for Socialism*, London: MacMillan.

Taylor, I. (1999) *Crime in Context*, Cambridge: Polity Press.

Taylor, P. (ed.) (1987), *Britain and the Cinema in the Second World War*, New York: St Martin's Press.

Taylor, P. (ed.) (1988), *Britain and the Cinema in the Second World War*, London: Basingstoke.

Taylor, W. (2005) *Review of Disciplinary Arrangements*, London: Home Office.

Tendler, S (1991) 'Big Mack's tough challenge', *Police Review*, 8, March: 484–85.

Thomas, D. (2003) *An Underworld at War: Spivs, Deserters, Racketeers and Civilians*, John Murray: London.

Thompson, E.P. (1980) *Writing by Candlelight*, London: Merlin.

Thurston, G. (1967)*The Clerkenwell Riot: The Killing of Constable Culley*, London: Allen and Unwin.

Tietjen, A. (1956) *Soho: London's Vicious Circle*, London: Allan Wingate.

Tomlin, M. (1936) *Police and Public*, London: Heinemann.

Travis, J. and Waul, M. (2002) *Reflections on The Crime Decline: Lessons for the Future*, New York: Urban Institute Justice Policy Centre.

Trodd, A. (1998) 'Introduction' to W. Collins, *The Moonstone*, Oxford: Oxford University Press.

Upton Sahm, C. (2005) 'New York revitalizes US policing', *City Journal*, http:www.cityjournal.org

Vahimaji, T. (1994) *British Television*, Oxford: Oxford University Press.

Van Maanen, J. (1973) 'Observations on the making of policemen', *Human Organization*, 32(4):407–418.

Waddington, P.A.J. (1986) 'Mugging as a moral panic: a question of proportion', *British Journal of Sociology*, 37 (2): 245–59.

Waddington, P.A.J. (1999) 'Police (canteen) sub-culture: an appreciation', *British Journal of Criminology*, 39:2: 286–309.

Wakefield, A. (2003) *Selling Security: The Private Policing of Public Space*, Cullompton, Devon: Willan Publishing.

Walker, D. (2002) *In Praise of Centralism: A Critique of New Localism*, London: Catalyst.

Walker, N. (1995) 'Defining core police tasks: the neglect of the symbolic dimension' *Policing and Society*, 6: 53–71.

Walker, S. (2000) '"Broken windows" and fractured history: the use and misuse of history in recent police patrol analysis' in W.M. Oliver (ed.), *Community Policing*, Upper Saddle River, NJ: Prentice Hall.

Walker, S. (2004) 'Science and politics in politics in police research: reflections of their tangled relationship', *ANNALS*, AAPS, 593: 137–155.

Wall, D. (1998) *The Chief Constable of England and Wales*, Aldershot: Ashgate.

Walsh, W. (2001) 'COMPSTAT: an analysis of an emerging police paradigm', *Policing: An International Journal of Police Strategies and Management*, 24:3: 347–63.

Warner, J. (1975) *Jack of All Trades*, London: W.H. Allen

Warner, J. (1979) *Evening All*, London: Star Books.

Weatheritt, M. (ed.) (2000) *Zero Tolerance: What does it mean and is it right for policing in Britain?*, London: The Police Foundation.

Welsh, A. (1971) *The City of Dickens*, Oxford: Clarendon Press.

Westley, W. (1951) 'The police: A sociological Study of Law, Custom and Morality', Ph.D dissertation, University of Chicago, Department of Sociology.

Westley, W. (1953) 'Violence and the police', *American Journal of Sociology* 59: 34–42.

Westley, W. (1970) *Violence and the Police: A Sociological Study of Law, Custom and Morality*, Cambridge, Mass: MIT Press.

Westmarland, L. (2002) 'Challenges of policing London: a conversation with the Metropolitan Police Commissioner, Sir John Stevens', *Police Practice and Research*, 3 (1): 247–60.

Whitaker, B. (1964) *The Police*, London: Penguin Books.

White, J. (1986) *The Worst Street in London: Islington between the Wars*, London: Routledge.

Whyte, W (1943) *Street Corner Society: the Social Structure of the Italian Slum,* Chicago: Chicago University Press.

Wiles, P. and McClintock, F.H. (eds) *The Security Industry in the United Kingdom,* Cambridge: Institute of Criminology.

Willis, E. (1964) 'Dock Green through the years', *Radio Times,* 17 September: 7.

Willis, E. (1991) *Evening All: Fifty Years Over A Hot Type Writer,* London: MacMillan.

Willis, E. and Hatton, C. (1960) *Dixon of Dock Green: My Life by George Dixon,* London: William Kimber.

Willis, E. and Graham, P. (1961) *Dixon of Dock Green: A Novel,* London: Mayflower Books.

Wilson, J. Q. (1963) 'The police and their problems: a theory', *Public Policy,* 12: 189–216.

Wilson, J.Q. (1968) *Varieties of Police Behavior: The Management of Law and Order in Eight Communities,* Cambridge, MA: Harvard University Press.

Wilson, J.Q. (1969) 'What makes a better policeman' in *Atlantic Monthly Supplement,* March: 129–135.

Wilson, J.Q. (1975) *Thinking about Crime,* New York: Vintage Books.

Wilson, J.Q. and Herrnstein, R.J. (1985) *Crime and Human Nature,* New York: Simon and Schuster.

Wilson, J.Q. and Kelling, G. (1982) 'Broken windows: the police and neighbourhood safety', *Atlantic Monthly,* 249: 29–38

Wollen, P. (1998) 'Riff-raff realism', *Sight and Sound,* Summer: 18–23.

Yallop, D. (1971) *To Encourage Others: Startling New Facts on the Craig/Bentley Case,* London: W.H. Allen.

Young, J. (1986) 'The failure of criminology: the need for a radical realism' in J. Young and R. Matthews (eds), *Confronting Crime,* London: Sage.

Young, J. (1992) 'Crime: the Maginot Line', in N. Abercrombie (ed.), *British Society,* London: MacMillan.

Young, J. (2000) *The Exclusive Society,* London: Sage.

Young, M. (1991) *An Inside Job: Policing and Police Culture in Britain,* Oxford: Oxford University Press.

Young, M. (1993) *In the Sticks,* Oxford: Oxford University Press.

Zedner, L. (2006) 'Policing before and after the police: the historical antecedents of contemporary crime control', *British Journal of Criminology,* 46(1): 78–96.

Zukin, S. (1997) 'Cultural strategies and urban identities: remaking public space in New York' in O. Kaltrop (ed.) *Cities in Transformation,* Avebury: Aldershot.

Zweiniger-Bargielowska, I. (2000) *Austerity in Britain: Rationing, Controls and Consumption, 1939 and 1955,* Oxford: Oxford University Press.

Index